Into the Forest Primeval

R. O. Fanjoy

Cover art: Ryan J. Pedersen
Book layout: Jim Fanjoy
ISBN: 9798740281971
Imprint: Independently published

My father used to tell great stories about his post-WWII adventures while hunting in the forests and diving in the Pacific Ocean during his young adult years in the coastal areas of Northern California. Retelling those stories became an eagerly anticipated oral tradition in our family. One evening while standing in my back yard in Montana to get some fresh air, I was reminiscing about my own adventures many years before and realized I needed to write down my own adventures to pass on to the next generation. My young adult years were spent as a young air force pilot stationed at Kincheloe Air Force Base in the Eastern upper peninsula of Michigan. Back then I spent every available moment in the surrounding Hiawatha National Forest which my friends and I referred to as the Forest Primeval. Like the Forest Primeval of Longfellow's Acadia, our forest primeval was also a dark and foreboding place. We rarely saw any animal or human sign as we traveled down poorly lit forest lanes covered by a heavy canopy of trees to get to our hunting or fishing destinations. Occasionally we would come across an abandoned hunting cabin or the remains of a wrecked rowboat on the lakeshore, but otherwise the forest had reclaimed any other evidence of life. Birds were not seen or heard and even the local deer and bear left little sign of their passing. On the days when I had flight duty, departing and returning to base over the vast tract of woodland provided no insight to what lay below. On the ground, each trip into the woods was a great adventure. What follows, with minor editorial license, are memories of good times with good friends and fellow pilots. And so begins tales of my time at 'the Kinch' and expeditions into the Forest Primeval.

R. O. Fanjoy
December 2017

Noodling, Night Fishing, and Other Diversions

As I became a young adult and moved into the work force, my total fishing experience consisted of bait fishing for sunfish in a local pond with my younger brother. My limited knowledge of fishing lore at that time included the secret of dipping worms in licorice-flavored extract (anise) to improve their tastiness to fish. I had picked up that tip from an ancient fisherman whom I had encountered on a solo expedition to the stocked ponds near our southern California home. I'm sure it gave the old codger something to laugh about for days, but I dutifully received such valuable information and went to the nearby store to buy a bottle of the stuff. I carefully explained the tip to my brother and amazingly, we actually caught a fish or two on worms that died a happy death by drowning in anise (my brother still says he remembers the anise trick fondly). In addition to my stocked pond experiences, I had experimented a couple times with a fly fishing rig during my days at college. Never caught anything, mind you, but did some experimenting that convinced me I would have much better luck with conventional tackle. So, when I received an invite to go fishing a few months after my arrival in Northern Michigan, I had no misgivings about the possibility of success, but the expedition offered an opportunity to get out of the house and inhale the sweet smell of the nearby pine forests. The evening I got the invitation, I was in the corner of the room nearest the door at a mandatory social event and wondering how I could gracefully slip out. I noticed a fellow sufferer standing a few feet away. He introduced himself as Tony and I still can't remember how the topic of fishing came up. He was a big, friendly, bear of a man and had been fishing in the local area a couple of times. He was looking for company the following weekend to scout out a couple of fishing spots he had heard about. He would drive and all I needed to bring was my fishing tackle and some bug repellent. The next day I went to the local Kmart and bought a fishing license. My old bluegill rig did not seem adequate for trout fishing so I also picked up a sizeable Mitchell 300 fishing reel and matching rod. Figuring the heavier the line, the better, I threw in a hundred yards of 14-pound test line. I didn't really think I would catch a fish that big, but it seemed like the heavier line might come in handy, just in case something significant came around. In addition, I picked out some small brass swivels, some number 10 hooks, and some split shot. I also found a couple of impressive looking silver spoons that might come in handy. Michigan fish were probably more selective than stocked fish, so it would not hurt to have some backup for worms! I thought about getting some kind of fishing vest or pack to carry my tackle. However, I had an old field jacket that would probably do the trick. The pile of stuff I had picked out seemed like way too much for the few times I would probably use it, but maybe the trip would go well and I would get additional use out of the stuff.

Saturday did not come soon enough and Tony arrived at my house in an old beat up rust-colored station wagon at sunup. Since my arrival in Michigan, I had taken a few trips into town, but had not investigated the back roads of the local forests. We soon cleared the outskirts of the military base where I lived and headed north on the main highway towards Canada. After a few miles, we turned west on US 2 and quickly left any sign of civilization, other than the occasional car heading in the opposite direction. The scrub pine forest and marshy lowlands on both sides of the highway were so thick you could not see more than a few feet into the interior. Tony explained that our destination was Whitefish Bay on the southern shore of Lake Superior. He had made a couple of earlier trips into the area and noticed several streams that ran inland from Lake Superior. He felt that we might be able to find some trout there even though it was mid-June. The steelhead run had ended the preceding month, but he had heard that the local streams still held some nice brook trout and small rainbows. We passed an abandoned air force Bomarc missile site near the small town of Raco. The "town" itself was nothing more than a sign announcing 60 inhabitants (they must have been in the deep woods somewhere) and a general store that looked closed. Then we turned north again towards Dollar Settlement, a small enclave of Chippewa tribe members. I had asked Tony about his fishing hat on the way out of base. He was wearing a black, wide-brimmed hat with a blue and white beaded hatband. He explained that some members of the Native American community that lived in the fishing area did not like outsiders and he said, "the hat will keep down the arrow fire." I figured that was unlikely since he was a six foot four inches tall, blond, blue-eyed Norwegian, but any extra insurance had to be good. Just a few weeks before, the newspaper spoke of locals firing on DNR agents who were removing illegal seine nets from the bay. No one was hurt, but tempers were high in the Indian community. As we passed through the few scattered houses of Dollar Settlement, I didn't see anyone who would cause us trouble, and noted that the village looked just like any number of small towns we had passed on the road. The exception was a large circular collection of telephone poles in the center of the village. Tony explained that the purpose of this arrangement was to hang up gill nets to dry when not in use. However, the subject nets were not in sight and probably in use on nearby Lake Superior.

The paved road ended at the Lake Superior shoreline and a small country store. We stopped for gas and collected a huge pile of snacks. There were cokes, potato chips, fruit pies, cookies, and any number of other less than nutritional foods. Tony explained that we had to have a sufficient pile of food to endure the long journey ahead through the Forest Primeval, whatever that was. He asked the storekeeper about local fishing success and was encouraged by the shop owner who said he had heard of a few fish caught in the nearby streams. We loaded our pile of goodies into the car and headed west from the store along the shoreline. The paved road turned to gravel after a couple of miles and glimpses of the lake shore could be seen through the trees on the right. On the left, the pine forest was as dense as it had been for the past twenty miles. We passed an occasional cabin and the silence of the woods was only broken by the steady click of gravel against the bottom of the car. I looked behind us and a thick cloud of dust obscured our passage and anyone who might be following. After a few miles, Tony slowed and pulled off the road near a sign that announced 'Pendill's Creek National Fish Hatchery'. He explained that sometimes a few fish escaped from the hatchery and remained in the feeder stream that ran downstream to Lake Superior. We parked in a small dirt parking lot near the hatchery and crossed a crudely constructed wooden bridge that led to the shoreline. Ahead, the forest gave way to a wide expanse of sandy beach, about ten yards deep. The view was breathtaking and we could see for miles in either direction along the shore of Whitefish Bay. As we walked along shoreline towards the nearby creek, I could clearly see the lake bottom for several yards from shore. At the mouth of the creek the bottom was sandy and barren—any fish present would have easily been seen—but we only saw sand, water, forest and birds. Far out on the Lake, two freighters could be seen making their way east towards the Soo Locks. After a few moments to stretch our legs, we headed back to the car, climbed in, and headed west again along the shoreline road.

I enjoyed talking with Tony about his youth in the Minnesota north woods that was so different from my own experience. He seemed to have a wealth of knowledge about the woods and waters and I felt like I was with a genuine fishing guide. He said he liked fly-fishing the best and found some good populations of trout in the local mosquito infested beaver ponds. I had never seen a trout before, but the way everyone talked about them, they must be a great fish to catch. He was especially interested in "brookies". The way he described them, they sounded like minnows with the strength of a shark. The opportunity to catch little fish did not seem very exciting, but I was caught up in his enthusiasm. After another twenty miles down the gravel road, we took a slight turn to the left and soon the bright sun of the morning disappeared under heavy hardwood growth on both sides of the road that joined overhead. Tony announced that we had entered "the Forest Primeval" and chuckled. It was a dark and spooky drive down the hard-packed dirt road that was barely wide enough for one car. He had been there once before and seemed pleased by the mysterious nature of the place. I, on the other hand, was especially nervous that this was a great place for an ambush—being shot at by arrows or guns had the same results! Soon we passed over a little bridge with a sign that read 'Naomakong Creek'. Nearby, an overgrown entry path was marked with a sign that said 'Naomakong Hunting and Fishing Club'. The trail led a few feet to a nearby weatherworn cabin. Tony said he had heard that the place

was a popular hangout for industrial barons from the Detroit area, back in the 1930s and 40s. Grass and brush grew up in the lane to the cabin and it did not look like the property had been used in a long time. We drove on a few more miles and passed over a bridge with a sign that read 'Angadosh Creek'. Tony said he had caught a few fish there on flies. The tiny flow of water that was visible did not look like it would support much of a fish population and was so overgrown that I could not imagine how to fish it with regular tackle, much less fly-fishing. Clouds of mosquitoes were apparent over the little stream and I was hoping that we would not be about to try our luck here. I was relieved as Tony continued on down the road. After a few more miles, we passed over another little bridge with a sign that read 'Roxbury Creek'. Tony announced that this was our destination as he pulled the car over to the side of the road. He had not been to this particular creek before, but had noted its presence on his DNR map. He pulled a map from the stack of papers, cups and debris that littered the back seat, to show me our location. I could see that this was the last creek flowing into the southwestern arm of Whitefish Bay.

The warm, pine scent filled the air as we got out of the car and assembled our fishing gear. I noted that the hard-packed dirt road was really sand, and that the sand flowed down the road edge into the boggy pine forest that lined both sides of the road. Tony said we probably should get some worms for bait and retrieved a shovel from the back seat of the car. We looked around for a likely place to dig and finally found an area that looked more like dirt than sand. There were many tree and brush roots in the area and pushing the blade of the shovel into the ground was difficult. We did manage to turn over a few shovels of dirt, but after about fifteen minutes of work, our success was limited to about a dozen anemic-looking red worms. Tony produced two light-blue metal tobacco tins to contain the worms and we headed off through the woods. Once we left the road and entered the woods, the trees and brush were almost impenetrable. It was difficult to follow the stream and we soon split up to find our way towards an open bank of the nearby stream. I headed towards what I hoped was north and the mouth of the stream. A compass would have been handy, but I did not expect one would be needed. Staying clear of the deeper wet spots on the swampy forest floor was easy enough, but the proliferation of brush and snags in the dense undergrowth threatened to tear my hip waders at every step. I finally found a clear patch of woods that led to the edge of the stream. The stream was not much. As far as I could see, it was only about eight to ten feet across. Although the surface of the water was about three feet below the sharply cut banks, it looked like the stream was only two or three feet deep in most place. This certainly looked like a place for the small fierce brook trout that I had heard about, but my fishing equipment looked better suited to deep sea fishing that this small body of water. I walked along the bank testing worms in little riffles and the infrequent places where floating brush had clogged the river. Although I thought I saw little minnow-sized fish dart out from under logs in a couple of places, nothing else was going on besides the occasional call of nearby birds and the crunch of my boots through the undergrowth. I was walking along the stream, making an occasional attempt at fishing, and wondering where Tony was, when I suddenly saw something shoot past me heading downstream toward the Lake. My first impression was that a large torpedo had been launched in the stream and was expertly navigating its way through the twists and turns of the little stream. There was no noise associated with the vision—just fast movement. My heart leaped in my throat and I rushed downstream towards the retreating mirage, completely forgetting the possibility of tearing my waders or tripping over some deadfall. I could not follow far because brush soon blocked my path along the bank and I cut through the woods to the next section of stream. When my path intersected the stream again, I looked in both directions, breathing hard and wondering if I had imagined such a huge fish in such a small stream. Just as I was about to move on, I saw the torpedo approach from the right, followed by another one. I quickly dropped my line in the center of the stream and watched the fish approach. Even under water, the fish looked huge. I had no idea what they were, but they were clearly fish and looked three or four feet long. I looked for Tony, but he was nowhere in sight. I leaned out over the stream to get a better look at the approaching fish in the crystal-clear water and one immediately shot past my position and the other one abruptly headed back upstream. I pulled in my worm and followed, crashing through brush and keeping my eyes glued to the departing fish lest I lose sight of it. I came around one of the many bends and saw the fish enter a small but opaque stretch of rapids. I slowed my pace to sneak closer to the stretch of water without spooking the fish. I was unsuccessful. No less than four fish torpedoes shot out of the riffle and headed downstream while another one headed upstream! I tried to stay with the single fish as it moved upstream and soon came to an area of the creek that was a little deeper--maybe up to four feet. A short thick log protruded from the western bank into the middle of the stream. I had not seen the fish go upstream past the log. I was also fairly sure that it had not gone downstream past me. The wine-colored water was not very clear in this section of stream. Again, I stealthily approached the bank and log, this time on hands and knees. As the log and water came into close view, I saw the nose of a huge fish retract back under the log. The only thing on my mind was that this fish was mine! From its position under the log, the fish could not see me and if I could be quiet enough, I might be able to catch it.

I took the old, drowned (and probably dead) worm off my hook and fumbled in my coat pocket for the tobacco can and a high-quality stand-in worm. As I picked through the moss I had put in the can, I uncovered two miserable looking worms that were barely larger than the hook. They would have to do, however, because this fish was not going to stay put for long. I threaded the worm on the hook and leaned out to dangle the line in front of the upstream side of the log. My thought was that Tony would never believe my story about this fish unless I had material proof. I was not even sure my tackle could handle this monster, and it clearly was not one of the brook trout he had described. I bobbed the worm for several minutes in front of the log with no luck. I could see the nose of the fish occasionally as he finned forward to hold his place in the current. He knew I was there and I knew he was there. It was a standoff. I could not see if my hook was going to the right place under the log and my concern for stealth soon evaporated, as I stood right over the log and peered into the stream. My frustration was building when I heard a snapping twig and turned to see Tony standing about ten feet away drawing on a pipe.

"Whatcha doin'," he said. I quickly explained what I had seen and he listened closely and nodded at each point. He approached the log and looked at the front side and then the back side. He said he wanted to try something and set his fishing pole against a tree. He went down on his knees by the log, set his pipe off to the side, and rolled up his shirtsleeve as I watched with curiosity. I didn't know what he was up to, but his knowledge of fishing in the north woods seemed comprehensive. He put his face close to the water near the downstream side of the log and slowly put his arm into the water. Deeper and deeper he went until his arm was wet up past his elbow, including his rolled-up shirtsleeve. Then, so quickly that I jumped, he yanked his hand out of the water holding a huge, bucking fish by the tail. He rolled back from the water as the fish slipped from his grasp and flopped on the forest floor. We both pounced on it and pushed/kicked it away from the stream that seemed to be its intended destination. The tension of the moment evaporated as the fish was safely secured and we both burst out laughing. When we were finally able to stop laughing, he explained that the fish was a steelhead trout. He took out a pocket-sized fish scale and measured it at 26 inches and six pounds. I had no idea such huge fish were found in such small streams. He said he didn't either. We cleaned the fish and carried it back to the car. He put it in a plastic cooler and we went back to look for more of these huge fish. Although we looked for another half hour, the monster fish were gone. Tony thought that they had come in at night to feed and headed back out into the Lake at first light to get away from predators like us. In any case, the fishing trip was done. On the way home, Tony explained to me that his technique was called noodling and used in southern states to catch catfish. He had read about it in a fishing magazine and had always wanted to try it. Down south, noodlers reach into the water under banks to grab sleeping catfish. The trick is to not grab anything else—like a water moccasin or alligator gar. Tony also said that fish in the salmon/steelhead family have a fixed tail structure, unlike other fish, that allows you to grab the fish in front of the tail and hold on despite the slippery skin. He read that in a book too. What he was unprepared for was the need for a firm grip to secure a solid piece of muscle that is bucking and wiggling to get out of your grasp. However, we had our fish and one fish makes a successful trip. That trip began a series of adventures that lasted eight years. Little did I know that many odd and unusual fishing adventures would follow.

Although Roxbury Creek was not one of our frequent fishing destinations, other Lake Superior streams were. In particular, Pendills Creek became the site of many odd fishing experiences and occasionally, as my old friend Keith would say, many limits were taken. On one particular trip to Pendills Creek, we arrived shortly after sunup and began the walk down the bank from the little dirt parking lot to see if any fish were in the river. This stream, like most on Lake Superior was fairly shallow and narrow. Features on the sandy bottom stand out clearly in the morning light. We immediately saw four or five large steelhead moving rapidly downstream and went our separate ways to try our luck. Although I did catch one fish of about three pounds after a few minutes of casting, the fish were easily spooked and soon headed downstream to the Lake. Tony and I rejoined to consider our options now that the morning was half gone and fishing appeared over at Pendills. We thought to take one last look at a couple of deeper holes and undercut banks on the stream to see if any fish remained. We walked the stream's edge for about an hour with no luck. It appeared that all good little fishies had made their way home to the big water. At the edge of the woods, on the inside of the last bend in the stream before the parking area, a very large log protrudes from the bank to about twelve feet from shore. The current here has under- cut the log and bank to a depth of about seven feet. Tony thought that maybe a fish would hide there and carefully approached the log to scan for signs of movement. I was ready to move on, but waited patiently while Tony slowly examined the log and nearby water. He acted like he saw something under the log, but when he got down on bended knee to take a closer look under the log I was certain it was for theatrical value. I was fairly sure he was playing with me, but he had jerked a fish out from under such a log on an earlier trip and I was not sure what he was up to. With this mindset, who was I to question his motives when from his kneeling position he looked at me and quietly told me to remove the fishing lure from the end of my line. He said to leave the snap swivel on and hand the end of the line to him. His serious, no-nonsense manner did not leave room for questions or delay. I removed the two thirds ounce blue and silver Cleo and handed the end of the line to him. He asked me to give him some slack. I did as he asked. Then, with the end of my line in his hand he submerged his arm near the back edge of the log and began feeling around. He announced, "Get ready!" I had no idea for what. He suddenly jumped up with a splash of water, and my line took off from under the log with the reel drag buzzing in protest. Up ahead, in the clear Pendills current, I could see a sizeable fish heading downstream towards the lake. I tightened the drag slightly and began to play the fish. It was no contest, because other than the log, there was no place for the fish to hide and it was unlikely that the 14-pound test line could be severed. After about five minutes, a nice silver steelhead trout of about eight pounds was on the bank. My line was not in the fish's mouth. My swivel was attached to a #3 Mepps spinner that was firmly embedded in the trout's dorsal fin. We laughed about that one a

while. Tony explained that he thought I needed a little excitement and he could clearly see the fishing lure embedded in the fish under the log. He was not able to close the swivel, but it somehow held until the fish was on the bank. Although not the most ethical or legal way to catch a fish, it provided a memorable moment in Pendills fishing.

One evening in early fall, we came across an elderly Native American man who was fishing from the bank of Pendills by a small fire. He had a nice stringer of large trout that he had taken using fresh spawn for bait. He explained that trout come into the stream after dark to avoid exposure to predators in the clear, shallow water. The fish usually left the stream before full daylight. He said his best luck at fishing was usually around midnight. I was surprised that a tribe elder would share such information, but he must have noticed Tony's hat and felt great sympathy—probably for me. We decided to come back and try this expert advice. We headed out to Pendills around 10 pm the next night and arrived to a nearly empty parking lot. There was one other car parked there, but no sign of a campfire or our friendly Chippewa angler. We felt our way down the path to the lake in the dark. As we approached the mouth of Pendills Creek, we could see two human shapes about thirty feet offshore in the dim moonlight. The hiss of outgoing line and splash of fishing lures betrayed the shapes as fellow fishermen. We waded out into the lake a respectable distance from the other two anglers. I shuffled my feet forward on the sandy bottom to sense any obstructions that might cause me to fall. I had no cause for concern, however, as the bottom was smooth, hard packed sand and the drop-off from shore was very gradual. We were able to move out a good fifty or sixty feet from shore before the water neared the tops of our hip waders. I could feel the freezing cold of the water through my insulated waders—cold enough to make the 35-degree evening air feel warm. The surface was glassy smooth and not a breath of wind stirred. The only sound was the whir of cranked fishing reels and the occasional plop of a descending lure. I held the pole with a gloved right hand and used my bare left hand to feel for the slight line tug that indicated an interested fish. I had to frequently cycle my bare hand into my coat pocket to get relief from the penetrating cold. Time passed slowly and the moderate cloud cover overhead partially screened a sky bright with stars and a harvest moon. I was pulled out of my reverie by the sound of someone's reel drag squealing in response to the pull of a fish and one of the silent shapes announced "fish on!" As a gesture of fishing etiquette, the other fishermen present reeled in the lines so as not to interfere with the action. There were no splashes by fish or angler, and the quiet remained intact save for the occasional buzz of reel drag or the whir of retrieved fishing line. Finally, it appeared that the fish had tired and the angler's partner turned on a flashlight in preparation to net the fish. Big mistake! As soon as the light hit the fish, it surged mightily and with a renewed shriek of the fishing reel, headed back out from shore. The angler told his partner to shut the damn light off and net the fish in the dark. Soon the fish tired and this time the fish was finally netted. We walked in to shore with the pair to see what was caught. It was a nice lake trout of about five pounds. I had not seen a lake trout before, and it looked much like steelhead we had previously taken, only darker. I was grateful for the excuse to escape the cold water and stayed on shore until feeling returned to my numb legs. The cold water was merciless, but we came to fish. I waded back into the lake and began casting again. Within minutes, there was a sharp tug on my line and I had a nice sized fish on. Seconds later, as I played the fish, I could see that Tony also had hooked one. Tony's fish broke off, but I landed mine by just backing onto shore and dragging the fish out of the water. As most other anglers probably know, this is not an especially good technique. As soon as the fish was

half way out of the water, it began flopping and the lure fell out of its mouth. I dropped the pole and jumped into the shallows on my knees to wrestle and shove the big fish up on dry land before it could escape. Luckily, the deed was quickly done and the fish was mine. Before the night was done, I landed two more lake trout and Tony caught one too. Then the clouds parted completely and the moon shone bright on the water. Fishing was over for the night as the school fled the shallows for deeper water. It was time to get back on shore and warm up. We spoke with the other two fishermen who said they had been doing the midnight thing for a couple of years with periodic success. They said that we should have been there the week before. Given our success of the evening, we listened in wonder about even better fishing success. After some final conversation, we all headed to our cars with the nights catch. It was 2 am and the workday would start in only a few hours.

From noodling to night fishing, every trip to Pendills seemed to offer the promise of a new experience. One evening in the fall moonlight, my friend Keith and I chased large steelhead up and down the shallow waters with long handled fishing nets for a half hour but only succeeded in getting wet. When we gave up and fished off the mouth with shiny silver lures, we each caught nice fish. There is surely a lesson there somewhere. During another trip to Pendills, in the dead of winter, we came across a group of fishermen on the thick ice surface just off the mouth. One member of the group was an old trapper named Henry, who invited us to try his spearing tent. We spent an hour on the cold ice, spearing large herring with lead-weighted fishgigs in fifteen feet of water and loving every minute of it. In the spring, just after the ice goes out from the shore, we found that we could float a canoe just off the mouth of the creek and catch a fine limit of jack salmon at dawn. I have fished in many bodies of water over the years, but Pendills Creek is the setting for some of my more memorable trips. Of course, there was the time on Munuscong Bay when I caught a pike with a girth larger that the six-inch hole I had drilled through the ice. Then there was the 50-inch alligator gar that I caught in a pocket of the Platte River on eight-pound test line. However, those are stories for another time.

Boat Fishin'

In the first place, I didn't want to buy a boat. Fishing from the river bank worked just fine and at that time my cash reserves were barely sufficient to afford a fishing license and a couple of new lures each season. But I had been softened up by a couple of boat rental adventures on Munuscong Bay with a friend during which a few decent sized fish had been caught, after endless hours of trolling. So, when my neighbor Keith suggested that we check out a "boat for sale" ad in the paper, I went along for the ride. It was just a couple of miles from where we lived to the rural house of a farmer named "J. White" who placed the ad in the local paper. We found the correct mailbox on a country road and bounced down the muddy driveway to a small two-story clapboard farmhouse with a patchy weed-covered yard that had not been attended to in some time. There was a small tricycle and a number of other toys near the back step and I could hear the loud barking of several dogs nearby. I was reluctant to leave the car and become the victim of some rabid dog, but after a few moments, it seemed that the coast was clear and we got out. When Keith knocked on the back door the frenzied barking of a pack of wild dogs began anew from somewhere inside the house. The man who came to the door squeezed outside while holding back several dogs of various sizes that seemed to have an interest in devouring anything or anyone they might encounter. Farmer White was a middle-aged fellow who explained that he had come on hard times and wished he didn't have to sell his boat and the few other things he had recently put up for sale. He led us out behind his house to a weather beaten old barn where a dingy looking metal rowboat sat on a rusty trailer. The ancient eighteen horsepower motor on the back of the boat looked like it had seen some hard use. While I examined the boat for holes and terminal injuries, Keith haggled with the farmer. The farmer said that although he had advertised the boat at $600 it was worth much more. He said it pained him greatly, but since we looked like a couple of descent guys he could let it go for around $550. Keith said that it looked like a great boat and he really wanted to buy it, but we only had $350. The farmer laughed long and hard. Even I could tell it was a forced laugh. I think he was actually angry. He said that there was no way he would ever let the boat go for less than $550. Keith said he was sorry we didn't have more money (he actually looked sorry!) but that he would leave his name and phone number with the farmer in case he changed his mind. The farmer said that his price was firm, but he took the piece of paper with the phone number.

On the way home we talked about what a great buy the boat would have been and how we could have put it to good use. We also talked about going fishing at a local hot spot the next weekend. We did not want to spend money for a boat rental, so it looked like we would be fishing on foot. It was a nice summer day and plans for the upcoming expedition were soon formed. The White farm and the fishing boat were quickly forgotten. Three days later, Keith stopped by my house to say the farmer had called and although the farmer hated to do it, he needed the money and would take our offer. We were very excited and immediately started making plans for all the great fishing adventures ahead. We went to the White farm that afternoon, money changed hands, and we headed home with our new boat.

Keith already had a trailer hitch on his car and I soon bought one for my truck so that either of us could tow the boat. The first order of business was to determine how we would share ownership. Since we usually fished together, boat usage was not a concern. Within a few minutes we struck on the plan that one owner could buy the other one out for the price of the original $175 share if we ever decided to dissolve the partnership. That was it. No paper was required and the deal was done. Since we lived next to each other the boat sat on the lawn between our houses, allowing each of us to bask in our new status as boat owners, a few rungs up the social ladder.

Work on upgrading the boat began immediately. The trailer was sanded and spray painted with a couple of coats of primer, followed by a coat of some paint that was left over from a duck blind painting project. When finished, we still had a couple of cans of spray paint left, so we painted the boat the same color. I supposed pea green was not the most attractive color, but we already had the paint and the color might work well if we decided to use the boat for a hunting platform. I was starting to think about many other possibilities for this boat. We could use it as a floating duck blind or as transport to islands in the river for camping or hunting. We could take our kids for boat rides and use the boat to learn how to water ski. Well, maybe some of the ideas were not well thought out yet, but the value of this boat would easily outweigh any complaints we might get from the home front about the cost. I mean, anyone could see that this boat was a bargain that should offset the somewhat less economical decision that Keith and I had made the previous winter to build an ice fishing shanty. That too was a great bargain, but many of our friends probably did not see it as such. It was true that we used so much wood

to build it that the lumber yard asked us if we wanted to open an account. And the shanty weighed as much as a small car, needed a tractor trailer to be moved to the lake, and was eventually turned into a tool shed. But all of that didn't detract from the ice shanty's potential. And the boat presented even more possibilities.

Keith had done repair work on small motors and trailers so he replaced and greased the wheel bearings and tuned up the old blue Evinrude motor. He registered the trailer and boat with the state fish and game commission and we were ready for action. Only one thing remained…a name. We talked about using our last names together in some way and, in the process, came up with "the Facker". We both laughed and knew immediately that was just right. The "Old Facker" was appropriately christened with a couple of sloshes from cans of Coors beer that afternoon (at the time Coors was not locally available, and using it for other than drinking was considered a great sin by many!). Although the name raised a few eyebrows, it was soon accepted by all.

Over the next several weekends we frequently took our boat to Munuscong Bay, a shallow body of water about 20 miles from where we lived. Although the bay averaged only ten feet deep and the water was very muddy, we regularly caught limits of walleye, bass, and northern pike. The only apparent setback in the operation of our new boat was that the motor would quit running several times during each trip...usually when we were no less than two or three miles from the boat dock. When that happened, Keith would remove the motor cover and tinker with the various misbehaving components while I passed the time examining the contents of my tackle box or taking a nap and hoping to not wake up and find that we had floated out to the main steamship channel. After endless minutes of tinkering and a few strong obscenities, Keith would usually get the cranky motor back in operation and we would once again be trolling across the more productive parts of the bay. There were a couple of instances, however, when the only option was to row back to the dock and take the motor home for more detailed repairs. If you were able to fish during those times it wasn't too bad (although the splashing of the oars probably scared every fish away for several hundred yards). If you were the rower, however, there was no joy in the situation. It takes a lot of strokes to travel a couple of miles.

On one of the first weekends that summer we planned a fishing trip on the St. Mary's River. That 75-mile long waterway flows along the Canadian border and connects Lake Superior and Lake Huron. Although much of the river is only a couple of hundred yards wide, the main channel is deep enough to serve the 1,000-foot long ore carriers that ply the Great Lakes. The river is big, fast moving water, but it is common to see small boats on its surrounding bays and tributaries so we figured the Facker would serve us well there. We awoke to a cool, foggy morning with visibility of only a couple of car lengths. After some discussion about whether or not it was too foggy to travel, the need to go fishing won out and we loaded our gear and headed out to the highway that would take us towards Sault Ste. Marie and the river, some 25-miles away. The fog we encountered on the way to town was really bad and we crawled along the highway at thirty or thirty- five miles per hour with three sets of eyes glued to the road ahead, expecting to get rammed from the front or the rear at any moment. With great good fortune we managed to find the correct off ramp and eventually the boat launch site after a grueling hour and a half drive. The launch site backwater area is protected from the main river current by two small islands that are covered with a thick screen of brush and small trees. The sun began to rise as we put the boat into the water and loaded equipment and snacks on board. At least the sun seemed to rise because it got somewhat lighter, but the fog got even thicker and the visibility was soon down to ten or fifteen feet. But we would not be denied our expedition by a little fog. Keith, as the most experienced boater of our group, took the position he would occupy on most of our trips, at the back with the motor. I climbed into the middle, and Tony pushed us off from shore and jumped in. The motor was very difficult to start and it looked like our expedition would be over before we could leave the launch area. I reached for the oars to row us back in, but after several starter-cord pulls and a little coaxing from Keith, the motor finally fired up with a blue gray cloud of smoke and began to purr its readiness to get us out to the fishing grounds. Keith put the motor in reverse to back us further away from the launch ramp and then put the motor into to forward gear with a resounding clunk. The cold fog quickly enveloped us as we idled along and I could barely see the shore of the nearest island, only ten or fifteen feet to our left. I pulled my hands into the sleeves of my field jacket and hunkered down in the boat, facing rearward into the gloom. Gingerly and ever so slowly, Keith guided the boat towards a channel somewhere ahead between the two islands that led to the main river. I could occasionally see the rough form of trees on the nearby bank and soon could see banks on both sides as we entered the narrow cut. I turned forward to watch for an opening that would indicate we were entering the main channel.

The St. Mary's River near our launch point is about a couple hundred yards across and frequented by Great Lakes freighters that are up to a thousand feet long and fifty to sixty feet wide. Although these ships are restricted to a speed of less than ten knots while in the river system, they put out a significant wake and present a navigation hazard to anyone foolish enough to maneuver a small boat nearby. We had heard the story of a small cabin cruiser that had been flipped by such a wake and sunk so fast that the owners barely had time to jump overboard and swim to shore. With this story in mind, we motored blindly along the southern bank of the river, and listened for foghorns or wave action that would indicate the passage of a large vessel. Our intention was to go across the river into a large pocket of water on the north side of the river known as Georgian Bay, just down from our launch point. Keith had heard from one of his fishing buddies that small mouth bass were currently spawning there. In addition, the latest Michigan Fishing report had advised that "many limits" were recently caught in that very area. Although state fishing reports were notoriously well out of date, we still considered them a good source of information. We idled along the south shore of the big river hoping for a view of the far bank, but the fog didn't lift. After a short discussion we decided to turn towards a direction that we believed to be north and head directly across the river to some islands near the main freighter channel. Our plan was simple, motor across at slow speed and listen carefully for any approaching ship traffic. So, with the memory of the sunken cabin cruiser on our minds, and the bright promise of hallowed fishing grounds as a reward, we started across. Every wake and splash in the water sounded like approaching doom. The crossing seemed to take an eternity. Finally, Keith could not stand the suspense of wondering if a big lake freighter was approaching and gunned the engine to maximum speed which was probably about eight knots with all of our combined weight and gear on board. And if not for Tony's yell, we would have rammed the bank of an island on the far side, about 50 feet later. Almost immediately there came the blast of a foghorn so near that we nearly jumped overboard. Out of the gloom passed one of the larger ore carriers, not 100 feet away. As our boat rocked gently in the wake of the passing freighter, we could see the name on the stern. It was the Edmund Fitzgerald out of Duluth, a boat that would become famous two years later for being sunk in a Lake Superior storm with the loss of all hands. We looked at each other in wide-eyed shock and shook our heads. We were surely either the craziest or the most determined fishermen on the river that day!

We were not exactly sure where we were on the river. Although we had seen this area a few times from rented boats, in the dense fog nothing seemed where it should be. We decided to slowly troll along a while keeping the nearby northern shore in sight. That would keep us from ending up in the main steamer channel again. When the fog finally lifted and we could see where we were going, we would motor off to fish in Georgian Bay. All eyes were on the proximity of the nearby shore and little attention was paid to trailing fishing lines. It was another hour before the fog began to lift. Visibility eventually went up to about 100 feet and we could see that we were near a couple of small narrow islands at the mouth of Georgian Bay, each about a hundred yards long and about forty or fifty feet in width. In the clear water, we could see the tops of thick weed beds about fifteen feet beneath the surface and decided to drop anchor about halfway between the two islands. Tony and I were using red and white three-inch daredevil lures and Keith was trying a shiny blue and silver spoon. After a few casts Tony called our attention to a dark, torpedo like shape that was following his line towards the boat. As he reeled in his line, the shape continued under the boat and out the other side. It looked like a really big fish. He cast again and suddenly his fishing pole bent with the weight of a striking fish. From the surging runs it began to make we thought it might be a northern pike of some size. We stopped and watched as he played the fish to the boat. Keith got out the net and soon we were examining a nice northern pike of about six pounds. We congratulated ourselves for our quick success and all began to fish in earnest. Soon I also caught a nice pike. Keith netted that one. Then Tony and I both had a fish on the line. Keith threw the net forward and said he had enough of assisting. He came to fish and we could net our own. We all laughed and the business of fishing began in earnest. Within a half hour we had boated six pike, the smallest about three pounds and the largest, a whopping ten pounds and over two feet long. We began to toy with the fish. Tony put on a fishing fly that resembled a minnow. Soon it was torn to shreds by an attacking pike. Anything that was red or resembled a minnow seemed to work. In the clear water, we watched as fish after fish glided beneath the boat on the way to a strike one of our lures. The fog, the dampness, Georgian Bay, conversation, nearby lake freighters, food, all were forgotten in the pursuit of fish. And then it ended almost as fast as it begun. We looked at our watches and somehow three hours had passed since we launched the boat. The fog had cleared so that we could see both shores and 14 nice fish on two stringers struggled and bounced against the side of the boat. It was time to go.

We proudly returned home as expert sportsmen who had defeated long odds to catch so many fish. Pictures were taken with our trusty boat in the background, and neighborhood children gathered in awe to stare at the toothy grins of huge pike. Word quickly went out around the neighborhood that fresh fish were available at Keith's house and we began to prepare about 30 pounds of fish filets on the picnic table in his back yard. A long line of neighbors soon formed to get their share of our catch and we saved out a few filets for ourselves. Our catch this day was northern pike, which are less prized due to their large number of bones, but it was hard to complain about success. As the last of the neighbors departed with their fish, we began discussing our next expedition. We talked about all the things we would do better and who would check the fog forecast and where the best fishing places were and how we would use our results to convince the spouses what a fine thing it would be to go out again soon. Our egos grew in the belief that our skill as providers would secure our family approval for many future fishing expeditions.

A few weeks later I was trying to organize another fishing trip, but Tony and Keith had to work. Tony asked if would take his visiting father-in-law and teenaged brother-in-law fishing. I figured I could handle this chore and made sure I had enough fishing gear and lunch fixings for the three of us. I hooked up the Facker, made sure the boat motor gas tank was full and loaded all the rest of the gear into the truck. I picked up the relatives at Tony's house and my first impression was that they probably had never been fishing before. They each had on slacks and button down collared shirt. I was wondering what kind of fishing they thought we would be doing. The father-in-law's gray hair was cut in a 1950s style flat top and he was smoking an oversized pipe that looked like it had previously belonged to Sherlock Holmes. He squinted at me through oversized bifocals, and I was reminded of a college professor who used to scrutinize my every move in class. The equally geeky kid brother immediately began asking a million questions and pawing through the fishing gear in the back of my truck. This was going to take a little extra patience on my part and would cost Tony big time.

On the drive to the bay the father-in-law talked about how beautiful the forest was. At least he had that right. Then he started asking questions about how safe the boat was and whether or not the weather would be good. He wanted to know if I had ever run the boat by myself and how far from town was the place where we would be fishing. I assured him that it was going to be a great day and we would have a great time. He grunted reluctant acceptance of my assessment. The brother started asking more questions, including whether we were almost there yet. I began wondering how hard it would be for him to accidentally fall overboard once we were on the water.

We arrived at the boat launch and the other two travelers stood by while I backed the boat down the gravel ramp into the muddy water, floated it off of the trailer, and tied it up to a rusty old boat cleat on the nearby dock. After parking the truck, I helped my companions into the boat, and was pleased that the motor started on the first pull. It had not done that before. I should have been suspicious, but why question success when a plan seems to be coming together. Once clear of the dock and marina area, I opened up the motor and the boat settled into a nice plane across the mirror-surfaced, muddy water. As I gazed back over the spreading boat wake, the dock and marina quickly faded into the distance. We continued out into the bay, and I scanned ahead for likely areas to fish.

Usually there are a couple of dozen boats working the bay, but today there was only one other boat trolling near the pine covered island in the middle of the bay. Seeing no need to disturb that fisherman, I angled the boat towards the northwestern shore of the bay, some three miles away. It was certainly a gorgeous day. The deep blue sky and scattered cumulus clouds were like something out of a Simpson's cartoon and the temperature was somewhere in the mid-seventies. On top of that, the noise of the boat motor prevented the kid brother from asking more dumb questions. I have heard that there is no such thing as a dumb question, but whoever made up that saying had not met this kid. He tried pestering me a couple of times as we rode across the bay, but I made it clear I could not hear him and he finally gave up. I was looking forward to a perfect day and thinking "look out fish, here we come!"

When we were about a hundred yards from the far shore, I slowed to trolling speed and helped my companions rig their fishing lures. We were using night crawler harnesses for bait. This lure includes a small silver spinner and a few colored beads. Behind that, a large worm can be stretched out on three hooks that are sequenced in tandem, about three inches apart. Once the other two had their lines in the water, I made my cast and we began trolling along the shore. The father-in-law soon caught a nice walleye and I think my stock as a fishing guide went up immediately. After landing the fish, he put another worm on this lure and resumed fishing. We trolled for another hour with the motor softly putting along and generating a thin oily cloud of exhaust that hung over the water to mark our passing. Time went by with a silence that was only interrupted by the occasional cry of a seagull or the whir of fishing line being cast. Occasionally I had to turn the boat around when one or the other of my guests managed to snag their hooks on the bottom. This was not an unusual occurrence in these shallow waters as we wanted to put our lures near the bottom where the fish were most likely to be in such warm weather. After a couple of hours, I passed out sandwiches and drinks. We continued to troll and shortly after eating lunch the motor started running rough. And then it quit abruptly. I was not concerned, because this had happened before and usually meant that the motor needed to be run at a higher speed for a few minutes to burn off excess carbon buildup on the spark plugs. I tried several pulls to get the motor restarted but with no luck. I thought about pulling the spark plugs to check them out, but had not brought any tools. This was not looking good.

After about fifteen minutes of trying to get the motor running again, it became apparent that my efforts would not be successful. I told the other two we would have to row back to the dock, some two miles distant. I changed places with the brother so that I would be in the middle rowing position near the oarlocks and positioned the oars for the long row towards shore. After a few minutes of rowing I had worked up a good sweat and the brother began to complain that he hadn't caught a fish and wanted to keep fishing. I explained that if the wind came up it could blow us away from shore into the main steamship channel so we needed to keep moving towards the dock. I told him he could troll while I rowed in. He cast his line while his father filled a pipe and began to smoke. The brother soon hooked the bottom of the lake and I had to turn the boat around and go back about a hundred feet to retrieve his lure. I began rowing towards the dock again. After two more course reversals to retrieve snagged lines, I told him if he hooked the bottom again, we would have to cut the line rather than turn around. At that point he reeled in his line and stowed his fishing gear, grumbling all the while. After a half hour of rowing a number of blisters began forming on my hands. Just when I was considering asking one of the others to row, I saw a boat approaching from the direction of the island in the middle of the bay. When it got close, the fisherman asked if we had a problem. We were saved! I explained our situation and he threw us a line. The tow to the dock was uneventful and I helped my companions out of the boat. We noted a freshening breeze that roiled the surface of the water as I backed the trailer down the launch ramp and then quickly pulled the boat onboard. We loaded our gear into the truck and as we headed down the gravel path towards the highway and home we could see a building thunderhead over the western shore of the bay. We had gotten off the water just in time. It was very quiet in the truck as we made the short drive home and I dropped off the visiting fishermen at my friend's house. I parked the boat in the side yard for Keith to fix when he got home from work. I was pretty worn out by the trip and felt that it would be some time before I volunteered to take anyone's relatives fishing again. The next day, after talking with Keith about the problems I had had with the boat, I decided to buy a new 15 horsepower motor. It was a lot of money, but this would be the last time we would have engine trouble with the Facker.

We decided that our next trip would be to another legendary fishing spot that we had heard about, the dangerous St. Mary's rapids. Almost every fisherman we knew had heard about catching huge trout in the rapids, but no one seemed to know anyone who had tried it. We had also heard reports that the rapids had contributed to several overturned boats and drowned fishermen in years past, but we figured those incidents occurred around the turn of the century when people were not as smart as we were. In any case, we had a good boat and would approach the whole thing very scientifically. The head of the St Mary's River is about two miles wide and just below the International Bridge which links the US and Canadian border entry points. To the west of the bridge is Whitefish

Bay at the eastern end of Lake Superior. Just to the east of the bridge, on the American side of the river, are four locks which lift and lower ships the twenty feet of height that separates Lake Superior from the St. Mary's River system. On the Canadian side of the river are two smaller locks that serve the same purpose. In between the two lock systems are the St Mary's rapids, a mile-long stretch of plunging, turbulent water that is expressly avoided by all traffic on the river. It was this stretch of section of the river that was reported to hold large numbers of huge trout and was our destination for the expedition.

We set off for the river a couple of hours before sunup and we very happy that there was no fog to deal with that morning. The drive into town passed quickly and soon our truck tires were crunching across the gravel parking area of the boat launch near Sugar Island. After using flashlights to load our gear, we quickly backed the trailer into the water, floated the boat off, and parked the truck and trailer. After a quick look to make sure all of our gear was in the boat, Keith got the motor going and we headed out into the dark. As we entered the main river channel, Keith brought the motor up to full speed and the chill of the resulting breeze washed away any lingering sleepiness. I pulled my ball cap down tighter on my head so it would not blow overboard and lowered my profile to avoid occasional sheets of spray as the bow sliced through the small waves generated by a light breeze from the west. Although there was not a cloud in sight, the sky seemed filled to overflowing with stars in the pre-dawn darkness. As we headed further west I could see the lights of moving cars along both shorelines as the towns on both sides of the border began to come to life in anticipation of the day ahead. Soon we passed the big hydroelectric plant on the American shore and also lights at the floatplane base on the Canadian side. Further upriver, the American lock system began to come into view and Keith angled the

Facker away from the American shore towards the center of the river and the rapids ahead. I could see two huge lake freighters near the American locks. One was just entering the open lock gates, headed upriver, and another lingered in the center of the steamship channel, awaiting its turn in the lock. Behind us, the sky was growing lighter with the approaching dawn as Keith throttled down the boat about a hundred yards below the bottom of the rapids.

We let the boat float back down river as we rigged up out fishing poles with bright silver spoons that resembled the minnows we believed the trout would feed on. It seemed to me that the current here was as fast as the top speed of our boat which was about eight to ten knots. Up in the rapids the surface looked smooth, but I could also see a heavy rolling wave motion that looked to be two or more feet from trough to crest. At the very top of the rapids I could faintly make out spots of white foam where the water crested over submerged rocks. This looked very scary and I was wondering if we really knew what we were doing. About that time, Keith said "here we go" and throttled up the motor all the way as we charged up into the rapids. I laid my fishing pole down and held on the center board of the boat with both hands as we bucked and surged our way up into the turbulent current. The further we went, the worse the bucking got and at each dip of the bow, wave surges threatened to turn us into a submarine. I looked back at Keith who had a maniacal grin on his face…either that or a combination of sheer terror and intense concentration. Just when I was sure that we were on the edge of disaster and could go no further upriver without striking some large submerged rock, he put the motor in idle and our forward speed ended. In an instant we were racing back down river with the surging current. Keith used the motor as a rudder to keep the boat pointed up river and thereby avoid swamping as we cast our lures. We were moving down river at such a speed that I could not imagine any fish that could swim fast enough to catch the lures. As I took up the slack in my line, I could see chunks of granite the size of a house passing swiftly by, only eight or ten feet below the boat. At least I hoped they were that far down, because I could not tell for sure.

The sense of motion on the rapids was very subtle until you looked at the nearby southern shore. By now, the sun was just beginning to rise and brought the rocky embankment, fifty feet away, into stark relief. There was not another soul around to either witness our rapid passage or potential demise. It only took a couple of minutes for us to float from our perilous position near the top of the rapids to the bottom end and into relatively smoother water. We reeled in our lines and took a moment to consider how to safely try another run. One of our immediate concerns was the potential for snagging our lures on the bottom of the rapids. At our floating speed, we would either have our poles (and us) yanked out of the boat or we would have all the line stripped off of our reels. We decided that each of us would have a knife ready at hand and if we struck bottom we would immediately cut the line. Keith brought the motor up to full speed and we charged up into the rapids again.

This time we had a little bit better sense of the conditions and although it was still scary to press upriver into the bucking current we were marginally better prepared when Keith cut the motor. We cast our lures and almost at the same instant, Tony and I were both hooked up with what felt like sizeable fish. Down the rapids the boat flew and although we kept our lines taut we were unable to gain any ground on the fish. As we reached calmer waters, I tightened the drag on my reel a little bit and was sooner able to move the fish to the boat as Keith readied our net. Shortly, a nice two-pound silver trout lay in the bottom of the boat. It was soon joined by its twin as Tony landed his catch. Things were looking up and we soon forgot the apparent danger of our venture as we made another run up into the rapids. On one run the motor died just as we started our float from the top, but Keith did not panic and was able to quickly get it restarted so as to keep the bow pointed upriver. We made run after run up the rapids and I began to relax a little and take in the surrounding sights as we made our way back up the rapids each time. I saw a canoe with two fishermen working the slower, shallow waters to the north where gravel shoals marked the Canadian side of the rapids. To the west, tiny vehicles on the International Bridge upriver from us clearly stood out in the morning sunlight. I wondered if the people making that crossing could see us and if they wondered what we maniacs were doing dashing up and down the turbulent flow.

After about twenty runs we had eight nice trout on our stringer, each weighing about two to three pounds. The last few runs had not yielded a bite and we figured it was time for one more run. By now we were getting comfortable with the ride upriver, but this time it looked like Keith was trying to go farther up than we had been before and I started getting nervous. I yelled at him my concern but he only laughed and continued on. As the bow began surging even more violently than it had during past runs, I could see the top of a large boulder sticking above the surface only a dozen feet ahead and the erratic current was nudging the boat that way. I yelled at him to cut the forward motion, NOW! To my relief he did so and down river we went. We cast lines with the near bank whizzing by. About halfway down I heard Tony yell from the front of the boat and saw his pole snap down towards the water. This was no fish, he had snagged the bottom. The shriek of his drag filled the air as line was stripped from his reel at a desperate rate. He groped for his knife with one hand as he fought to hold on to his pole. He knocked the knife to the bottom of the boat and fought to maintain his balance as the boat rocked in the surging current. I leaned forward to retrieve the knife and lost my balance, falling off my seat into the bottom of the boat. Keith screamed at us to quit moving around. With all the rocking and our backward-speed I expected the boat to turn over at any instant. And then, just when I was sure we were goners, Tony's lure came free from the bottom on its own and we were moving into calm water. As Keith steered the boat out of the main current, my heart was beating like a jackhammer as I carefully got up from the bottom of the boat and resumed my position on the center board. Nobody said anything for a few moments. Then Keith said he thought he probably had enough fishing for the day. He got no arguments and we turned towards the launch site. The trip downriver was uneventful and we saw a number of other boats trolling their way up and down the river in the mid-morning sun. We loaded our gear up at the boat ramp and made a short stop for a hamburger on the way home. As we filleted the fish on the picnic table by my house, we quickly pronounced the trip a success, with no mention of any near disasters that had occurred. We had met the mighty rapids and caught several nice fish, and somehow that was all that was important.

We made other boat trips to the rapids over the next few years. The Facker also carried us on Lakes Superior, Michigan, and Huron as well as several rivers and smaller lakes. We even took the boat into Canada on one fishing expedition. It was at various times rigged with homemade downriggers for deep water fishing, outfitted with side panels to hunt ducks, loaded with lumber for transport to a distant duck blind, or burdened with bouncing children for family boat rides. In each of these incarnations, the boat served well and needed little maintenance save for an occasional washing out of accumulated mud, weeds, and the various odd and ends that result from heavy use as a fishing platform. Three years after our initial fishing trip, Keith moved to Nebraska and, as agreed, bought the boat from me for his share of the original purchase price. I kept my new motor and he kept the old one. I watched out my kitchen window as he towed the Facker from its parking place in our yard for the last time. I saw the Facker again several years later. It was collecting dust in an old barn at Keith's new house. I am not sure it had been used in many years.

There are still days when I am wandering along a shoreline and spot a small fishing boat working its way along far out in the water. The fishermen on board are quiet as they cast a line or reach down to find a new lure or select a handy beverage. I wonder if they are new to boat fishing or are motoring along in an old and trusted friend. I imagine that their boat motor sometimes acts up and they curse at it while deciding if it is time to sell their problems to someone else. Those are decisions you never have to make if you are walking the shore. As I make my way further upstream, I wonder if today's paper has any boats in the classified section....

Survival Training

The small convoy of cars, trucks, and vans made its way west in the early morning light, the crisp mountain air generating just enough chill to encourage the use of heaters. Highway service areas and other signs of civilization had become less frequent as we drove up from the valley floor on the highway into West Virginia. The chatter of the group of boy scouts in each car reflected excitement about the coming adventure while the adult drivers merely looked forward to a chance for relief from stresses of the work week. Every year the scouts had planned a survival-themed campout at one of the public campgrounds near our community. This spring, however, one of the fathers had offered the use of some remote mountain property for that purpose that was at least 20 miles from any sign of civilization. The adults had held meetings with the boys over the previous two weeks to discuss primitive camping and methods to find water and food. The scouts seemed eager to test their knowledge of survival skills in a 'real survival situation'. In the truck with me were Greg, a 16-year old who was designated as the youth leader for the event, and Robb, a 12-year old tenderfoot scout. Greg was a quiet teenager who was looked up to by all the younger boys and since most of the boys on this trip were fairly young, this was going to be a big test of his leadership.

Each scout could bring a sleeping bag, a canteen, a

pocket knife, a small first aid kit, matches, and an 8 foot by 8 f00t sheet of thin plastic to be used for a ground cloth or shelter construction. It was recommended that they bring a poncho or jacket in case of rain. There were boxes of food for the adults in the back of my truck as well as a large tent and other camping equipment. The adults intended to spend their weekend in a somewhat more comfortable fashion than the boys.

After a couple of hours, the lead vehicle in our convoy turned off the highway onto a sparsely graveled road that climbed steeply up a hillside dotted with clumps of wild flowers and small bushes. I slowed to put a little distance between my truck and the dust cloud generated by the vehicles I was following. After a short distance we entered an area of thick forest and the road leveled off somewhat. The chatter of the two boys abruptly ended as they peered through the windows hoping to catch a glimpse of any woodland critters. We continued into the hilly forest, slowing frequently as the narrow road twisted through shadowed stretches where I could occasionally see the vehicle ahead. There were few clear spaces beside the road, and those only provided a view of a few yards into the woods. After three or four miles the gravel ended and the road became rutted dirt that was overgrown with grass and weeds. It looked like it had been some time since anyone else had come this way.

Just about the time that I began to wonder how much further it was to the camp site, the road ended abruptly at a small clearing that provided just enough room for the vehicles in our convoy. Two of the vehicles had only come along to provide transportation and as soon as they unloaded their passengers, they turned around in the tight space and headed back down the mountain. I climbed down from my truck and moved a little way into the trees to stretch my legs and get the lay of the land. I could hear some distant birds calling, but the overall sense was one of quiet. The peaceful forest sounds were interrupted by the sounds of a dozen boys behind me who were milling around the cars, ready for some activity.

Harry, the adult who owned the property, said that it was a short hike into the camp site. We assigned boys to unload and help transport the adult camping equipment. Some of the boys groused about having to carry more than their own equipment, but soon we were ready to go. We formed up in a single file with Harry leading the way and headed north. The short distance ended up being a half mile, but we soon arrived at the location where the adults would camp. Two adults remained there and began to set up our tent while the other adults walked with the boys another quarter of a mile through the trees to a hillside that was designated as the survival camp location. The trees were less thick here, but there was a lot of downed timber that the boys could use to construct shelters. At the bottom of the hill was a small stream where the boys could get water and nearby there were plenty of rocks and bare ground where they could construct campfire rings. Greg, the boy leader, decided where the latrine would be located, well away from cooking and sleeping areas. After pointing out where they could fill their canteens, we showed the boys how to use water purification tablets, and reminded them how sick they would get if they forgot to do so. We told the boys to pair up for shelter construction and then we headed back to the adult campsite.

There was the smell of wood smoke in air as we arrived back at our camp and one of the adults had a coffee pot merrily bubbling away while he was starting to cook a late breakfast of eggs and bacon. The men had already set up our large field tent and the only camp chores that remained were to unpack our personal gear and to collect firewood, which we did while the cook finished up. Each of us then dished up a plate of food and found a place to enjoy the meal. We sat around talking and taking in the fresh pine smell of the forest for a couple of hours and by then it was nearing lunch time. We gathered up several bags of survival rations that we brought for the scouts and headed back down the trail to examine their progress. As we arrived at the boy's camping area, it was apparent that they had been waiting for us and were hoping we had brought them something to eat. We had, after a fashion. We told them we had their lunch, but before they could eat they needed to get cooking fires going. After a few minutes of grumbling about who would collect firewood and who would actually start the fire, each group settled in to their individual assignments and began to work on starting their cooking fires. We sat back to watch with no small amount of amusement. After a short time, it became apparent that the fire building skills of several boys needed great improvement. One pair of boys used a whole box of kitchen matches before they finally got a fire started.

After about a half hour of false starts, the twigs and small branches in several cooking fires were crackling away and a blue grey cloud of smoke settled over the area. Young hands intently fed additional branches into the flames and now that most of the boys had their fires going, and the others were making good progress, we produced their first survival meal which consisted of three dozen eggs, two pounds of bacon, a loaf of bread, and a sack of oranges. They were also given a sack of potatoes and some granola bars for later meals. When we were asked about cooking and eating utensils, we reminded the boys that this was a survival situation and that they would have to improvise. We sat back to watch them consider the problem. Soon, a couple of boys began to whittle short sticks that could be used for forks. Decisions were made on how to divide the food and other boys were assigned to be cooks or to maintain the fires. The group decided to cook bacon and toast on sticks, but could not figure out how to cook the eggs. We suggested that they cook them on flat rocks that could be found near the stream. Several boys headed down to the creek and soon returned with several flat pieces of slate. Some looked to have been freshly washed in the stream and others were covered with dirt and forest debris. A piece of slate was taken to each cooking fire and supported above the flames on a ring of large round rocks. The cooks began to cook bacon and scrambled eggs at each site, but after a few minutes heated slate began to explode at one of the fires, sending shards of rock and pieces of scrambled eggs in all directions. Some of the creek water had found its way into cracks in the slate and when heat was applied, the pressure had no place to go. The result was like several small hand grenades going off in quick succession and a rapid departure of all nearby cooks. Although no one was hurt, several boys had welts on their arms where they had been struck by flying slate, and scrambled eggs were splattered all around the campsite. When the fireworks ended, one of the leaders led the boys back to a cooking fire and demonstrated an alternative way to cook eggs, using half an orange rind as a container to make a kind of poached egg. This method was not as popular, and I think the boys preferred exploding rocks for the entertainment value.

After lunch, one of the adults took the boys on a walk through the nearby woods looking for signs of small mammals and good locations for setting snares and deadfall traps. After the hike, the boys gathered in a clearing where several logs had been placed for seats. Then an adult demonstrated several methods of making animal snares and deadfalls. Although we did not plan on being in the woods long enough to have much success, we encouraged the boys to try their luck at catching animals for food. We planned on showing them how to clean and cook any small game they caught as a supplement to the other food we had provided.

I found some shade under a tree near the clearing and settled down in the leaves with my back against a stately oak tree to listen to the presentation on making traps. The fresh forest air and warmth of the afternoon sun were perfect incentives for a short afternoon nap. In the clearing, Harry was explaining how to make a figure-four trigger. He was explaining that this type of trigger worked very well with a deadfall trap for small animals who were seeking shelter near a game trail. I thought about the hamburgers and other tasty food that we would be making at the adult camp site that evening, glad that our menu would not include rodents. I shifted my position in the leaves to get more comfortable and pulled down the brim of my hat over my eyes. I found myself thinking about my own air force survival training a few years before where catching small mammals was a daily challenge. Like our present location, my survival training site was also in the mountains, but it was colder, wetter, and more remote. I could almost remember the feel of the mountain mist floating through the trees as I huddled around a small campfire trying to capture a little warmth. I was in a group of military pilots who had been abandoned in the remote woods to master the lessons that could possibly save our lives should we have to bail out of a crippled plane over remote or enemy territory. During that training, there was no nice tent and camp equipment nearby and there certainly wasn't much food. We were starving. Our animal traps had not produced after four days and we only had found plants and bugs to eat. I remember the consuming hunger and the need to find food.........

• • •

The morning chill lingered as my friend Keith peered over the edge of the granite outcropping at the game trail ten feet below. He could hear the voices of the other fifteen members of his survival element as they crashed through the brush to his west. The air was still and that was good as his scent would not disrupt the ambush he had planned. Only his eyes and the top of his head were visible from below the ledge. The base of the vertical rock on which he lay was alongside a well-worn game trail and only five or six feet from a swiftly flowing stream. The steady rush of water over the rapids just downstream masked any noise of approaching animals. His view of the trail to the north was partially blocked by a weather-beaten dogwood tree whose pink-capped buds were just starting to show, but only moments before he thought he had seen motion in that direction. Only his eyes moved as they flitted back and forth between both ends of the trail below his position.

Earlier, he and the others in his survival training group had awoken hungry in their makeshift shelters and had gathered to search the woods for something to eat. They had not eaten more than a few plants and grubs over the last several days. They had hoped to catch a squirrel or rabbit during the previous night, but the snares were empty again. Each man in the group carried some kind of weapon that he had constructed from native materials. Most had spears, some with small knives firmly attached to the business end by lengths of dried vine. Some had clubs. One had a home-made slingshot. With a week's growth of beard and accumulation of grime, the group looked like some kind of post-apocalyptic mob as they formed into a skirmish line and then ghosted through the trees in pursuit of something to eat. There had been an attempt to corner a squirrel earlier in the morning, but that animal escaped to the top of a tall tree and chattered its anger at the hunters far below. They moved on.

A half hour into the foraging expedition, one of the group saw motion ahead and the shape resolved into a small doe which moved just fast enough to stay out of reach of the pursuers. The deer was missing the lower half of one of its hind legs that may have been shot off by a hunter or lost in an encounter with a predator. Although driven by hunger, the group quickly tired of chasing the deer which continued to maintain its distance ahead of the hunters. They gathered to discuss options. Keith suggested the deer could possibly be driven into an ambush. He had seen a well-used game trail along a nearby stream and believed he could ambush the deer there if the rest of the crew could drive the deer in that direction. Since no one had a better plan, Keith headed towards the ambush site with instructions for the group to keep the deer in sight but not drive it in his direction until he had a few minutes to get into position. After a short jog through a stand of hardwood trees the river came into view and Keith found a suitable overlook above the trail where he could wait in ambush.

Now, as the sounds of the other men moved closer to his position, Keith realized he was not sure how to actually attack the deer if it approached on the trail below. He had a small knife with a two-inch blade, little more than a pen knife, but maybe he could jump on the deer, holding it down until the others arrived with their more substantial weapons. But he had no more time to think, because the motion up the trail resolved into the three-legged deer which limped towards his position. The deer's focus was over its shoulder, back up the trail towards the men who were herding it. Keith moved from his prone position to a crouch. He got a grip on the edge of the ledge with his left hand while holding his open penknife in his right. The deer was oblivious to motion from above as it shuffled down the trail, intent on its pursuers. And then the deer was below and Keith leaped.

He landed on the animal's back and fought to get an arm around the deer's neck, but an unexpected consequence of his leap was that his forward motion carried both him and the deer into the stream where the shock of the icy cold water immediately cut through his concentration on holding the deer. The small deer was much stronger that he had anticipated and he realized that the deer's thrashing hooves could do some serious damage. He tried stabbing the deer in the neck with his penknife, while trying to maintain his position on its back and thereby avoiding the kicking hooves. At the same time, he was having trouble keeping his head above water. He got in a couple of stabs with his pen knife, but the only effect was the deer struggled even more violently and he was coughing from taking in water as his head went under again. After two or three times underwater, he was sure the deer was getting the best of the situation, but then he could hear shouts and felt the pressure of feet and hands around him as the other members of his group splashed into the water to help. He managed to get his head above water again and saw the largest man of the group brandishing a large hunting knife and yelling for Keith to hold the deer still so he could stab it. In fear for his life, more from the eager group members than the animal, Keith released the deer and, coughing up water, splashed to the nearby bank and safety. Meanwhile, five members of his group were able to dispatch the deer in a fairly brutal but efficient manner. There would be venison on the menu for the next several meals, and that thought overrode the cold and pain he had endured from bouncing off the rocky stream bottom.

My friend had related this tale to me after returning from military survival training in the mountains north of Spokane, Washington. And a couple of weeks later, I left for my own two weeks of survival training in the same general area. My group received classroom training at a nearby military base that began with an orientation to basic survival skills and included a demonstration of signaling methods as well as instructions on how to make cooking fires and sleeping shelters. The following day we were taken by bus, about one hundred miles from the base, to a remote area of the Selkirk Mountains. In preparation for the cold and damp weather, we wore typical winter flight gear that included thermal underwear, a flight suit, a flying jacket, gloves, and a knit cap. We would have parachute material with us at our camp site since we were simulating surviving in the mountains after parachuting from a crippled aircraft. We were allowed to bring with us waterproof matches, a small flashlight, and a small metal band aid can that could contain as much first aid and survival equipment as we could cram into it, including fishing line and hooks. The whole experience struck me as typical outdoor training given to boy scouts so I was looking forward to it.

The bus bumped and jerked its way up the rough gravel road into the mountains and stopped at a remote alpine pasture with some standing water. We could see patches of snow in several places under the shade of pine trees. We exited the bus and it left, leaving us wondering where our campsite was located. There were four or five instructors with us who broke us into groups of about 15 men each and then each group began a several mile trek further into the mountains over fairly rough terrain. We arrived at a place designated as our campsite which was located on the side of a mountain in some heavy timber and had obviously been used many times before. In a central clearing, grass and weeds had been trampled down to bare dirt and a ring of soot covered rocks marked a well-used campfire location. The young airman who was assigned as our instructor in survival skills hung around for the first day to insure we got shelters set up properly using branches from trees and silk from several parachutes. We were also provided with compressed military sleeping bags which would normally be present as part of the seat pan survival kit that was attached to your parachute. As the airman went through his introductory briefing he said that the snow and the rain would keep us wet much of the time and we should remember to take off all our clothes before crawling into our sleeping bags at night. Evidently, just the preceding month, a major who had crawled into his sleeping bag with wet clothes had been found frozen to death the following morning. That got our attention, and although no one wanted to take off clothes in the chilly night air, we found that after we did so, we quickly warmed up in the sleeping bags. It was not toasty warm, but it was bearable.

On the first day at the mountain camp, we were provided with canteens and water purification tablets, about ten potatoes, ten onions, and a live rabbit in a cage. The instructor made a big deal about not getting attached to the rabbit, because it would be needed food. We were told that this food would have to be supplemented by foraging in the woods for plants, small animals, and other edible things. We were shown how to make snares to catch rabbits and squirrels. The instructor showed us grubs and bugs in the area that were edible, but I thought I would probably starve before eating anything like that. We were shown a couple of edible plants and I quickly figured out that trillium, which tasted a little like lettuce, was going to be a mainstay of my diet until I could find a nearby general store.

Our survival training group was made up of fifteen men, and although most were young, fit pilots, there were also a few support officers who did not look to be in very good physical condition. By virtue of his senior rank, a captain from supply was put in charge of our group. For the first day or two the group followed the captain's directions, but it soon became apparent that he was not a very good leader, had no practical outdoor skills, and was not in very good shape. On the third day, we received a visit from one of the training staff who gave the captain a map and told him to move the group to a different location, five miles away, for additional training in first aid and rescue signals. The staff member left and after we all looked at the details on the map and it was oriented with a compass, the captain announced that we would follow a fixed compass heading direct to the next location to save time. We climbed up hills through thick brush, slid down rock strewn slopes into valley bottoms, waded across creeks, and generally became more miserable as our fearless leader frequently checked his compass bearing while huffing and puffing from exertion. Sometime later, we were climbing through knee deep snow on a shaded mountain side when several members of the group asked to look at the map. After a discussion of alternatives, the captain and two others wanted to continue the direct course, but the rest of the group had had enough and the result was a full-fledged mutiny. The party would follow the contours of the hills to the training site, which would take a little longer, but would greatly reduce the level of physical exertion. The captain reluctantly agreed and we changed course. We arrived at the site in good time and after that, the captain had plenty of help in making decisions that would best serve the entire group.

During the return to our camp that evening from the first aid training site a storm moved into the area and visibility went down to a few yards in the mountain mist. We were cold and soaked when we arrived at the camp area. A couple of men tried to start a fire but were not successful and we crawled into our sleeping bags, sans wet clothes, and went to sleep hungry. The next morning sounds of grumbling permeated the camp as each man put on still damp clothes and wandered a short distance from the shelters to take care of their morning toilet. Two guys were able to get a roaring fire going and everyone soon gathered around. After that, food was on everyone's mind. The potatoes, onions, and rabbit had been rationed out over the first three days, and supplemented them with some edible plants, but we had been unsuccessful with our snares. Men started drifting away from the fire and headed into the woods to check snares or forage for anything edible. I and another man had been talking about fishing in a stream about a half mile from camp and we headed in that direction. We had spotted some small trout in a couple of pools during one of our earlier hikes and the idea of eating fish for the next meal sounded a lot better that eating bugs or plants.

There was not a breath of wind as we walked down a game trail towards the creek and our wet flight suits and boots were drying quickly in the morning sun. Except for rumbling stomachs, we felt pretty good being out in the woods. Soon the stream came into sight and I parted ways with my companion. He headed upstream and I headed downstream to find a good place to fish. After walking a hundred yards or so, I came to a bend in the stream where the bank looked to be undercut, providing shelter for what I hoped were a number of hungry fish. I found a nearby dead tree and after a lot of pulling and pushing managed to break off a decent sized branch to serve as a fishing pole. I trimmed it into shape with my pocket knife and rigged it up with fishing line and a hook from my band aid can. I still needed bait, and found a nearby rotten log. Upon rolling it over, I found several bugs and a couple of very anemic looking red worms.

I crept up to the undercut bank and lowered my baited hook into the current. Nothing happened. I bobbed the hook up and down a couple of times and there was still nothing. I checked the hook and the bait had obviously fallen off. I baited the hook again with a wretchedly anemic worm that was barely larger than the hook. Upon lowering the hook again into the water, there was a terrific jerk that almost pulled the branch out of my hand. Then the line was still. I raised the line out of the water to see that the hook and bait were gone. The knot I tied had not held, and I only had five small fish hooks with me. I got the second hook out of the can. This time I was very careful to tie the hook on the line with several overhand knots. I have never been very good at tying knots but this would have to serve. I went back to the bank dropped the newly baited hook into the water. After a couple of bobs on the line, there was another yank and I lifted a nice eight-inch brook trout out of the current and onto the bank. As soon as flopping fish hit the bank, the hook came out and it flopped back towards the stream. I was starving and dove on the fish, almost smashing it flat. It quit flopping. It still looked edible, and I put it in the leg pocket of my flight suit, just in case it came back to life.

Over the next hour the fishing continued to be very good. Looking into the clear water, I could see small trout periodically leaving the undercut bank and rushing upstream to a small section of rapids to feed. I lost my bait several times, but did not lose another hook. The nearby rotten log provided a steady supply of worms and my pockets were soon stuffed with six or eight small trout. The members of my group would be pleased with my success and I would be the hero of the day, especially for those who were tired of eating bugs! After a half hour or so, the fish seemed to lose interest in my bait, and I decided to take a break from fishing. I was lying in the grass, peering over the bank at several small fish that were not interested in my bait and watching them dart back and forth in the current. The sun was very warm now and I was in kind of a peaceful, half sleepy state. I heard the cry of a red-tailed hawk and shielded my eyes to see one circling high above. The only other noise was the gurgling of the stream. I wondered how my partner was doing upstream. The fish were plentiful at my location and I assumed he was doing equally well. I soon fell asleep. I dreamed of a story my friend Keith told of fishing during survival training. He said he was taking in the surroundings when he looked about 100 yards downstream, and noticed that a large log that had fallen across the stream and beyond that there was something large moving out of the brush line. He lifted up a little higher above the grass to see better and realized the shape was that of a good-sized bear who was now walking along the far bank towards the log. The bear was walking upstream with his nose in the air, sniffing.

He is kind of a nature freak, and so he watched the bear with great interest, feeling privileged to see such a sight, and with no concern for the bear's intentions. It seemed to be sniffing all around, but primarily focused upstream. He wondered what it smelled. And then, as he watched, fascinated, the large black bear approached the log and nimbly made its way across the stream. He was thinking that there was no way he could have done that without falling into the water. What an amazing creature. The bear was still sniffing the air as it dropped from the log to his side of the stream. It was coming up stream. And the distance between it and Keith began to close. About that time, an icy chill ran up his back as he realized the bear smelled him…and the fish he had caught and jammed into the leg pockets of his flight suit. He was frozen in position, not wanting to attract the bear's attention, as it continued to sniff in his direction while closing the distance to 75 yards, then fifty yards, and at about thirty yards, adrenaline kicked in and he jumped up, and began sprinting upstream as fast as he had ever run, knocking small tree branches at of his way. He ran/hopped along, yanking trout out of his pockets and throwing them over his shoulder, all the while hoping that the bear would find them tastier than a hunk of human backside. He covered the first fifty yards upstream in world class time, throwing fish in every direction and getting raked by branches. At some point he looked over his shoulder expecting to see drooling fangs, but all he saw was the rear end of the bear as it galloped off in the opposite direction. He slowed to a stop, gasping for breath, and leaned forward to rest his hands on his knees. The bear was clearly as spooked as he was. However, he was not about to go back and look for the fish he had tossed. I woke up from the dream and headed back to camp, watching my back trail all the way.

When I arrived at camp, my fishing partner had already returned with a dozen nice trout and the group was setting around the fire, roasting the trout on sticks. There was a polite inquiry about how I had done and in the bottom of my flight suit pocket I pulled out two tiny six-inch trout. Although not much to look at, everyone was happy to have a little real protein for lunch.

We spent a quiet week in the survival training camp and were not pleased at the end of that time when one of the instructors informed us we would have a land navigation exercise that night. At the appointed time, just before dark, we were given maps with directions on how to complete the route. We were told that during the hike, we should simulate traveling in a hostile area and make as little noise as possible to prevent detection. We were to complete the course in two-man teams who would follow a narrow canyon to a location where we would be given further instructions. When someone tells you there will be further instructions later, you can always plan that those instructions must involve something unpleasant or you would have them right away. This was certainly the case with our night navigation course. Unbeknownst to us, we were being led into the second phase of our survival training…capture, internment, and mistreatment by the enemy.

My partner and I decided not to be in a rush the trek and let the other groups head out first. We spent some time looking at the map by flashlight to identify the best way to use the terrain to mask our presence. We even talked about using mud to camouflage our features but decided not to. Finally, a half hour later, we headed out, following the same route most of the other teams had taken. After about a mile, we heard noises and yelling up ahead. We could see lights moving towards us through the trees and also hear vehicles. My partner signaled that we should climb into some nearby bushes for concealment. The lights and vehicles drew closer and I could hear men yelling instructions in English with a foreign accent. Spotlights moved back and forth across the bushes where we were hidden and then stopped, centered on where my partner and I were crouched. Footsteps came toward us and then someone yelled for us to get up and put our hands on our heads. At first, I wasn't sure we had been seen, but then it was apparent we had as a large man in a strangely camouflaged uniform came to within ten feet of us and continued to yell at us to stand up. We finally did so and immediately were manhandled by several men who tied our hands with plastic restraints and put a cloth bag over each of our heads. We were shoved along from behind for several yards towards a lighted area that I could faintly make out through the mesh of the bag. There were more loud voices ordering people to shut up and to move. Soon a piece of rope was thrust into my hand and I was told to hold on to the rope and keep moving. I was able to lift the bottom of the bag up a bit and could see that I was in a long line of 'prisoners' headed towards a lighted compound. About that time a guard began to verbally abuse someone up ahead who was similarly looking under his bag. I dropped the edge of my bag immediately so as not to draw that kind of attention.

Eventually we arrived at a destination and members of the prisoner line were separated. I was pushed along until I could feel concrete flooring underfoot. I was then shoved into a space and, with a lot of screaming from the guards, told to take off all of my clothes but to leave the bag on my head. I was told stand at attention, and that if I sat down there would be punishment. Then a door was slammed shut and I was alone. I stood there naked, in the dark with the bag on my head. After I time, I lifted the bag and, by the light coming under the door, could see that I was in some kind of small closet. My clothes were gone. There was a metal pot on the floor, but I was not sure if it was a container for food or relieving yourself. Periodically, I could hear guards banging on other nearby doors and yelling at other prisoners. Frequently I could hear them yank open a door to see if the occupants were still standing. By the screamed accusations, I could tell that some were not following orders and it sounded like those were then roughly hustled away for punishment. I don't know how long I was in the closet. It could have been hours or days. Once, there were sounds like a bucket of water had been thrown at someone nearby. Endless minutes passed as I wondered what would happen to me.

Eventually, everyone got to experience punishment. There were several forms. Sometimes you were slammed around although never struck. You were made to assume positions of physical stress until you lost all feeling in your extremities. The worst punishment was the collapsible box. After what seemed to be hours, I was taken from my closet and manhandled along with the bag still on my head until I was I felt I was in a different room and forced into a box-like structure. Then the sides of the slatted box were compressed to force me into such a small ball that I couldn't move anything. After I was fully compressed, the guards secured the sides of the box in a fixed position, turned out the lights, and left me in the box in a locked room. In a few minutes I began to lose all feeling in my limbs. I could occasionally hear other prisoners screaming from someplace nearby and crying to be let out, but I could not tell whether the guards responded or not. When I was finally let out of the box after a long, long time alone in the dark, my arms and legs hurt terribly as circulation was slowly restored and I had to be assisted to stand. I was then taken back to my isolation closet with no further explanation. At some point I forgot that these activities were part of training or why I was in this situation. It had become too real and scary.

After a day or two of isolation and related mistreatment, I was put into the general POW camp population with the about fifty other prisoners. The rules of the camp were very restrictive and we slept on cold cement floors when we weren't being roused for inspections or to make sure no one had escaped. Food was infrequently provided and consisted of some nasty smelling gruel and dried up bread. Periodically we were taken out of the compound and interrogated. We ordered to provide information about our military duties, our units, and our fellow prisoners. When we only provided name, rank, and serial number, we were either put in positions of stress or threatened with other, unspecified mistreatment. We were also told that if we provided information about camp leaders or escape plans we would receive good food and a pleasant rest area separate from the others. During the period of our imprisonment, guards frequently came into the compound to rough up prisoners and some individuals were taken away for an extended period.

We were told that if we attempted to escape we would be punished. There was a double perimeter of fence around the camp topped with razor wire, and we were told there were mines between the rows of fencing. Handlers with guard dogs patrolled the perimeter. We were told that no one had ever escaped from this camp and to try was futile. However, as a concession to the training environment, if someone should escape they were to go to a telephone pole a few hundred yards south of camp where there was a phone that they should use to report their escape. When the individual did so, they would receive special good food and care for a day before going back into the prisoner compound. After the abuse we already had received, no one really believed any of this. As it turned out, our escape committee successfully helped two of our number escape. They were found missing at the next roll call and guards were sent to hunt them down while we were all punished with heavy physical exercise. We found out later that one individual did make his way to the phone and call in and he did receive special treatment. He told us this when he was returned to the general prisoner population the next day. The other man did not believe the guards and disappeared into the woods. The guards looked for him and we could hear the bullhorns calling his name and promising safe conduct if he came out of hiding. While they were looking for him, he hiked ten miles to a highway and hitchhiked back to the main base. After the prisoner training ended and we had returned to the host military base, we heard that the escapee was given a failing grade for the prisoner course and made to repeat it. I think that must have been a rumor put out by the instructors to prevent similar events in the future. To the rest of us, that guy was a hero.

After a week in the POW compound, we were 'repatriated' and a bus arrived to return us to the main base. Upon arrival, everyone in our group wanted the same thing...a hamburger and coke, a shower, and sleep in a real bed. The next morning, we were assembled to hear a debriefing on the training we had received and then went our separate ways to return to our home stations. The man who had escaped the compound was noticeably absent from the debriefing.

• • •

I was glad that I never had the opportunity to use the skills I had learned in survival training, particularly the prisoner training. But wilderness survival training was still useful stuff to know and the boys seem to be very interested in everything they were learning this day. I noticed that the scout leader was wrapping up his lesson on making animal traps and the boys were getting up to go to their next location. I too got up and followed the group down the hill to where the boys had erected their shelters. A couple of the shelters were very well done and I was sure they would stand up to any amount of bad weather. Unfortunately, several others had not received much attention and if it rained, they occupants would be in trouble. But it was not forecast to rain so the adults decided not to harass them very much about improvements. Shelter construction could be a discussion for the follow up meeting after we returned home.

As darkness approached, we left the boy scouts and headed back to the adult camp for the evening. Their shelters were complete and we would check on them in the morning. The adult camp was a place of pleasant conversation after dinner as we stared into the dying embers of our campfire. Encouraged by a few yawns, we eventually drifted off to the tent and our individual sleeping areas. I tucked into my sleeping bag and began to enjoy the night sounds outside. Judging by the loud snoring on the far side of the tent, at least one adult was clearly way ahead of me in his sleep cycle. Unable to doze off, I revisited my earlier thoughts on survival training. In the 1970s, new military pilots could expect to deploy over the Pacific Ocean enroute to the war in Southeast Asia. In addition to mountain survival training we also had to complete water survival training.

• • •

The small group of pilots from our base traveled to Miami, Florida for the week. There was a military water survival training facility located on the shore of Biscayne Bay, just a few miles outside the city. After a restless night's sleep in a military barracks, we assembled for a day of classroom instruction on the use of water survival equipment and what we could expect if we had to abandon and aircraft over the ocean. Then it was time for some 'hands-on training'. We first received a half day of refresher training on parachute landing technique. This training consisted of jumping off a platform that was six feet above a pit, lined with a fairly thin and ineffective layer of sawdust. When the instructors were satisfied that we could fall without breaking any major bones, we graduated to an apparatus that suspended us from a parachute harness. We were attached to the apparatus while standing on a wooden platform about ten feet above the ground. Then the instructors had us jump off the platform to land on a hard dirt surface. The instructors held on to one end of a long rope that was attached to the apparatus above our heads. The instructors could somewhat ease the speed of our descent to the ground by maintaining a grip on the rope. Their commitment to easing the rate of descent, however, was suspect as the number of bruises on my body would attest.

That afternoon, we progressed in our training to a swimming pool where we practiced jumping off a three-meter diving board fully clothed as well as swimming and floating while wearing a flight suit and combat boots. We also practiced getting in and out of various one-man and twenty-man life rafts. Although getting in and out of rafts was not as easy as it looked, we were taught techniques to help with the process. Then we were transported to the shoreline where we were to ride a 500-yard zip line that ended in a tidal basin. Our parachute harness was attached to the starting point of the zip line on a platform at the top of a small hill. The 45-degree descent down the zip line ended in a fairly dramatic impact with the water that was repeated until the instructors were satisfied that we had demonstrated a proper water entry. This training was actually pretty fun and most of us were sad to see it end. We were told we would have an actual water survival exercise the next day. We were told to wear flight suits and combat boots, but not to bring anything else with us except our band aid box survival kits. We would be getting wet.

We assembled at the marina the following day and boarded a PT boat which had been modified with a large helicopter landing platform on the back. We were issued a helmet and a life preserver vest. Both smelled very moldy and had apparently had been used many times. We were advised that sometimes the life preserver vest did not inflate when activated and we should be prepared to manually inflate them. It sounded like they were telling us that some of them had been purposefully made to malfunction. I hoped mine would work since I could not imagine the difficulty of manually inflating one while trying to tread water fully clothed and dealing with an entangling parachute and waves.

We were told that over the years, many pilots had successfully bailed out over water, only to drown because they could not get untangled from their parachute which was being drug by high winds. As a result, we would this day receive special training that would help us avoid that problem. Anything to prevent drowning sounded good to me, and I was eager to have this training until I learned how it would be conducted. Each of us, in turn, would be connected to a parachute harness that dangled from vertical metal arm at the rear of the boat. Then the arm was swiveled out over the end of the deck so that the trainee (read victim) dangled twelve or so feet above the water. When the boat was brought up to about ten knots speed, which approximated how fast the wind could drag a parachute over the surface of the water, the instructor would trigger a mechanism that dropped the trainee into the water where he was drug at the end of the harness line, beneath the water. It was the job of the trainee to somehow arch his body and plane to the surface. Then the trainee was to activate the parachute harness manual release, thereby disconnecting from both the entangling harness and the boat. Then the individual would be picked up by a following speed boat and brought back aboard for a second attempt. If this sounds like trolling for sharks while trying to drink most of the water in the bay, that is exactly what it was for me.

After we were dropped from the boat and hit the water, we were not allowed to release from the parachute line until we planed to the surface and received a visual signal from the instructor. My first attempt went OK, but on the second attempt, despite my best efforts, I could not get my head above the water to see the instructor's signal and after drinking several gallons of salt water, I finally just pulled the manual release. I was still coughing up water when they hauled me aboard, and the instructor gave me a look like he was sure I not received his signal to release, but let me get by without a repeat attempt. After all the trainees had practiced the 'shark attraction maneuver', we assembled on the back of the boat for instructions about the final activity of the day.

We were going to parasail about 2 to 4 miles offshore and then be cut loose to survive on the open water for the rest of the afternoon. After donning the life preserver vest and helmet, we were to be connected to a parasail harness and a one-man life raft seat pack. We would then be hooked to a 500-yard nylon line trailed off the back of a high-powered speed boat. The boat was the kind with lots of muscle, and designed to yank the arms out of the socket of any water skier who got this boat by mistake. At a signal from the PT boat captain, the speed boat would take off and as the slack in the line was taken up, the trainee was to start running towards the end of the deck. The first trainee took about three steps and was then yanked off his feet. At that point he quit running, a big mistake, and shortly came back down to bounce on the deck twice on his side before he disappeared over the end of the deck. Luckily the speed boat finally got up enough speed to prevent him hitting the water and he soared into the sky as the speed boat headed out to sea with him in tow. After about ten minutes, the speed boat roared back to our position and the next victim was hooked up to a parasail harness. Several other launches followed and then it was my turn. The instructors helped me into the parasail harness and the life raft seat pack. They had me back as far as I could away from the edge of the deck and hooked me up to the speed boat line. Then, at a signal from the instructor I began running. My feet were still running as I was yanked into the air and it probably looked pretty funny. There was no way that I was going start this thing by being dribbled across the deck! The takeoff was exhilarating and the wind was whistling through the parachute risers over my head as I soared into the air and the speed boat turned out to sea.

I bent my head back to see that the parasail was fully inflated and doing its job. Then I looked down the nylon line at the speed boat far below. It looked like it was only an inch long as it smashed through the water, creating a foamy white wake on the dark blue seas. I twisted to my right in the parachute harness and could see the shoreline behind falling behind. In front, well ahead of our path, I could see a couple of large oil tankers in the distance. This water survival stuff was suddenly very cool and I was enjoying the ride. My wet flight suit and boots were starting to dry out in the breeze and about the time I was wondering how far out to sea we would go I was startled as the boat released the line and I began a rapid descent to the water. The parasail was not rigged to provide an excess of lift, but rather to drop like a conventional parachute once forward motion of the speed boat ended.

At this point the training from the previous day kicked in. At release, we were supposed to check that we had a good chute, and then release our raft seat pack which would deploy and inflate the raft as it dropped to dangle at the end of a twenty-foot line below me. We were then to point our toes towards the water, fix our eyes on the horizon rather than the water below, cover our parachute quick release rings with our hands (but on penalty of actual death not expose the quick release triggers!), and prepare for water entry. Should we accidentally pull the quick release rings before hitting the water, the result would be instant release of the parachute canopy and a dead drop to the water from whatever altitude we were at. I did all of these things and heard the raft inflate as it dropped to the end of its attaching line. I was looking at the horizon and mentally preparing to pull the quick release rings when I hit the water. It seemed like I was falling pretty fast, but I dared not look down and kept my eyes on the horizon. Just about the time I was tempted to look anyway, I hit the water and went maybe ten feet below the surface. I pulled the parachute release rings as I sputtered to the surface. My life raft was only a few feet away and I swam to it, forgetting that I was attached to it by a length of line and could have just pulled it towards me. My adrenaline was kicking in and unlike the difficulty I had with raft entry at the swimming pool, I had no trouble climbing aboard. We were told to expect a hole in our raft and be prepared to use the raft repair kit located in a pouch inside the raft. Luckily, my raft was in good shape, but the left side of my life preserver was deflated so I located the manual inflation valve and pulled it out to inflate that portion. Now I was lying in the one-man raft, soaking wet, with a couple of inches of sea water in the bottom of the raft and wondering what to do next. I could see some boat traffic in the distance, but I was all alone in the gentle swells in the middle of the bay.

I looked through the contents of the raft pouch and saw a signal flare. We were told to only use it in case of a dire emergency. It was not specified what a dire emergency was, but we gathered death should be imminent or something like that. But here I was, floating around in the ocean in a very tiny raft that barely held my lanky frame, a warm sun was shining overhead and I felt like I could stay that way all day. I used my hands to bail out what little water there was in the raft. I was tempted to get out the fishing line and hooks in my survival kit, but since I didn't have a fishing pole and could only imagine the hopelessness of trying to land some huge fish with the line tied to my finger or leg, I decided not to. After all, in the ocean it seemed to me that everything was either shark sized or grouper sized. If I left them alone, they would leave me alone!

About a mile from me, Leo, one of my fellow pilots, had been floating in his raft for a couple of hours and was getting bored. He too had brought his fishing equipment with a couple of small shiny lures and figured he could catch something to show the others when he got back to the launch site. He tried fishing for about an hour but was not having any luck. The portion of the bay where he drifted was only 35 to 40 feet deep and the water was crystal clear so he figured he could spot some fish. As his raft moved along in the current, he could occasionally make out some junk or structure on the sandy bottom. He saw something that looked like an old tractor tire down there and began splashing along using his hands as oars to try to get a better view. Just then he spotted the shadow of his raft moving slowly along the bottom a little ahead of his position. As he was thinking about how fast the raft was moving along in the current, he realized that there was something odd about the shape of the raft. Instead of being smoothly oval-shaped like a raft, it looked like there was a log-like projection on one side. He had been using his arms as paddles but they were certainly not that long. He was puzzled that the shape was not what he expected and followed the line of sight from the shadow on the bottom up to the raft and leaned over to look directly under the raft. What he saw, hanging a few feet below him was a six-foot barracuda, motionless in the shade of the raft, its long jaws sporting a forest of teeth.

Leo quickly yanked his hands out of the water and pulled his feet to his chest, almost overturning the raft. He carefully peeked over the side again and the barracuda was still there. The latex material of the raft seemed to offer little protection but for a few minutes Leo felt like if the Barracuda could not see him or detect movement, he should be OK. But then again, this seemed like one of those emergency situations they mentioned on the boat, so he fumbled in the raft pouch for his emergency signal flare. He removed the safety cap, pulled the igniter ring and held the flare aloft where it produced huge billows of orange smoke. After a minute or so, the flare stopped making smoke, and the large orange cloud moved slightly downwind in the gentle breeze. For several minutes, nothing happened, and Leo wondered if the instructors were really monitoring the trainees that were strewn across the bay in their small rafts. Then he began to hear the throb of a large diesel motor, and saw the distant shape of a PT boat headed his way.

The PT boat arced into the wind and pulled along-side his raft, the swells from its bow wake causing the raft to rock dangerously close to overturning. As it drew near, he looked up at the deck, maybe fifteen feet above his position, where two crewmen leaned over to ask him what his emergency was. He explained that there was a huge barracuda floating below his raft in a menacing fashion, and that he needed to be pulled onto the PT boat. One man, the first mate, asked Leo if he wasn't a little old to be afraid of a little fish. However, he gestured to the other man to dive into the water and check it out. That man, outfitted with a dive mask, snorkel, and swim fins, jumped from the deck into the water, gripping his face mask tightly with both hands. After rising to the surface, began swimming around the space between the raft and the boat, breathing noisily through his snorkel. Then the man did a surface dive and disappeared from sight. The man exploded to the surface a few seconds later and thrashed madly for the dive platform on the back of the PT boat. As he hauled himself aboard, he announced "there is a big damn fish down there!" At that, the mate had Leo paddle his raft to the dive platform and then he and his raft were hauled aboard.

At my distant location from Leo, I saw none of this action, but about the same time I heard the beat of an approaching helicopter. Soon, a rescue chopper came into view and a line was dropped to recover me from the water. The man in the chopper doorway indicated that I was to get out of the raft and swim to the rescue collar which I then pulled over my arms and head. I gave a signal that I was ready, and the crewman hauled me up and into the chopper. We then flew off to 'rescue' four other trainees from the water. After a short flight to shore, the chopper dropped us off at a landing pad and we were assembled for a briefing before being released to travel to the barracks for a shower and some dry clothes. The following day we left the training site for our return home.

• • •

Back at the scout camp, I was trying to remember who the other guys were that went with me on the training exercise, but at some point, my tired mind gave up the exercise and despite the loud snoring in the tent, fell asleep. It was about five or six in the morning when the first clap of thunder sounded. I lay there listening to the wind come up and could see bright flashes of lightening through the tent walls. That went on for maybe a half hour and then it was like someone had turned on a shower full blast as a deafening rainfall began hitting the roof of the tent. I heard one of the other adults in the dark say, 'that's not good'. I said, 'we better go down and see how the boys are doing, some of those shelters were not put together very well.' Another adult said, 'they will be fine, it's a good experience for them. Go back to sleep.' I lay there in the dark for a few more minutes. The rainfall seemed to be getting heavier. I was nice and warm in my sleeping bag and I had no interest in going out in the rain, but for some of those kids it was their first experience with weather while camping. Grumbling, I got out of my bag and pulled on my clothes and rain gear. Two other adults were doing the same and we stepped out into a full-fledged mountain downpour.

We walked down the trail to the hill overlooking the area where the survival shelters were located and came to a stop. Below us, on the hillside, it looked like a disaster scene. We could see the flashlights of eight or ten boys who were wandering around aimlessly in the dark and heavy rainfall. We headed down the hill and the first boys we came to included Greg, the teenaged leader who was on his knees with two boys ineffectively trying to shield him from the rain with their ponchos. As I stood watching, Greg lit a dozen matches trying to start a fire in a pitiful little mound of soaked twigs. I asked him what he was doing and without looking up he said "making a fire to get warm.' After watching him use up the last of his matches, each one extinguished by the falling rain, the other two adults and I gathered up all the boys and took them back to our campsite where we set up a large tarp for shelter and underneath it started a fire with the dry wood we had collected the previous day. The boys stayed there, trying to dry out their wet clothes by the fire, until the storm had passed and with the coming day, the sky began to lighten to the east.

Later that morning, under a warming sun, we cooked a large breakfast for the entire group and then went back down the trail to assess the shelters one final time. Most of the shelters had partially collapsed and the ground and sleeping bags within were soaked. Two of the shelters had remained dry, despite the heavy rainfall, and they belonged to four of the youngest boys who apparently had paid good attention when we discussed the potential for rainfall. Some of the older boys looked embarrassed after seeing what the weather had done to their constructions. It was time to head home. We disassembled all of the shelters and animal snares, and carried all the gear we had brought to the sites, both wet and dry, back to the vehicles.

The ride home was very quiet and most of the boys quickly fell asleep. For the adults, we felt like the survival training weekend had been a success. However, I hoped that like my military survival training, their training would never be put to a real test. I am not sure what lessons the boys took away from that weekend, but I still remember what I learned from my own training. First, always take plenty of food when you go into the woods; second, don't get captured by the bad guys; and finally, never go fishing in a raft when the fish are bigger than you.

Strategic Alert

My first flying assignment was during the height of the Cold War. Part of that assignment was serving on strategic alert tours in support of nuclear armed B-52 aircraft. Typical alert duty meant that you were confined to an alert facility or 'mole hole' for seven days, after which you got three and a half days off. What this meant was that at least once a month you were on alert, twenty-four hours a day, ready to run to your aircraft and takeoff within a few minutes. The stress of being notified at any time of day or night by the sounding of a klaxon hour, that nuclear war might be imminent, was very debilitating. What this meant was that you spent about a third of your life living on alert. No one liked that duty, so as a result, there was no shortage of volunteers for temporary flying duty for several weeks to remote locations around the world.

For the first couple of years, my alert duty was served in a fenced compound of three-bedroom trailers, located at the east end of the runway. Several trailers were available for alert crew officers and two were reserved for boom operators. The bedrooms were very cramped with barely enough room for a small bed. Crews brought food that could be prepared in a small kitchen and the living room contained three reclining chairs and a television. Just outside the trailer compound was a small visitation facility where crewmembers could meet with their families. The heavily loaded KC-135 tanker aircraft were located about fifty yards away so we were always able to sprint to the aircraft and get them started for takeoff. We were also allowed periodically to travel to nearby portions of the base as long as we had a working radio with us by which we could be notified of needed alert response.

It was a matter of pride as to which crew could respond to an alert the quickest and get their engines started, and in some cases taxi to the end of the runway in preparation for takeoff. When the klaxon sounded we would sprint to the aircraft climb up the entry ladder and strap into position. Then the crew chief on the ground would connect to the aircraft interphone and clear us to fire explosive cartridges in each engine to begin the start sequence. This process was much quicker than positioning a pneumatic starter cart under the wing and then moving it after the engines were started. The cartridges were about the size of a large coffee can and created huge clouds of smoke when then were fired. After engines were up to idle power, the crew chief would pull the wheel chocks and come aboard for the taxi and takeoff. When ten or more of these large aircraft all were starting at once, there would be a huge cloud of smoke that blanketed the area, loud engine starting noises, and the potential for an accident was significant. In one instance, the crew chief forgot to pull the chocks on his airplane and the pilot not knowing why the airplane was slow to respond when he pushed up the throttle, pushed the power up much higher than normally needed, at which point the airplane jumped the chocks and nearly collided with another taxiing aircraft before he could reduce power and apply the brakes.

Sometimes on a cold morning the tires would be partially frozen to the pavement requiring excess power to get the airplane to move. Military policemen were installed in telephone booth-like structures near the aircraft. On one alert, the jet blast from a departing tanker sent the structure, with policeman inside, bounding across the pavement. Luckily, other than a few cuts from broken glass, the individual was unhurt. After than instance, the structures were tied down with reinforced steel cable. I think the sentries were still nervous every time we had an alert with engine start.

After my first year on alert duty, the decision was made to move the tanker crews to the alert facility (mole hole) near the west end of the runway to be collocated with the bomber crews. I do not know if this decision was made to build closer comradery between the crews or because the bomber crews were jealous of our more relaxed trailer set up. We were not happy with the change, but soon settled into our new digs. The mole hole was so nicknamed because all the sleeping areas were underground with access tubes that led directly to the nearby parked aircraft. Above ground, the mole hole had a kitchen and dining area, a small theater for showing movies or training films, a recreation room with pool tables and a ping pong table, and several study rooms to

review materials for upcoming flights. We did have to admit that this was a pretty nice setup, we just did not want to share it with the bomber crews who we viewed as prima donnas.

One major negative was that there was not a nearby family visitation facility. Across the road from the secure alert area was a small park with three picnic tables for that use. This was a poor substitute during inclement weather although you could set in the family car when they visited. This situation helped us understand the bomber crew jealousy about our previous alert location with a family visitation facility.

We knew we could expect at least one simulated alert exercise each week. For effective training, the command staff would try to surprise us with one of these no-notice exercises, and as part of the game, the crews would try to find out when this might occur so we could make a good showing of our readiness. These exercises were conducted during daylight hours due to the safety aspect of taxiing aircraft at night. A big clue would be two or three staff cars with senior officers cruising around the area of the mole hole to observe the exercise. Such exercises were precoordinated with Strategic Air Command Headquarters in Omaha, Nebraska. Personnel there would be responsible for sending a message that would alert the local command post to initiate the exercise and remotely sound the Klaxon. When someone saw staff cars nearby, the word would go out and crews would gather in the mole hole tunnels and hide so as not to be observed by the commanders. On occasion the 'sneaky' commanders would hide somewhere near the east end of the runway and then speed to the alert location when the Klaxon was sounded. We would respond to the aircraft, and depending on instructions from the command post, stand ready, start engines, or some cases even taxi to the end of the runway in readiness for takeoff.

The fact that these exercises never happened in hours of darkness was key when in the early morning hours, I was awakened by the sounding of the Klaxon and all the lights inside and outside the facility were turned on by the on-duty facility controller. Most of us slept in our flight suits and many with flight boots on. I sat up in bed confused by the noise of the klaxon and running feet. My navigator who slept in the bed across from me had jumped up and ran into the door and bounced off. He did this twice more before he became awake enough to open the door. By then we were all running for the airplanes. Outside in the still night air as I ran to the aircraft there was the sounds of running men, and cursing. I was not quite awake and had run about fifty yards when I realized I was almost to the nearby takeoff end of the runway. I stopped, reoriented, and then sped back to my aircraft where the boom operator was unsuccessfully trying to get the ladder in the crew entry chute. Together we got it in place and climbed aboard. I strapped in and heard the cartridges firing on the airplane to my left. I quickly ran the abbreviated checklist and pushed the selector switch to fire our cartridges and the engines began to wind up as my copilot climbed into his seat. We quickly completed the taxi checklist and I looked at the navigator who by now was in his seat and decoding the message from the command post which said to stand by with engines running for the next message. This had never happened before and in the back of my mind was that we were really about to go to war. After about twenty minutes waiting for the next instruction, we were told to shut down engines, replace cartridges, and remain in the aircraft for further instructions. Staff cars with commanders were finally arriving on scene and they were mostly dressed in civilian clothes. As I looked out the aircraft window to finally take in the scene with all the nearby stadium lights now turned on, I could see items scattered between the alert facility and the aircraft. There was a couple of jackets, a cap, and even a pair of boots. Clearly, most crewmembers were sound asleep when the klaxon went off. After about an hour, with dawn approaching, we were told to secure our aircraft and could go back to bed. Most were too wound up to try that and went in the dining hall for coffee and an early breakfast. We found out later that an exercise scheduled for 4pm that afternoon was mistakenly read as 4 am. As a result of that goof up, all training activity for the day was cancelled and we were left alone for the rest of the week.

A couple of years later, we were flying back to the base from a month-long temporary duty trip to Spain. About 100 miles out from the base, on the command post radio, we heard what sounded like an actual alert being broadcast at our base with instruction to taxi to the end of the runway. My navigator confirmed this was the 'real deal' and we immediately contacted local air traffic control for instructions. They told us to begin a holding pattern at our current location over Lark Erie. We did so and then we tried to figure out what are options were if this was a real alert. We had enough fuel for about another hour and looked at potential landing airfields in nearby Canada. If this was the prelude to a nuclear strike, we would not have a base to land at in the US. After about ten minutes of holding, ATC called to say we would be cleared to land at our home base and we turned in that direction. After landing, we found that all the alert aircraft had returned to parking and we were directed, along with all other crews on base, to prepare our aircraft for alert. Whatever the international situation was, things were still not sorted out by our higher command headquarters. It turned out later that the Israeli and Arab world had gone to war and since it was unclear how the USSR would respond, someone at a high level decided we needed to be ready to go war. After about 36 hours with all crews on alert, it was decided that we could go back to our normal stance and my crew was allowed to go home for some well-deserved, post-TDY rest.

The actual big test to see if we were ready for our nuclear alert mission is the annual Operational Readiness Inspection or ORI. Although we usually knew within a few weeks when this would occur, it was initiated when a general and his staff arrived on base unannounced and advised us that the flying exercise would occur in 24-36 hours. Until then, the inspectors tested the crews about knowledge of their assigned mission and inspected all aircraft and facilities for readiness. The base was a bee hive of activity as every tanker and bomber on the parking apron was being readied for flight. Engine cowlings were removed as last-minute checks were made by maintenance personnel. Maintenance 'bread trucks' scurried between airplanes for last minute checks of avionics and delivered extra parachutes, engine parts and supplies that would be onboard in an actual launch. Refueling trucks topped off fuel tanks. As the time for actual launch neared, crews arrived in blue busses and download personal equipment and inflight food and drink. Copilots did an external inspection and then climbed aboard to join the rest of the crew running the pre-flight checklists. Radio checks were made with command post and between aircraft who would be flying in formation. Then everyone waited nervously for a message from the command post that would direct the actual launch. After about a half hour that message was transmitted and the ramp was filled with the sound of engines winding up to idle power. Soon the message was received to taxi to the end of the runway. There was a lot of nervousness as no one wanted to be the crew that messed up and caused our base to fail the inspection. As twenty plus large aircraft waited on the taxi-way for the instruction to launch, engines running, a voice came over

the radio. It was George C. Scott giving his famous Patton speech...' Now I want you to remember that no bastard ever won a war by dying for his country'. My copilot and I looked at each other wondering what the heck. Then we were given the order to take off and the speech continued on the second radio as we began to roll toward the runway. We about to do a MITO (minimum interval takeoff) which results in aircraft being about ten seconds apart on the runway. One aircraft is just lifting off, one is halfway down the runway, and one has just begun its takeoff roll. This is a dangerous procedure with smoke from the preceding aircraft obscuring your view of his position and the runway in general. In addition, as soon as you lift off you hit the wake turbulence of the preceding aircraft which requires back and forth full throw of the ailerons to maintain a semblance of level flight and not hitting the ground. After getting a hundred feet or so off the ground, you begin a very slight bank to get clear of the wake turbulence while maintaining a position clear of the preceding aircraft. All this while listening to George C. Scott tell us about going to war. We never did find out who was doing the illegal radio transmission but it sure had us pumped up. The rumor mill said one of the bomber navigator was doing it with a tape recorder smuggle onboard. This was not confirmed as the culprit would surely have been in big trouble. And surprisingly it was not brought up by the inspectors after the flight. The actual flight involved one thousand plus mile simulated navigator leg and refueling of our mated bomber. Then the bomber broke off and navigated to his simulated bombing target while we completed our navigation leg and returned to base. A few days later we found that all mission activity was outstanding and our base was recognized with a 'well done'.

Life on alert can be boring but sometimes little events do much to break up the boredom. When you are grounded for medical reasons such as a cold. You get assigned all kinds of weird duty. One time that happened to me and I was assigned to do the annual inventory of the Officers Cub. In addition to counting all the furniture and various pieces of equipment and the food and drink had to be inventoried. It was bone chilling cold in the walk-in freezer as I inventoried each pork chop and frozen veggie box. Then it was on to the bar where every bottle of booze had to be inventoried as well as how many shots were left in each opened bottle. It was an all-day task and I was glad to be done.

One of the pilots was assigned to attempt a penetration of the alert facility as a test of the security. What he was not told was the several military policemen had recently been decertified for failure to do a proper job guarding. This was a big deal and could result in demotion or worse. One of our pilots was issued a security access pass for the alert facility with a picture of an African American crewmember who was six foot three inches tall and weighed 230 pounds. The Caucasian pilot was barely five-foot four inches tall and weighed about 140 pounds.

He drove up to the gate and when the guard approached the pilot passed his badge to the guard who studied it briefly and handed it back. Then seemed to pause as he realized there was a problem. The guard, who has been since know as shaky Jake, drew his pistol and pointed it at the pilot's head. The pilot said he gun was shaking so badly he later said he thought he was about to die. After getting spread eagled on the ground, a hidden inspector appeared and gave the 'all clear.' The pilot did not get sick again, with resulting special duties, for a long time.

On another instance, the security folks used an extremely attractive female lieutenant who was granted access to the alert facility, but not to any other area. She told one of the bomber crewmembers she had always wanted to see the inside of a bomber. The hapless crewmember was foolish enough to grant her wish which resulted in his courts martial and permanent removal from flight status.

Recounting my time in the mole hole, I ended up serving about 150 weeks on alert in my early career. I think it was important duty, but the strain on families and mental health as well as not being able to actually fly, has never received the public recognition it deserved.

The Big Bang

It was a late December afternoon and the sun was going fast as we crept through the old growth forest, the dry snow squeaking underfoot. Fresh deer tracks were everywhere, but the only sign of life was a crow calling in the distance. I could occasionally see my hunting partner, Don, off to my right about thirty yards, his focus intent on the woods ahead. We had agreed that I would follow the deer tracks and he would stay off to one side to spot any deer that might pause to watch the back trail. I was not very confident our strategy would pay off, but the alternative of sitting in the cold by a tree, did not seem to have much merit. In any case, either method beat the heck out of spending the weekend in the house.

Regular deer season had been over for a couple of weeks and when Don called to ask if I was interested in heading south for a special season hunt, recently announced by the DNR, a little walk in the woods and the opportunity to escape the early stages of cabin fever seemed like a great idea. I had not hunted with Don before, but his knowledge of deer hunting, in general, appeared acceptable. You can also tell a lot about a prospective hunting partner by the care with which he handles firearms. After only a half hour of covertly watching which way my companion's muzzle was pointed, I was satisfied that I could relax and enjoy the hunt.

Dressed in heavy clothes for the subzero weather, I was already sweating from the hike in and wondering whether or not I should take off a couple of layers. If we were to get lost in these woods, however, extra layers would be welcome. It was overcast and the light was going fast. The occasionally flurries drifting through the pines reminded me of the snowstorm that was supposed to come in overnight. Don had a crude map of this area of state land, but it was not very detailed and my attention was divided half between following the deer tracks and half on the location of my truck about a mile behind us. I shifted my .348 Winchester from the sling position down to port arms and checked for the umpteenth time to make sure I had chambered a round and the safety was on. The choice of the big gun was determined after checking the weather forecast and the fact that the scope on my .270 Remington had fogged up the last couple of times out in cold weather. The .348 had open sights, but there was not much chance the shooting distance would be very far, so it seemed the right gun for the outing. The snap of a branch off to the left reminded me Don was still moving and as I looked, he was shaking his head in embarrassment at the sound. It did not seem to be a big deal since the loss of daylight would end our stalk in a few minutes and I did not hold out much hope for last minute luck. I fumbled with my heavy gloves to grab the sling and swung the rifle back up on my shoulder as I ducked under some low branches and continued up the trail. I was reminded that the old gun had been around a long time, but could not remember the last time I had used it. It had been buried in my hall closet for some time.

The Winchester had been in my possession for many years. I first saw it when I was about 14 and my father had opened a steamer trunk left in his care by a military buddy from the Korean War. A good friend, Barney, had left the trunk in my dad's care and headed off to explore the world. My dad had not heard from him for several years. Dad had unsuccessfully tried to contact him and was now going through the trunk to see if there was anything important inside before finally turning the contents over to Goodwill. My dad carefully stacked old clothes and shoes off to one side for disposal. At the bottom of the trunk he found a couple of photo albums and a handsomely hand tooled leather gun case. Inside, wrapped in oilcloth, was the most beautiful gun I had ever seen. My dad said Barney had talked of using the gun to hunt bear in Alaska. It was a lever action .348 and I was reminded of the rifles used in all the western action films I had ever seen. After putting the gun and other apparently important items back in the trunk, my dad closed it up, stored it in the basement and I forgot about the gun. As the years went by, no word was heard of Barney's whereabouts.

When I turned 21, as a last fling before joining the military, my best friend Crawford and I decided to go on a deer-hunting trip in the Pacific coast mountains of Southern California. Neither of us had done much more than hunt rabbits with .22s, but it seemed like a great idea. He would borrow his dad's old .303 Enfield and as I considered where I might borrow a gun, I remembered the .348. My dad agreed that I could use the gun and we were set. We spent the week before departure getting Crawford's old Willys Jeep in shape for the trip. Crawford had a large footlocker that we filled with canned goods from our respective houses and a few pots and pans. I went to the local store to buy a hunting license and some cartridges for the .348 and found that none were available. After trying three sporting goods stores with no luck, one of the clerks suggested I visit a gun show that was being held in a neighboring town that weekend. I did so and found a booth that sold a wide variety of shells, including ones for a .348. I did not know the .348 was an uncommon caliber and was accordingly shocked at the price for a box of 24 cartridges…nearly $40! However, the limit on deer was only one a year, and at one shot per deer, I figured a box would last me a good long time. Now we had everything we needed for the hunting adventure of a lifetime.

The old Willys huffed and puffed up into the Cleveland National Forest about 40 miles from where we lived. Our plan was fairly simple. We would go high up into the mountains on the main highway, find a dirt road off to one side, follow it a couple of miles, and set up camp. And that's what we did. After about four miles, the primitive dirt road we turned off on ended at a roughed-out parking area already occupied by six cars. Nearby, several tents could be seen and a number of men in hunting clothes lounged around campfires, cooking their midday meals. We had hoped for a little more isolation, but if all these professional-looking hunters were here, the place should be perfect. We spotted a small clearing about fifty yards west of the parking lot and began to set up camp. As we finished putting up our tent, I watched three men who had been setting by a fire in the next camp as we arrived. They were loading their gear on an apparently matched set of ATVs and getting ready to head into the woods. Actually, what caught my attention were their shiny new Fifth Wheel trailer and camp accommodations that looked like something out of the LL Bean catalogue. Everything they had looked fairly pricey. I was wondering how they got the big comfortable trailer up the dirt trail. I reflected on our flimsy canvas tent, trunk of canned food and street clothes. Maybe we could learn something from these guys about how to get our deer.

About an hour later, we heard a couple of loud gunshots a short distance off to the south …and then there were several more. When the shots continued for another five or ten minutes, we concluded that a deer was not being shot to pieces, but that an informal firing range was in operation. Since neither of us had shot our guns before, we figured it best to go do a little target practice before heading into the woods. We took our guns and a box of bullets from the back seat of the jeep and headed towards the booming of the guns. As we walked down the trail to the makeshift firing range, the loud reports made me wish I had brought some kind of earplugs. We soon arrived near the firing line and saw seven or eight men shooting, from a standing position, towards an embankment about 100 yards away that was littered with paper targets of various sizes and a few cans and bottles. Although the continuous gunfire seemed sufficient to drive all wildlife from the forest, the report of one gun in particular seemed much louder. When I remarked on that, a man standing nearby said with no small amount of reverence that the gun in question was a seven-millimeter magnum. I gathered that having such a manly firearm was a big deal. I was just glad I did not have to shoot a gun that loud and was well satisfied with my ancient lever action. What I needed was the kind of gun that made the ricocheting noise I had heard in all the old western movies. Now that was a cool sound to have working for you and one that would certainly impress the other shooters!

Crawford and I found places on the firing line and loaded our rifles. I had practiced loading in camp so as not to embarrass myself while in view of seasoned hunters. The heavy report of guns on the line continued and I could see a few hunters were skilled at hitting the distant bottles and cans. The strike of bullets on the paper targets could not be seen from our position, but every now and then I could see an eruption in the dirt that indicated paper targets were also getting some attention. I put half the box of shells in my pants pocket, but quickly decided the weight was too much and put them back in the box. The .348 rounds were unlike any bullets I had seen before and considerably larger than Crawford's .303 rounds. The lower two thirds of the cartridge were half again larger than most rifle bullets. The top half of the lead slug ended in a blunt silver tip that would surely do in the largest, meanest werewolf. The dealer who sold me the cartridges told me that .348s only came in 240 grain slugs which were designed to stop bear or moose dead in their tracks. I just hoped a well-placed shot would not completely disassemble the smallish deer that I had seen in this area. I managed to load five rounds though the side port in the Winchester and lever a round into the chamber. Working the lever action put the external hammer at full cock and I lifted the rifle to sight on a distant can. I heard the loud bang somewhere off to my right that was probably Crawford's Enfield getting into action. I wondered if there would be much kick with my shot. The rifle had a two-inch rubber pad on the end of the stock and I found myself wondering why a pad that big was needed. I had a momentary image of the kick from the gun sending my 135-pound frame flying, to the entertainment of the others on the firing line. My concentration, however, returned to the Winchester and the target. I remembered shooting instructions I had read in a hunting magazine that focused on breath control. As I drew in and held a short breath, I began to squeeze the trigger. It seemed like the rifle fired almost immediately. I do not recall any kick, but the most vivid memory was of a shock wave that went out ahead of me in the dust for about thirty feet. That and a ringing in my ears that blocked out all other noises. I may have hit the target, the dirt bank, or the next county, but I could not tell you for sure. Pine needles were raining down from all nearby trees. As my ears stopped ringing, I noticed all the shooters on the line were looking around, obviously trying to figure out which gun had just fired. I found myself looking around too and tried to locate the magnum shooter we had observed earlier. Soon, the shooting started again and I could sort of hear once again, I levered another round in and lined up another shot. When the gun went off this time, I was even more aware of the shock wave, the ringing in my ears, and even the apparent strike of the bullet a few feet from a can at the bottom of the target wall. Unfortunately, I was aiming at a bottle about 20 feet higher. Men on both sides set their guns down. One walked over and asked what I was shooting. I told him I had a .348. He said he had heard of the caliber and wondered why I would want to take a gun that big deer hunting. He wandered away muttering and shaking his head. At that point, I felt like I had just demonstrated that I was a new guy hunter and wondered if everyone there was thinking the same thing. In any case, I did not think my ears could take anymore ringing so I unloaded the gun and set down by a nearby a tree to watch Crawford finish his practice. When he was done, we headed back down the trail. On the way, he remarked on the huge bangs from my end of the line and wanted to know if it was the seven-millimeter magnum. I told him "probably", not realizing he was referring to my own shots.

We had lunch. It was not much and with the dry air and high temperature, we were not very hungry. To add to the discomfort, the pine needle carpet in the camp area did little to keep down the dust that continually floated in from arriving and departing cars of hunters. I was terminally thirsty and glad we had remembered to bring a five-gallon water jug and canteens. It was so hot that the flies had quit flying. We had come to hunt, however, so we slung canteens, gathered up our rifles and headed down the dusty trail to the north that appeared to be the direction to the hunting grounds. I could still hear banging from the firing range and wondered how far we would need to go to get out of range of the sound of gunfire that was probably scaring off any nearby deer. We wandered a mile or so up the road and soon put on our hunting faces as we crept along with what must surely be great stealth. In reality, the jungle grapevine had already announced the arrival of nimrods and that all local animals should take up a key vantage point to observe the entertainment. We soon left the road and approached a small knoll covered by huge closely spaced boulders. After climbing up to check the view, we found that we could cover the area quickly if we jumped from boulder to boulder. I was feeling particularly agile until I followed Crawford in a jump across an eight-foot gap. As I made the leap, I noticed a huge timber rattler stretched out on the cool earth below. The next three jumps were made after carefully checking what lay below.

After crossing the boulder field, we continued north for about another hour. On the way, we found a shady area where we stopped for a drink and a moments rest. I mentioned the snake in the boulder field to Crawford but I do not think he believed my story. In any case I was not eager to go back to camp with a second tour of the boulder field. We soon topped a small hill and were treated to a great view of an open meadow about three hundred yards across to the next group of woods. As we scanned the view for any sign of deer standing idly by, waiting to be shot, I noticed a distant hunter on the far side of the meadow. About that time, he seemed to raise his rifle, point it our way and then a puff of smoke appeared. The gun's report arrived about the same time as the shot hit the trees ten feet above our heads. We both hit the ground and rolled down the backside of the crest. About the time we stopped to catch our breath, there was another report and another shot hit the trees at the top of the hill. We both yelled loudly for the hunter to stop shooting, but shortly thereafter, there was a third shot. At that, we looked at each other, got to our knees and both fired a shot up over the rise in the general direction of the incoming shots. We lay on the ground for several minutes trying to decide what to do next and hoping we had gotten the attention of our apparent assailant. We could not imagine how we were mistaken for deer, so the hunter was either blind or intent on causing us some harm. There were no more shots. After a few minutes, we cautiously got to our feet, but there was no sign of the hunter. We had had enough for the first day of hunting and headed down the backside of the hill to make a roundabout approach to camp.

We finally arrived back at our camp about an hour before dusk. We could see two of the well-equipped hunters reclining in chairs near a campfire. We decided to ask about their success and maybe get some pointers on where we might spot some deer. The two hunters appeared to be middle-aged and well relaxed in comfortable chairs by the fire. They were sharing a bottle of whiskey and offered it to us. We said no thanks, but maybe later. After some small talk, I noticed the third man in their party had not appeared and asked where he was. One of the men said he was still way out in the woods. He related a story about how the third guy, who also was the owner of the trailer, ATVs, and most of their gear, had wandered into a swarm of bees and had been stung so badly that his eyes had swollen shut. They said after that he had become irrational and would not let them help him. They had returned to camp a couple of hours earlier and went down to the highway to call an ambulance. Neither man seemed overly concerned about the third hunter or returning to the woods. We excused ourselves and went back to camp to cook dinner. About two hours after dark, the arrival of an ambulance and a park ranger's pickup truck was announced by flashing lights and a rolling cloud of fresh dust. The rescue team asked for directions from the injured hunter's companions who then returned to the fire as the rescue unit headed out. It was some time later that the rescuers returned and placed the injured man in the ambulance. As the ambulance headed back down the dirt road, we marveled at the lack of concern from the hunting companions.

The next morning, after a short and unsuccessful hunt, we decided we had had enough of the dusty woods and our first deer hunting adventure. The campsite of the injured hunter was empty and it appeared that the man's blue-collar hunting companions had taken his expensive equipment back down the mountain. We never did hear the final outcome of the events from other hunters in the area, but the story of the trio's incident was commonly known. As we drove down to the highway, we decided to go down the west side of the mountains to a nearby beach. Let me tell you, the cold clean Pacific Ocean never felt so good. We spent the night camping at a nearby state park and then headed home. The .348 was cleaned and returned to my dad's closet. Many years later, when he had finally given up on ever hearing from Barney, my dad asked if I wanted the gun permanently. I was glad to take it off his hands to add to the other guns that I owned. From that point on, it received a good cleaning every fall but was rarely taken from its case.

I was remembering the gun's unremarkable history and the hot weather hunt so many years ago as I crept through the woods. The rifle's darkly blued action and rough wood stock made me feel like a grizzled old mountain man from the 1800s. Just then, I heard a low whistle from Don and a rustle in the heavy brush to my front. Don looked like he was moving around to get a clear view of something. At about the same time I caught a glimpse of brown bounding through the woods about eighty yards ahead that was clearly a medium sized deer. I tried to get a good sight picture, but the brown kept disappearing and reappearing behind the heavy growth. If I did not take a shot soon, however, the deer would be out of range. I thought I had a sufficiently clear path to shoot and I began my trigger squeeze. The huge concussion from the big gun disrupted the silence like a low altitude sonic boom. Clumps of snow rained down from every tree in sight. I could no longer see the deer and wondered if my aim was true. It was fairly certain that I was on target and feeling pretty good about the shot. Don hollered over, "did you get him?" About that time, about sixty feet ahead, a small barren sapling, about fifteen feet tall, slowly began to fall and hit the snow with a muffled thump. It was quiet for a minute, and then Don's loud voice drifted my way with, "Well, that one will be easy to clean". We walked over to examine the sapling that had been cleanly snapped off by the round and then continued to where the deer had been. There was no evidence that the deer had been hit and that the tree had been the only recipient of the powerful silvertip slug. It was almost dark, the cold was setting in, and the season had come to an end. As we made our way back up the snowy path to the car, I reminded myself that I really needed to get the big gun out of the case more often! And I wondered if Barney ever really went hunting for bear.

The Orange Crate

As someone used to a warm climate, I view ice fishing as a sport practiced by crazy people or old folks with too much time on their hands. With all the really good and personally rewarding things to do on a winter day, it is hard to believe that someone would actually go outside in subzero weather, of their own free will, and sit for hours over a hole that they drilled through several inches of ice. The "sports" up north practice this activity for endless hours, hoping that some luckless fish will wander by and be sufficiently motivated to attack a half-frozen minnow or shiny metal spoon. Although you can probably read about any number of innovative punishments meted out by our judicial system, it seems like this ice fishing business might have potential as one of the more creative penalties. With these thoughts in mind, and nothing but time on my hands, I agreed to venture forth into the bitter cold and try my luck on the frozen waters of Munuscong Bay with my friend Keith.

Keith was my next-door neighbor and a short, stocky north-country outdoorsman, who had brought home a nice limit of perch and walleye the previous weekend. He seemed to be very knowledgeable about the whole business of ice fishing and when he talked about the prospects of what we might catch on our trip, I became concerned about the utility of my little Zebco rod and reel. My experience with fish was in inches and ounces—Keith talked about fish in terms of feet and pounds. He said that I should bring all the warm clothes that I had and that he would take care of the fishing gear. That worked for me since the part about being warm was the most important thing on my mind. As we discussed the plan over the phone, I looked out the window at eight inches of fresh snow on the ground, and at the prospect of more that was clearly apparent in the large dry flakes floating down from the low cloud deck that filled the sky in all directions. When I mentioned the weather, Keith seemed pleased by the prospect of more snow and said that now would improve our traction on the ice. My thought at the time was that traction is a curious requirement for sitting over a hole in the ice, fishing pole in hand, but I knew him as an expert on ice fishing matters. I agreed to meet him at six o'clock the next morning, and let the matter of traction drop without further question.

Our departure the next morning was a little delayed as we struggled to hook up his snowmobile trailer to the back of his car. As we finally rolled out of the driveway, I poured myself a steaming cup of hot chocolate from a big green metal thermos and turned to see how the trailer was tracking behind us. The view out of the back window was almost obscured by a huge light-orange colored wooden box that was lying on its side on the back seat. It looked like the kind of box a kitchen appliance might come in, and the open top was facing the front seat. I could see three large white plastic buckets and all kinds of other material crammed inside. Among the items were several extremely short fishing poles with normal length handles but lacking any apparent fishing reel. There was also a large collection of what looked like two-foot commercial fireplace kindling pieces. These pieces were grouped in sets of three, and joined by a short bolt. With each set of pieces there was a two-inch metal spool filled with heavy fishing line and a long, flat metal strip that was topped by small red plastic flag. One of the buckets was tipped on its side and I could see that it contained some metal fishing lures and other assorted debris that looked like leftovers from garage cleaning day. I was positive that most of the stuff actually was junk, but I also knew better than to say so. Keith had a solid reputation for being able to turn a pile of junk into any number of hi-tech applications, such as brain surgery instruments or jet aircraft. You see, my friend Keith believes that every item in our world has more than one future and is just waiting for the right person to come along and identify its true potential. Many people choose to make fun of Keith's innovations, but those who know him value highly his unique ability when something breaks and they either cannot fix it or are too cheap to buy a replacement part. Because of Keith's reputation, I was aware that he had identified the true purpose of the strange pile of materials in the back seat and that these items were critical to our fishing success.

As I tried to imagine the utility of this strange collection of fishing gear, Keith explained that we were going after jumbo perch, and had a chance to catch a northern pike or walleye. He told me of a northern pike caught the previous week that weighed in at fourteen pounds and I wondered if I could possibly catch such a fish. Keith said that the fish we are after became most active early in the morning and late in the afternoon. However, he said that fish could be caught anytime during the day because the cold water increased their metabolism and resultant need for food. I could certainly relate to that insight since at the time I already felt cold and hungry and wished that I had not left my lunch on the kitchen counter as we departed for the lake. However, I nodded at Keith to show my understanding of his insight, even though I was sure that his words represented the typical fishing hype of the sort that preceded the "you should have been here yesterday" speech to be given later in the day. My thoughts were drawn to the warm bed and toasty flannel sheets that I had so reluctantly left for a chance at such fun. My wife was probably right when she mumbled 'jiel gfflk hs dkdfj' to me as I had banged around in the dark. Being extremely familiar with my wife's expressions of support for my endeavors, I suspected this translated to "Have fun out there and I think you are crazy to leave this warm, cozy bed. Snore."

After a short delay while negotiating some glare ice at a stop sign in the little town of Pickford, two wrong turns, and twenty miles of freshly plowed county roads, we finally slowed at a hand lettered sign that announced "Dan's Resort - Modern Cabins and Quality Fishing for the Discerning Sportsman." As we turned off the main thoroughfare, I could see some buildings up ahead through the light snow that had begun to fall. The woeful condition of the ten guest cabins we passed on our way down the lane made me wonder what discerning sportsmen might choose to spend the night at this place. Just past the cabins, wisps of smoke were swirling through the trees from the chimney of a lime colored residence with attached garage. Two late model cars were parked in the driveway, and about half a dozen snowmobiles littered what must have been the front yard. A gleaming black Artic Cat was parked near the garage door with its engine cover up and a wide variety of tools were scattered on the packed snow nearby. I assumed that this was the proprietor's residence. We continued to the end of the lane where the road opened up to a lake-side parking lot, a collection of portable ice shanties, and a decrepit double wide trailer that was marked by a sign that announced "Offise - Bate". It appeared that we had arrived at the launch point for our ice fishing expedition.

This spot seemed to be the focus of several "discerning sportsmen" who were unloading gear from nearby cars. I was immediately encouraged that we were not alone in our efforts to wander out on the ice to fish such miserable weather. I hoped that the presence of other lost souls would add respectability to the day's efforts, even though I fully intended to keep this mindless adventure secret from my office mates or others who might have previously held my character in some esteem.

When I followed a small group of anglers into the bait shop with my partner, I was drawn across the room to a patch of warm air near a medium-sized pot-bellied stove in the far corner. This was a clearly a popular spot and I had to elbow my way into a tight circle of eight other fisherman who had the same idea as I did—to store up a few mega blasts of heat that might last for the few minutes from when we exited the building until we could convince ourselves to go home. As the heat soaked in, I looked around and took in the grit-covered plank pine floor spotted with drying trails of melted snow that had been tracked in from the entry to the stove and the cash register. There were a couple of display racks loaded with fishing lures and other items near the center of the room. Near the wall closest to the lake there was a long counter topped by an ancient looking cash register. Nearer, the wall behind the stove was covered with dozens of old, curling pictures showing guests at the resort and their catches. The pictures had a common theme --a smiling Joe

Average and his many oversized fish. The dates penned at the bottom of most pictures seemed old, but the message was clear— "*There be Monsters here*!" In addition to the pictures, there were a couple of calendars depicting extremely healthy and barely dressed young women advertising Sunny Day Motor Oil and Stihl Chain Saws. A middle-aged man with a heavy beard and a red plaid shirt and another who looked like he belonged in an old folks' home were busy analyzing the relative merits of the calendar models. At the end of the room away from the lake, there was a gigantic fish mounted on the wall. The fish was flanked by a couple of snowshoes that looked old and worn enough to be rejected by the Smithsonian Museum. There were also several rusty animal traps on the wall, including one that was probably large enough to catch and hold a bull elephant. Although I was not aware of any nearby candidates for such a trap, I supposed that the trap and the fish mount were oversized imitations designed to provoke comment and critical analysis. Then again, both looked authentic.

The mounted fish looked to be almost four feet long and could have weighed as much as thirty or forty pounds. The more I looked at the fish, the more real it looked, but I decided that to be unlikely, given its size. It was mounted with its mouth wide open and could have inhaled a two-gallon milk jug with no difficulty. I asked one of the fellows at the stove what kind of fish it was and he announced that it was a local record Northern Pike taken four winters prior. He rather huffed out the information while rubbing his hands together over the stove and indirectly looking at me as if he thought that I must have been locked in a closet for some extended period to not be aware of this obvious bit of local legend. I still was not sure if this fish was real or an oversized plastic simulation. However, I am sure such a question would have clearly identified me as a novice adventurer and unworthy of other useful information. It was not so much that I did not want to believe the authenticity of that wall mount. My concern was for the miniature fishing poles in the back of Keith's car and my realization that they might be more appropriate for use as fish toothpicks rather than having utility for catching man-eating sea monsters.

Near the cash register a beefy, ruddy-faced man was methodically picking small brightly colored fishing lures up from the counter and placing them in small clear plastic bags. From the talk around the stove, I found out that the man was the owner/operator of the resort and known as Big Al. Big Al was warmly dressed in several layers of wool and the red flannel underwear he was wearing was exposed at his neck and wrists. His cracked and calloused hands and wind burnt face reflected many hours and days spent in the wind and cold. His insulated brown canvas pants and green suspenders were engineered to contain a significant waistline that was surely the result of expert and sustained efforts at the dinner table. One of the fishermen who had been leering at the calendars said that Big Al had owned the resort for about 14 years, since the death of the previous owner, Dan, in a boating accident. It appeared that Al, like the owners of General Motors and American Airlines, believed that generations of satisfied customers would be drawn back by a trusted name. Either that or the initiative to correct such details as an out-of-date entry sign did not fit into the man's work routine. Looking at the weathered man behind the counter who had just finished packaging the last of his lures, I imagined the latter was more likely.

In addition to the pot-bellied stove, a big kerosene heater near the cash register added heat to the room and to a mangy old dog with mud-caked hair that was sprawled about six inches away. The dog seemed oblivious to activity in the room and the entire length of his damp coat emitted a curtain of musky steam. The pungent smell of wet dog hair mingled with the cigar smoke and the smell of men too long in the field causing my eyes to water. It was a forgone conclusion that the dog was alive, although its eyes were closed and no movement or breathing was apparent. As I watched, the noxious vapor from the dog's coat seems to intensify and I expected his fur to spring into flame at any moment. I wondered what Big Al's reaction would be to such an event. His total attention seemed to be focused through a pair of granny glasses on a shiny lure that he was manipulating with his thick stubby fingers. I noticed that Keith had finished looking at the fishing gear displays and was talking to Big Al.

I reluctantly left the comfort of the stove and joined Keith at the counter. Keith had put on his game face and was about to get down to serious fishing matters. There was a lot of water out there, although much of it was frozen, and it was important to find out where the fish were before we started fishing. There is a time-honored ritual associated with getting the latest fishing information. One just does not walk up to a perfect stranger and ask where the fish are located. First, you have to prove yourself worthy of such closely held secret information. If it is determined otherwise, then the information you do get is probably going to be misleading at best. Knowing these rules of the game, and the protocol associated with verifying his worthiness, Keith had begun with a little light conversation on fishing lures and past fish caught before he asked the key question, "how are they bitin?'". This innocent question was designed to reflect one's membership in fellowship of local sports who will guard all fishing secrets with every means available. In the fraternity of true fishermen, such commitment is a given.

Big Al looked up from his work, hesitated a moment

and through clear blue eyes sized up my friend. Although he was probably registering sales potential, the storeowner assumed the guarded tones of helpful and friendly co-conspirator. I could hardly contain my excitement because I knew we were about to get "the secret information". Big Al said that several fishermen had come in with limit catches shortly before we arrived. Although it had been slow all week, a recent low front and changing wind direction had pushed many big fish back into the bay. This was the insider information we had hoped to hear. As I listened, I knew that my chances of catching the mate to the big fish on the wall had just increased ten-fold. I imagined the strength required to resist the heavy pull of such a fish as I heard Keith ask what kind of bait the fish were biting on. This was clearly an important question and the look in Big Al's eye told me that we had now passed the test as real customers who deserved every bit of expertise the old bay man could provide. It never occurred to me that his purpose in providing us with fishing information and equipment might be different from ours.

Al looked at the countertop before him and the array of fishing lures tacked to the wall behind him as if to remind himself which ones had been more successful. Surely, he was not remembering which lures had been on display the longest or which of those had been the poorest sellers? After the briefest of pauses, Al selected a medium-sized, lime-green metal spoon from among several arrayed on the counter (it seemed like there were dozens of this particular variety of lure). He said that the locals had been knocking them dead on the spoon that he called the Big Al Special. He said that just last Monday, a guy named Bob Jones had brought in an eight-pound walleye on a light green Big Al #5, just like the one he was showing us. It had two big yellow eyeball dots on one side and a pair of blue lightning bolts on the other. Al said that you should stick a big old silver minnow on each barb of the lure's treble hook and then you were ready to fish. According to Al, the rig resembled a fish about to inhale the minnows and was strong incentive for any nearby fish to join the feast. Now we were talking about results and this information collecting process seemed to be almost too easy! After some quick mental calculations regarding the number of lures I might lose to snags and thirty-pound pike teeth, I decided that I would need no less than half a dozen of these beauties to guarantee a limit catch. However, my old friend Keith did not get a reputation for shrewdness by accident, and despite the clever tactics of the old salesman, asked what the price difference was between the Big Al #5 and the generic lure of similar design on the wall behind the counter. Big Al allowed that the lures on the wall were only $2 each, but that they were easily damaged by striking fish and fishermen did not have the same level of success as with the Big Al Special. He said he could give us the Big Al lures at only $4 each even though they sold in town for $5. Faced with such generosity and honesty, we decided to buy three lures each and asked him to hide a couple more away behind the counter in case we needed to come back in for replacements ("Feller caught one nearly 25 pounds this morning, need any steel leader?"). After dropping about $30 each on lures, a bucket of silver minnows and snack food, we were ready to catch our limits. We said our goodbyes to Big Al and the pot-bellied stove and stepped out into the frosty morning air. I had only taken two steps towards the car when I suddenly realized that I had lost all the heat I had acquired during my 15 minutes in the fishing store. This was a bad sign.

We unloaded the snowmobile and a metal skid from the trailer and placed the large wooden box from the back seat onto the skid. The skid was a discarded car hood with a v-shaped connecting bar welded to one end, another of

Keith's inventions. When connected to the snowmobile, it could transport a fair-sized amount of equipment. We both put on insulated coveralls, heavy boots, knit caps and mittens. I felt like an astronaut about to take his first spacewalk. Keith told me that the surface of the lake could be a little rough. I would need to sit in the wooden box and keep our equipment from spilling off the skid on our way out to the fishing area.

I got into the cramped confines of the box and Keith wedged me in with various fishing gear so that there was no room to move. Luckily, it would be a short ride out to the designated hot spot. The last piece of gear in the load was the two-gallon silver minnow bucket that just fit on my lap. As I peered down into the bucket, my frosty breath quickly dulled my view. I had to blink several times to clear away the ice crystals. The small silver minnows seemed quite content in their temporary habitat and I wondered if they knew they were about to be piranha bait.

Keith pulled the rope starter up on his old Skidoo and the engine roughly came to life. I settled my face as deeply as I could into the collar of my snowsuit as we left the parking lot for the trail out to the lake. I looked ahead and past Keith's outline and tried to steady the sloshing minnow bucket on my lap. Through the sting of incoming snow, I could make out the vague shapes of a few ice shanties near the shore. To my surprise, we did not stop, but continued further out onto the lake's surface, quickly leaving the shore behind. All I could see was white as the sled picked up speed. The ride was generally smooth, but every now and then, we hit a slight bump. The sharp jolt of the box and skid hitting the ice surface made me glad for the cushioning effect of the extra layers of clothes I had put on. We were beginning to move pretty fast, probably around 35 or 45 mph, and I considered yelling at Keith to slow down, when we became airborne over a particularly large mound of snow.

It seemed like everything happened in slow motion as the sled, the driver, the loaded skid and me all drifted through space and began to roll. As the various parts of this airborne circus reentered the earth's gravity and impacted the ice, things flew in all directions. I tried to stay with the box but felt myself floating away from the gear, the box and the minnow bucket. There was a very hard jolt and muffled thump as I hit face down on the snow, along with the rain of fishing equipment and splash of water from the ice bucket. I lay there a couple of minutes, tentatively sending signals to various parts of my body and hoping the return message would announce that all parts were still connected and functional. I tentatively moved each limb and all seemed OK. I lifted my head and could see Keith lying about ten feet away. The sled and skid were on their sides, still connected, about 20 feet further. After wiping the snow from my eyes and nose, I sat up and could see Keith start moving. We confirmed we were OK and both began laughing in relief. Then we remembered the minnows. As we looked for the bucket, we realized there were minnows flopping everywhere on the ice. Many were already frozen solid. Keith spotted a nearby set of recently abandoned holes in the ice and ran over to break through the thin ice and get water in the bucket while I ran around putting minnows back in the little water left in the bucket. Although we had lost about half of the minnows, the rest seemed serviceable. We righted the sled and climbed back aboard to resume our journey. I suggested to Keith that he might go a little slower, but I think he had already arrived at that conclusion. In any case, we only went another 100 yards before arriving at a spot he had heard about, nearly two miles out on the lake.

We stopped and began to set up our fishing equipment offshore from a finger of land that Keith called Sunk Car

Point (I did not need any reminders that we were not walking on land). My discomfort at being so far from shore caused my speech to accelerate and I began asking all kinds of questions about ice fishing techniques and the weather. What I really wanted to know was how the ice could support cars, a heavy snowmobile, or two Pillsbury doughboy-shaped fishermen in heavy winter wear. I wondered if I could get my overalls and heavy boots off in time if broke through the ice and headed for the bottom of the lake. Sensing my unease, Keith told me that there were only a few cars and snowmobiles out on the lake at the time, but that there are usually dozens—he said I should not worry because the ice was probably at least six inches thick---in most places. He told me that just last winter he saw a Winnebago on the ice for the whole day. I nodded eagerly, wanting to believe. Then he said that the motor home began breaking through and the owner had to drive onto a small island that he pointed to about a half a mile away. Keith said "it took them until mid-summer to build a raft and float it to shore, har, har." I could almost see the cracks beginning in the ice around us.

We were a long way from shore and I was thinking that I could just accidentally wander a little closer as Keith began to assemble the fishing gear. The three white buckets were stuffed with junk that he began to sort through. He announced that we had to drill some holes and started to assemble sections of bent pipe. After the assembly, I watched him attach what looked like a small shovel face to one end of the contraption. He informed me that the device was a genuine Swedish ice auger and that it would make short work of our drilling.

About fifteen minutes later, when we finished drilling the first hole I was drenched in sweat. Keith announced that we needed about ten more, spread out in an area about 200 feet across. This was short work? As we broke through the ice at each spot, the cold clear water surged up the hole and stopped near the surface of the ice. With a long handled dipping spoon that he produced from his collection of gear, Keith dipped ice chips from the water and I could just make out the sandy bottom of the lake, about ten feet below. After finishing the drilling, Keith reached into a white bucket and pulled out a pile of two-foot long wooden sticks. He began to assemble the pieces into what he said were "tip-ups". He unfolded each tip-up into a crosspiece that sat on the surface of the ice and a vertical section with a small metal reel on the bottom end. He explained that the spool only held about twenty or thirty feet of line and was inserted down the hole in the water. After baiting a short section of line from the tip-up with a minnow, he bent a metal strip that extended from the top of the vertical piece of wood down to connect to the spool. On the end of the metal strip nearest the water was a small red plastic flag. He then sat the device over the hole with the reel and baited line extending down the hole. I could easily see the minnow swimming just beneath the bottom of the hole. The idea was that when a fish bit the minnow, the flag would go up and you would know when to run over and pull the fish up through that hole. In theory, it sounded great and I could hardly wait for my first flag. We positioned each tip-up and then got out our mini-fishing poles for two holes at the center of our spread. The little poles had no reels and looked to have about twenty yards of heavy line wound around pegs that projected from the handle. I remembered the conversation in the store about whopper fish and thought that we were not even close to having the right kind of tackle.

Keith returned from the snowmobile skid and brought the orange box with him. It was about 2 x 3 x 5 feet and looked like it could be used for a bench, although it was on the small side for that. Keith informed me that the box would serve as our ice shanty and we should begin to fish.

Having seen several ice shanties near the shore that were essentially tool shed-sized buildings, I was thinking that I had misunderstood him. But he told me that we needed to sit real close together on upended white buckets, next to a couple of holes drilled through the ice, and we pulled the orange box over ourselves.

It was pitch dark inside the box except for the surface of the ice. Outside of the box, sunlight penetrated the surrounding ice cover and my view down the freshly drilled hole was very good. Almost immediately, the view began to cloud up as the hole began to ice over. Keith dipped the ice chips from the hole with his ladle and suggested we get some heat going to relieve the bone chilling cold. I could not imagine what he had in mind, but he dug out a can of Sterno and lit the petroleum jelly concoction that it contained. It actually did feel a little warmer. Like from minus twenty to minus ten degrees. We baited our short poles with silver minnows and dropped them down the holes. I watched the minnow swimming around at the end of my line. Did it have any idea that something big and bad might soon come calling? As I looked down the hole, I remembered the tip-ups we set outside on the open ice.

To take my mind off the cold I attempted to look through one of the pin holes in the box to check our luck. The orange crate had several nail holes across its sides, including a few that were accessible from my current scrunched up position. Although the holes were drilled to permit an unrestricted view of the surrounding territory, they also provided access to jets of the bone-chilling breeze from outside. Somehow, I lined my eyeball up with an appropriate hole to see the nearest tip-up and was rewarded with an ice pellet in the eye. After several minutes of blinking away the pain, and in utter disregard for personal safety, I put my other eye to the hole and was just in time to see a flag pop up about 100 feet away. I announced this information to Keith who let out a whoop, yelled "fish on" and hurled the orange crate up and away, at least ten feet into the air. Caught up in the moment, I quickly followed him as he waddled/sprinted to the distant flag.

Keith slowly pulled the device from the hole, bringing up with it a crust of clear ice from the surface of the hole. I did not see him react to any lurking monster fish; in fact, there was no fish at all. He told me that the bait is gone and that we would have to reset the device. After about fifteen repetitions of this activity in the next hour, I came to firmly believe that this ice fishing business was some water bound version of a snipe hunt, and that I was the goat/victim. I will say that the activity did have some entertainment value and added warmth to an otherwise boring morning.

We had been setting on the ice in the dark for several hours, and I was deep into a cold induced coma-like state. As my mind drifted off to warmer places, I was alternately back home in bed, setting on the beach watching the waves roll in, or basking in the heat of the radiator from my position in the back of some classroom. Someone was gently snoring and it became apparent that it was probably me. Deep in this pleasant state of mind, I clearly heard my partner say "Uh oh".

Now there are normally only a few things you can do to guarantee my full attention, but hearing those particular words while sitting miles offshore, on open ice, in the dark, is one of the winners. I felt the tingle of blood draining from my face since his utterances could only me one of a few things. Each of those things was very bad. Either he had seen something that means the ice is about to quit supporting our weight, he had just realized he has lost his car keys, he remembered a meeting he was supposed to attend, or nature had called in its most severe form and he realized he would never make the shoreline.

In the darkness of the box, I peered at his face (about six inches away), wondering which catastrophe was about to befall us, but I could see that he was intent on the hole between his feet.

Even at this close proximity, I could not see what was drawing his attention and tried to learn over closer to see what spectacular activity his minnow was performing. About the time I could almost see directly down the hole, Keith raised his short fishing pole sharply and was rewarded by a strong tug that pulled the tip of his rod down to the surface of the ice. I was wondering how big a fish must be that would pull with this force. Keith announced that it is a big one. I had already figured that out. As Keith tried to gain line on the fish it quickly became apparent that I was the impediment in this close quarters battle.

The orange crate and I both went flying as Keith attempted to maintain his attachment to the fish with the light fishing line wound around his pole. Just before I was elbowed out of the way, I caught a glimpse of something going by the bottom of Keith's hole. The green scaly hide that was endlessly gliding by covered the entire six-inch diameter of the hole, with no hint of head or tail. Maybe it was a cousin of the Loch Ness monster…like the huge Muskellunges that I had been reading about in the paper. Maybe a cross between the two…I can see the headlines, "Fishermen subdue Messie through hole in the ice." I sat down on the open ice, and watched the back and forth battle as Keith tried to retrieve line and then lost ground. The problem was that he could not get the head of the fish started up the hole to pull it out and the fish did not appear the least bit tired.

After what seemed like half an hour but was probably closer to five minutes, Keith said he thought the fish was almost ready to land. Suddenly, the line parted and with a long string of expletives, Keith fell back on the ice. We spent the next ten minutes trying to decide what had just happened. We believed that our near miss was a fish of monstrous proportions...probably at least twenty pounds and three feet long. It had been a close battle and only frayed fishing line prevented our success. Yes, that would be our story and we would stick to it!

We rebaited our poles, pulled the orange crate over ourselves again and hoped for more action. I looked through a nail hole and saw that the sun was low in the sky, and we could feel the temperature dropping even colder. At the bottom of the hole, my minnow floated limp and lifeless. The flame over the last of the Sterno sputtered out and we agreed that it was time to head home.

Wordlessly we loaded the orange box and our equipment onto the skid and headed for shore. On the ride in, through the light blowing snowflakes, I could see the twinkling of small lights that began to appear in the scattered cabins along the shore. To either side for several hundred yards, the headlights from a few dozen snowmobiles and cars joined us in our retreat to the shore and safety and warmth. As we jolted and bounced our way up the short path from the shore to the parking lot, we saw several stiffly moving figures moving near vehicles in the gathering gloom. We made short work of loading up our gear and then headed into the bait shop to get a cup of coffee for the road.

It appeared that little had changed in the shop since we left many hours before. Maybe there were a few more puddles of melted snow on the floor, and several more fishermen seemed to be huddled in groups near the stove. We could hear stories being shared of fish caught, fish lost, and friendly fun being poked at Tom or Bob or KJ. I looked for the waterlogged old dog, but he was nowhere in sight. He had obviously thawed out and had gone off to do some important dog business. Big Al was at the cash register listening to a tall, thin fellow as we walked in and the man was wildly gesturing and talking in an excited voice. We dumped our excess minnows in the big tank in the back room, got a cup of coffee, and began to thaw out in the pleasant if sweaty smelling warmth. Al was still at the cash register and packaging a fresh lot of #5s for his display rack. A group of fishermen waved to Al as they headed out for a little night fishing. I shuddered at the thought of returning to the lake in the darkness and falling temperature.

Al walked over to join us by the stove and asked how we did today. Keith told him that the action was slow, but that we did OK. Somehow, Al could tell that our luck was not too good and seemed determined to leave us with a little good news. He said that we should return the next day and the fishing was sure to improve. "Most people did pretty good today…a guy was just telling me that he heard some guy caught a 32-pound Muskie." Keith, ever the collector of important information could not help but ask where such a major catch occurred and with what bait. Al moved over to the window and pointed out towards the distant shoreline. "Well someone left an orange crate out there about two or three miles today and the guy was fishing in the open right about the same place. He was using one of my metal shad lures and the fish just about pulled his hand off!" After exchanging glances, Keith and I looked back at the stove. Keith said, "Sure was cold out there today". We thanked the owner for the information and headed out into the night. As we climbed into the car, Keith muttered a muffled "Damn!" I could tell that it would be a quiet drive home.

Long Cold Nights

I was thinking about complaining because it has been unseasonably cold this week. There has not been any significant snowfall, but the wind was especially brutal on these February days when I went out to warm up the car. It had been colder, but not here and not now. It is easily much warmer than it must be in Alaska. I have nothing personal against Alaska. The raw beauty and unspoiled nature of the landscape is very inspirational, especially for an outdoorsman like me. However, every time I have been there, save one, it has been in February. And then the world record extreme temperatures and endless nights have made me wonder why anyone would ever choose to live there…even if there is big money to be made working on the oil pipelines or with the fishing fleets.

The purpose for our deployments to Fairbanks was to support military flights over the North Pole to and from Europe. The shorter distances of that route cut the transit time by at least a third. My first flight to the region provided a big hint that there were also disadvantages of operations from Alaska. I had returned from my first long term deployment to Southeast Asia only a month earlier and felt like I was ready for any challenge. My performance had earned some measure of confidence from my aircraft commander and when he told me to make sure that our cargo and passenger preparations were complete for our departure the next day, I was pleased with the responsibility. I was already at the aircraft when he arrived just before engine start and our crew chief helped him load his equipment on board. Passengers and cargo were already onboard. Engine start and taxi were uneventful and as the tower cleared us for takeoff I felt a measure of excitement about the upcoming deployment. The flight across Central Canada was scheduled to take six hours and I was ready to try out my newly acquired mastery of international radio procedures. Although we had received a heavy snowfall earlier in the week at our base, and the outside temperature was around 25 degrees, the runway had been plowed shortly after the snowfall and was now dry. Winds for takeoff were calm and the liftoff was smooth. After retracting gear and flaps we settled into a climb profile and I made initial radio contact with Soo Radar Control as we made the turn towards Canadian airspace. I called for the crew to check their oxygen systems passing ten thousand feet and the only checklist item left was to reset our altimeters passing eighteen thousand. As we passed thirteen thousand feet, I was checking the fuel panel to decide how to configure it for cruise when I heard the pilot gasp. I looked over to see a stunned look on his face and followed his focus to his forward windscreen that had just gone from transparent to an opaque craze of tiny pieces. Only the aircraft pressurization was keeping it intact and in place. He leveled the airplane and lowered his seat to duck down behind the instrument panel…it looked like the shattered window could fly into the airplane at any time. He started a turn back to our home airfield and told me to declare an emergency with air traffic control. I did so and began the checklist procedures to dump most of our fuel overboard to reach a reasonable landing weight. Those procedures went quickly and automatically as we transited the eighty or so miles back towards the runway. The control tower advised us that emergency equipment had been scrambled in preparation for our landing. This was the first time I had been in an emergency situation and I wondered what would happen if the window disintegrated and came into the cockpit. The pilot was also thinking about that and transferred control of the aircraft to me to make the landing while he hid behind the instrument panel. Luckily the winds were still calm and I made a fairly respectable landing, to our great relief. We taxed back to the parking ramp and shut down engines, followed by a line of fire trucks and ambulances. Maintenance vehicles met us at the parking space and they unloaded an army of personnel to look at our failed window. They soon determined the failure been caused by a short in the window deicing system. We were just glad to be back on the ground safely and headed off to the operations building. I was thinking I could spend another night in my own bed and we would reschedule our departure for the next morning. Wrong! As we finished up the post flight paperwork from our short adventure, the pilot received a call and was obviously not happy with what he was hearing. The window would be replaced over the next hour and after a three-our cure time for the sealer, we would be cleared for another departure. Although we had already been on duty for six hours, our allowed crew duty day was 20 hours with special approval, our cargo was needed, and we would be taking off again. The crew was not especially happy with the situation, but on the other hand, deployments meant that you were not at home station and did not have to put up with the daily boredom and training that made up our usual routine.

We rounded up our grumbling passengers four hours later and ran through the checklists for another engine start and taxi. The second takeoff was again uneventful. As we once again passed the memorable thirteen thousand feet, I closely watched the window expecting another problem and wondering if this time the safety glass would explode into the cockpit. We continued our climb and soon got back to the normal operations of completing checklists and identifying navigation waypoints. As we leveled off at 31 thousand feet, the pilot set the throttles to hold our target cruising speed of 450 knots. The crew chief came forward and asked if anyone wanted coffee. The pilot did, but I pulled out a can of coke that I had stuffed into my helmet bag. I finally relaxed and made my initial contact with Minneapolis Center as we approached Canadian airspace. Then we got another measure of bad news. Center advised us that Canadian air traffic controllers had just gone on strike and American flights would not be allowed to enter their airspace. Center asked us if we planned to return to our departure airport. We told Center to standby and tuned up the other UHF radio to contact our command post. After some discussion about how much fuel we had on board, the officer on duty said that we should continue west and that he would get back to us shortly with further instructions. At the time we had about 150,000 pounds of fuel on board which would be good for about 14 hours of flight if we chose to do that. Otherwise we would be dumping another big load of fuel to get to landing weight. Big environmental impact as well as big dollars! After a few minutes the command post called back with the decision. The planning staff had determined we had enough fuel to get to Fairbanks by way of the west coast. The decision seemed unbelievable at the time. I had flown an eight-hour leg in the Pacific between Hawaii and Guam and that seem to take forever. Now, we were being told to continue with what looked like a flight of over ten hours. The pilot seemed unfazed and told the command post that we would call back when we arrived in Alaska. We advised Minneapolis Center of our intentions, our navigator spread maps and enroute charts out over his table to plot our new course, and we settled into the normal routine that is part of long flights over relatively uninhabited parts of the northern tier states. After about an hour, I noticed that the pilot appeared to be uncomfortably squirming in his seat. After a few minutes of this, he told me had had a vasectomy the day before and wasn't feeling very good. He said he was going back to the bunk in the main cabin and that I should send someone back to get him if anything unusual came up, but no later than the west coast, about four hours away. I was surprised that he would leave me as the only pilot for such a long duration, but he did not ask my opinion and left me and the navigator, another fairly new crewmember, in the cockpit to press on into the late afternoon sun. I adjusted my seat to get the sun out of my eyes. The navigator said I should follow the HL500 highway in the sky all the way to the coast and I advised the center of our plans. We basically would be going west until we arrived off the coast of Washington State. Then we would go north to Alaska. I thought "cool", just like the song. I could do this. It was warm in the cabin. We had the heat turned up because the air conditioning system was acting up and the passengers in back had been complaining about the cold. I was very comfortable and I had things in hand. I was THE PILOT. I remember passing through North Dakota and entering airspace over Montana. There was very little air traffic and radio transmissions from center were very infrequent. My navigation instruments showed that our track was centered on the airway and the airspeed was wired on 450 knots. I felt comfortably pleased with being in charge. The next thing that happened is that I realized the air traffic control center was calling our flight on the emergency frequency and I was sort of asleep. I sat bolt upright and gathered my fuzzy thoughts together to answer the call which was to change radio frequencies to the next center down the route of flight. I had no idea how long I had dozed off. It could have been a minute or half an hour! I remembered the pilot was in the back sleeping and I was in charge. The airspeed had fallen off by 50 knots. We weren't close to stalling, but the impact on navigation calculations could be potentially huge. My attention next went to our location relative to the airway. The head wind was pretty much on the nose of our aircraft, but if you are off track by more than ten miles, center can issue a violation and you can lose your pilot's license! Somehow, miraculously, we were barely within ten miles. I made a course adjustment and then turned to look at the navigator and ask why he hadn't said anything. He was sound asleep with his head on the table, snoring away. I immediately woke him up and then sent him back in the cabin to get us some coffee. I was extremely shocked and was wide awake for the rest of the flight.

When we reached the west coast, the navigator went back to get the pilot who arrived in the cockpit looking refreshed and alert. He asked how things were and, after

exchanging glances with the navigator, we assured him that everything was fine. About 100 miles off the coast, we made our turn north and the hours that followed were uneventful. About 200 miles from Fairbanks we called their command center for local weather and were advised that visibility in the area was unrestricted with calm winds. The temperature was a balmy minus 40 degrees. We took turns leaving position and going back to the cabin to put on mukluk insulated boots and heavy parkas in anticipation of the cold after landing. The landing was uneventful and as the cargo door was opened, a blast of cold air surged into the cockpit that took our breath away. We quickly completed our checklists after engine shutdown and went down the passenger ramp to a waiting crew bus. I had never been so cold. Snow drifts were piled up 15 and 20 feet high on the edge of the parking ramp. That was a unique sight, but the cold was the enduring and invasive thing that held your attention. After a debriefing with local staff officers about the flight, we called back home to let people know we had arrived and then were taken to our temporary housing. My impression was all activity on the base seemed to be done underground or inside of buildings that were heavily insulated. There were above ground tunnels between most of the buildings we saw. We were advised that exposure outside on some days, even for a few minutes, could result in fatal frostbite to the lungs. After a few seconds of walking between the crew bus and the debriefing building, I was already a believer and settled in for a long boring time indoors.

We flew two or three times a week while in Alaska, usually four to eight-hour missions towards the North Pole or shorter missions over land in support of fighter aircraft who flew from Anchorage. The days passed slowly and when our month there was over, I was glad to return home. During our time in Alaska, we visited the local Base Exchange store several times and bought some things to bring home to our families. I bought a Mouton cape for my wife and also a nice six by eight-foot tapestry depicting bears in a black and gold forest. We had also taken orders from people back home for King Crab. At that time of year, ten-pound boxes of crab sold for a ridiculously cheap $8. We had taken orders for 240 pounds and as we readied for departure, the truck arrived with our seafood which the crew chiefs carefully loaded into external keel beam bays where the outside air would keep the boxes at a chilly, minus thirty degrees. After a six-hour flight home we radioed the command post from about 200 miles out to advise them to call the people who had ordered crab to meet us at the airplane. That was when we found out that an unusual winter storm system had closed down military airports all across the northern tier and we would have to divert further south. Our destination soon changed to central Ohio where the temperature was fifty degrees. It was Sunday, it was warm, and we had 200 pounds of King crab that would soon thaw and be spoiled. We called the command post at the Ohio base and told them that this was their lucky day. They should put out the word that there was a half price special on King Crab that would be landing at their base shortly and individuals should report to the parking area. We ended up selling about two thirds of the load and giving the rest away. It was an end to the trip that certainly seemed fitting, given the way the deployment started.

Two years later, I was once again deployed to Alaska. Now I was a newly minted aircraft commander and was assigned to an equally inexperienced crew. The one concession to our inexperience was the navigator who was ten or so years older than the rest of us, senior in rank, and extremely cynical about his chances of survival with his new pilots. The Major announced to us the first day that we should not volunteer for anything and he intended to pass his time reading in his room. Although we listened, pilots were made to fly and build hours. Alaska was the place to do that with frequent flights of long duration. Our deployment was uneventful (six hours through western Canada) and there seemed to be no problem that we couldn't handle. Ah, the confidence of youth. Our first mission was scheduled for three days later and we were to be a spare aircraft for a long distance refueling of a flight of RC-135 reconnaissance aircraft. It was a planned as a late-night takeoff. This seemed to be a silly way to look at our departure time, because it was always night in Alaska during February. There were two primary tanker aircraft and we were to stand by at the end of the runway, in case one of the other aircraft could not get airborne. The preflight briefing was given by the aircraft commander of the lead RC-135. He was a Lieutenant Colonel and seemed very experienced. I paid close attention because we would fly as a primary aircraft later in the week. Our part in this mission was to start engines, taxi out, and ten minutes after the airborne aircraft reported they were in good shape, we would taxi back in and head to our quarters for the night. As the crew bus drove into the parking ramp, I could see a lot of activity around each of the airplanes involved in the mission. Yellow heater tubes snaked into all engines and open cockpit doors. The temperature change in the cockpit was distracting. We had been briefed that it was minus fifty degrees outside and we got on the crew bus wearing heavy thermals, parkas, mukluks and subzero mittens. In the cockpit, with external heaters blowing hard, the temperature was more like 120 degrees. We suffered through, knowing that the bitter cold would take over as soon as the tubes were pulled for engine start. Aircraft heaters in those days were extremely inefficient on the ground and the cold would be with us until we were safely airborne and the heating systems would begin to operate at a reasonable level of efficiency.

As we finished our pre-start checklists, we heard the pilots of other aircraft on the radio as they announced that they were beginning their engine starts. We called in to announce that "the spare" was starting engines. As the aircraft began to taxi out, we fell into line at the end. We were loaded with over 150,000 pounds of fuel, but with the extremely long runway and cold temperatures, all aircraft should easily get airborne. I listened carefully to the radio chatter and soon it became apparent that one of the primary tankers was having electrical system problems. Such problems are fairly common in temperature extremes, and he turned off on a side taxiway to head back to the ramp for maintenance. A few minutes later, the command post called to tell us the problem was unworkable and we would now assume his flight duties. He was scheduled to be the first tanker with a four-hour flight time and we were glad to fill in to get the flight time and experience. Flight lead called for takeoff clearance and soon we, the lead tanker, and two other tankers were in the air and heading north.

As we settled into the climb, I could see rotating beacons on the other three aircraft in the formation, spaced a mile apart in trail, and the flight leader called to confirm that all aircraft were airborne and in formation (no rearview mirrors!). Everyone acknowledged and we eventually leveled off at cruise altitude in trail formation with the two RC-135s leading the way. As we headed north into the clear midnight sky, the inhabited parts of the ground fell behind and soon the only light sources to be seen were the stars and the rotating beacons of the other aircraft. The copilot and I were momentarily distracted by an amazing display of northern lights, but we were quickly drawn back to the job at hand to maintain our position at one mile behind the other tanker. As we approached the northern Alaska coastline, my navigator reported a fault with our number two generator (we had three) and that it was offline for good. I reported that to the flight leader and we droned on into the night. A little later the navigator reported that the primary compass system was also not working. This was a big deal because north of 60 degrees latitude (we were approaching 80 degrees!) magnetic compass systems do not operate well and without our primary compass we would be dependent on our navigator's dead reckoning which was based on celestial observations taken through a sextant out of the top of the aircraft. I was thinking that we were supposed to offload fuel to the receiver aircraft and turn around at about two hours into the flight so we should be OK. Soon we were at the initial refueling point and the big receiver aircraft announced over the radio that they would be drifting back behind us to get fuel. At about the same time, the other tanker passed on that he wanted to check his refueling system with one of the receivers before we gave our offload and headed back. Looking out the copilot's side window, I could soon see one of the receivers move up behind the other tanker. After about ten minutes of trying, the other tanker advised that his systems were not working and he would be heading home. This was absolutely the worst news. Our four-hour flight had just become an eight-hour flight. In addition, we did not have enough fuel for both of the receivers and for us to get safely home. I discussed options on the radio with the pilot of the lead receiver and he advised his mission was absolutely critical. After a few more minutes, the decision was made for us to give as much fuel as we could to both and then turn around for home. They, in turn, would adjust their mission profile to land earlier than planned. We quickly figured out that the two receivers could share about 80,000 pounds of our fuel if we began refueling immediately. That would leave us with enough fuel to get home with about an hour of flying time to spare. We gave the first receiver 40,000 pounds without problem. That receiver then took a position about a half mile off my left wing while his buddy came in for gas. About then we were bounced around fairly severely by what felt like a pocket of turbulence. Unfortunately, the number three engine fire light came on at the same time. We ran the emergency checklist to cut off that engine and put out any fire. When the copilot looked out his window at the engine, he said he couldn't see any flames so it was probably OK. I asked the receiver pilot to take a look. His report moments later was not very comforting. He said he could see through the engine nacelle from front to back. The entire inside of the engine was gone! We told

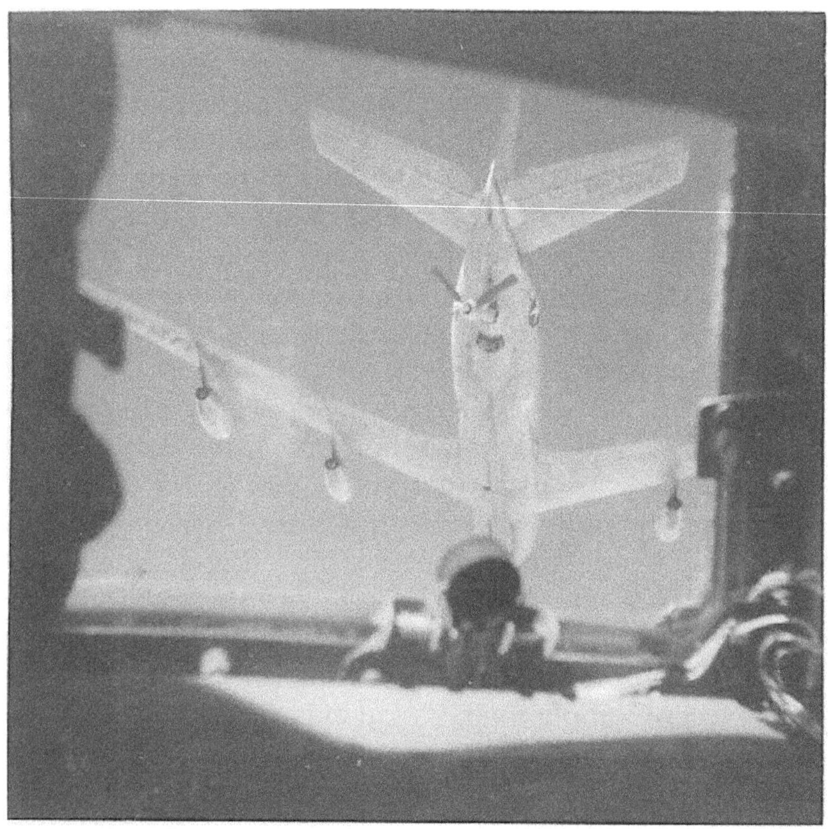

him we were done refueling for the night and turned for home. The lead pilot directed his wingman to divert to the nearest recovery base and said he would continue with his mission. He gave us our current position coordinates from his much more accurate navigation system and soon we were alone as we made a 180 degree turn towards home base. At that time, we were about two and half hours from land with an additional hour to our base.

My confidence level was still pretty good. The airplane seemed to be flying well on autopilot, we had lost an engine, we had lost two of our three electrical generators (one was on the failed engine), and the pressurization system was acting up, but all in all we felt good about safely returning home. I tried to call the command post on HF radio to let them know of our problems, but the electrical interference made contact impossible. On we went into the night, hopefully on track for an uneventful three engine landing. About a half hour later the navigator advised me that his celestial observations did not seem to match up with the position he had calculated using dead reckoning. When I asked what heading he wanted me to fly, he said he wasn't sure, but we should try to stay on our current course. He would try another observation in a few minutes. Now I was concerned! This far north, a mere ten degree heading error could make us miss the entire Alaskan landmass completely and either end up over uninhabited northern Canada, flying down the middle of the Pacific Ocean, or worse, enter Soviet airspace west of Alaska. A crew from our base had almost done that very thing two months prior. At that time, Soviet fighters scrambled to intercept the wayward aircraft and only the presence of American fighters launched from western Alaska had saved the day.

Another hour and more went by and we were no more confident of our position. We felt we should be nearing the Northern Alaska coast but the aircraft radar showed no land ahead at the hundred-mile limit of our equipment. Now our fuel status started to become a concern. I tried the HF radio again, but all I could hear was static. In desperation, I tried transmitting on our UHF radio, in the blind, calling for any station to acknowledge. There were a few remote early warning radar stations in this part of the world and maybe we would get lucky. After my third transmission and trying to hide my anxiety from the rest of the crew, the radio crackled to life and a sleepy voice asked who was calling. It was one of the Green Pine Radar sites and we had just gotten the duty controller out of bed. His voice was like a lifeline from heaven. He asked our track and position, and said it would take a couple of minutes for the radar to make a complete sweep to confirm our position. Less than a minute later he said he thought he had us radar identified about 150 miles from land. He had us make a little turn and confirmed our position. We were saved!

The remaining flight time was more or less uneventful. As we traversed the airspace over Northern Alaska, I was finally able to contact our command post on one UHF radio while on the other radio the copilot advised Fairbanks approach control of our emergency situation and requested vectors for descent and landing. We soon had course guidance from navigational radio ground stations and began our descent. The miles to final approach for landing seemed to take forever. We had plenty of fuel and the remaining operational systems on the airplane seemed to be working. I was just glad to get safely home. We advised the approach controller that we had the runway in sight from about twenty miles out. We would just take a visual approach and we thanked the civilian controller for his help. The radios were quiet for a minute and then the controller asked if we were sure we had the runway in sight. We had just told him we did, but again I said yes, at our twelve o'clock for about fifteen miles. He said we needed to turn right about ninety degrees if we want to land at the military base. Yikes! We were lined up on the civilian runway in Fairbanks! The euphoria of safety vanished in a moment. I begin a turn to the west and profusely thanked the controller for his help. I noted a tone of sympathy in his voice when he said he would stay in contact until we were safely on the ground. We landed without incident and taxied clear of the runway. After stopping on the taxiway, several maintenance vehicles approached the airplane and I climbed down from the cockpit to view the damage to our number three engine. There was no engine in the number three nacelle, but otherwise the airplane looked OK. I climbed back on board and we taxied to the ramp. After shutting down the remaining engines, we left the airplane to the maintenance personnel and headed into the operation building to report on our adventure. It had been a long cold night.

I didn't wake up until late the next day. It was still dark outside at noon, but it was time to get up. After breakfast at the Officers club, I walked through the underground tunnels to the operations building. When I got there, I checked the scheduling board to see which flights we would be assigned for the remainder of the week from those for which we had volunteered. To my surprise our name had been wiped from the volunteer board. The duty officer said that our navigator had removed our crew from that list earlier in the morning. He said the Major did not want any more drama with an inexperienced new crew and the last flight was enough for him. I thanked the duty officer and told him to put our crew back up for daily missions. We got a call later that day to tell us we would be flying again in two days. I could see that our navigator, John, was puzzled about how that could have happened but I did not enlighten him. I checked the schedule board a couple of times each day for the remainder of our deployment to make sure we had not been deleted again.

Two days later, our flight went off without a hitch. It was scheduled for a refueling of F4s from the Anchorage area. We had a senior air refueling technician on board for the flight, since our "baby boom operator" needed training in refueling fighter aircraft. After our last flight, we were relieved that we were only going a couple of hours to the west, over land, and then return. It was scheduled to be a fairly short flight with eight F-4 receiver aircraft. We leveled at our refueling altitude of 27 thousand feet and the copilot began setting up his fuel panel for the offload. The two boom operators headed to the back of the aircraft to check their systems. If we had a problem with our systems, we were to radio back to the base and they would launch the spare tanker that was standing ready by the end of the runway. However, this day the boom operator reported all looked normal in the back. Soon we heard the F4 flight lead check in on the Anchorage Center radio frequency. The center controller advised that our receivers were at our twelve o'clock position for 100 miles and should be in contact with us shortly. A minute later we heard the call from Eagle lead to Texaco 21, our call sign for the day. I passed control of the radio to the navigator who would coordinate the join up. Our closure speed as we headed toward the fighters was around 900 knots so timing for the turn was critical. At 21 miles separation on our radar scope, the navigator directed me to make an immediate left turn of 180 degrees. Half way through the turn, the copilot said he had the receiver formation in sight and that the boom operator should have them in sight shortly as they fell behind our aircraft. As the receivers closed with us, the fighter leader directed two aircraft to our left wing and one to the right, while he moved in to get his gas. The second group of four aircraft stayed about two miles behind us in trail. We had 115,000 pounds of fuel reserved for the formation of fighters and it was up to the flight leader to decide how that was divided up. I could hear the senior boom in the back coaching our boom to a successful hookup and soon the copilot positioned the switches to transfer 10,000 pounds of fuel to the leader. The offload went well and the flight of four moved well off to the south of our position so that the second flight of four aircraft could take fuel. One of the second group of aircraft was obviously new because he came towards us too fast and the boom operator called for a breakaway. A breakaway means that one of the receivers is about to collide with your aircraft and you want to quickly move away. I shoved the throttles forward and we accelerated ahead of the closing fighter. When we were well clear, the boom said we could slow back down and he cleared the plane back in for fuel. The boom said he almost hit us and it was a few minutes before the adrenaline level of everyone on board went back to normal. After two or three more tries it was apparent that the F4 pilot just wasn't skilled enough to refuel and the flight leader directed him to return to base. We refueled the rest and gave a top off to the first four. Then the seven remaining receivers headed off to the gunnery range to try their luck there. We were ready to call it a day, and headed for home.

We called the base to get the local weather from about 200 miles out. When we left the weather was cold but the sky was clear in all directions as far as you could see. The command post controller received our report of a successful refueling and then advised us of the local conditions. He said that a light breeze was blowing the plume from the local heating plant towards the runway and creating an ice fog over the center of the runway. We could orbit at altitude and wait to see if the winds might shift. A quick look at the fuel panel confirmed that we had about 20 thousand pounds of fuel left, enough for maybe an hour or two of orbit time and landing. I told the controller we would try an approach to see how bad the weather was and maybe consider diverting to Anchorage, a couple of hundred miles to the west. He advised that Anchorage was below minimums and would be so for most of the day. I asked what other runways could be used and he said everything in Alaska was closed. Uh oh. We decided to try an approach and sure enough, the ice fog covered the runway and we could not see the runway when we got down to 200 feet landing minimums. I asked again how long the weather forecasters thought it would be before the runway would clear. They were not sure. By now we had unsuccessfully tried to see the runway and were climbing through 3,000 feet to go back and orbit a short distance from the runway. I asked on the radio where the closest serviceable runway with acceptable weather was located. The answer? Spokane, Washington, several hundred miles away. For about two seconds a really cold chill went up my spine. Then I went into the "save your butt" mode. I pushed the throttles up to climb power, told the navigator to give me the most direct heading to Spokane and told the copilot to get in the performance charts and determine what altitude and airspeed were the best we could do for fuel economy. The navigator said to fly a 210 heading and he would give me a more precise heading in a few minutes. The copilot quickly came up with a best altitude of 41,000 feet, our aircraft maximum ceiling, and around 240 knots airspeed. I got there as quickly as we could and then began the first of many recalculations to see if we could actually make it. As we left the area, the base controller wished us good luck. The tone of his voice sounded like he thought we would need more than his good wishes. It was a long way to the next gas station and although we had heard of a way to reverse refuel a tanker aircraft from a B-52, there were no such aircraft in this part of the world at this time.

I reminded the navigator that we needed the most direct course he had ever plotted to Spokane. I was fairly confident his experience would take care of that part of the deal. Now we just needed to have a little luck with the winds and fuel burn. The next hour of flight was nerve wracking. We managed the fuel panel like it was heart patient and the least miscalculation would be fatal. Finally, we got within radio range of the base at Spokane. The local people there had been called about our problem and were ready with any help they could provide. Unfortunately, their report of rain showers at the field and a 400-foot overcast ceiling was not the help I was looking for. We were probably going to get one shot at the landing and I did not want to think about the chances of success if we did not make it on the first attempt. The copilot and I had figured out that if we pulled the throttles to idle and started down from 41,000 feet at about 110 miles out, we might not have to use much fuel for the last part of the flight. We did so, and I also delayed gear and flaps until well inside the final approach fix to minimize drag. It was one of my better approaches, and with emergency vehicle lights flashing on the nearby taxiway, our main gear gently touched down and we turned off at the first taxiway. I felt like I had aged ten years in the last few hours. We shut down the inboard engines on the taxi in and somehow had enough fuel to get to parking. Maintenance personnel later told us that when they checked our fuel tanks, we had maybe another fifteen minutes before the engines would have begun flaming out. We spent the night in officers' quarters at Spokane and had an uneventful return to Alaska the next morning.

By this time, my navigator had had enough of hair raising adventures and the rest of us were ready to agree with him. As did the schedulers. For the next ten days, we roamed the base tunnels, read endless paperback books, watched TV on the only base channel, and tried to find new items to buy in the same stores, day after day. I had brought some college homework for a labor relations course on the deployment and I actually got motivated to do some reading and writing. We were ready to go home, but our deployment had another ten days to run. We were assigned strip alert in a facility at the end of the runway. The job was to be ready to launch on a moment's notice if someone in Alaska had an inflight fuel emergency (and they were flying an aircraft that we could refuel). No one ever used this service and we settled in for several days of boredom. We sat there in the alert lounge, day after day. Outside the temperature dropped to minus sixty degrees. Preflight of our cold soaked airplane every morning was more painful than I can ever describe.

Finally, with five days left, we got another mission, sort of. We were to be the backup for two aircraft that would transport classified material early next morning to the lower United States. At the time of our deployment, the Vietnam War was in its final stages and the latest intelligence information needed to be flown back to the headquarters in the US to be used for mission planning. An aircraft would arrive at our Alaskan location fresh from Southeast Asia and then the materials they carried would be transferred to two of our aircraft and be flown to military headquarters near Washington, DC, and Omaha, Nebraska. On the day of our new assignment, the incoming aircraft radioed ahead his arrival time and the two aircraft plus us as spare started up in preparation for taxi. One of the primaries immediately radioed with an engine problem and just like that we went from spare to second primary aircraft. We would be going to Washington, DC. Our remaining two aircraft taxied to the end of the runway to await the landing plane. About the time the arriving aircraft reported he was on final approach, the other tanker radioed to say that his hydraulic system was not working and he would be taxiing in. Seems like we had been here before, but this time at least we were taking a flight back to the lower states and could look forward to spending a night in the warm quarters at Andrews Air Force Base. It was not to be. The Command Post radioed that the material was absolutely critical to the war effort, and we would be going to Washington, and then on to Nebraska where we would spend the night. By now the big transport aircraft was in the landing flare and after touchdown he taxied back to a position behind us on the taxiway. The supervisor of flying joined our little assembly and received a couple of large taped boxes and the courier who climbed down from the arriving airplane. The SOF brought the courier over to us and our boom operator helped the courier stow his baggage and find a seat in the back. We closed the hatch, got clearance to taxi onto the runway and departed without further incident. We leveled at 35,000 and headed southeast towards Canadian airspace and on to Washington. The mission was high priority and we felt good about being part of it. I pushed up the airspeed to about 475 knots with the thought that faster was better. The flight took about seven hours, the sky was clear, and the further south we got, the more daylight we were able to experience. This was a very welcome change from the continual night time at our temporary Alaskan home. Washington Center passed us off to Andrews Air Base controllers and soon we were on final approach. We were advised that we should taxi to the parallel taxiway after landing and personnel would meet us who were authorized to receive the classified materials. After landing we cleared the active runway and stopped on the taxiway. There was no one in sight. We asked the control tower if they knew where our contact person was. The tower didn't know, but they said they would make a couple of calls to find out.

After fifteen minutes of setting there with engines

running I decided to taxi in to the ramp and get a fuel top off for the next leg of the flight. We did so and after engine shutdown the refueling pit personnel appeared and topped off our tanks. We were trying to decide what to do next when a staff car finally appeared. Our courier deplaned to check the credentials of his contact. About then I noticed that our courier was strapped with a rather large pistol. I guess that made sense given the nature of his business. The gun was easily much larger than the .38 revolver my navigator had concealed in his pants leg pocket to protect us from hijackers. Anyway, the courier gave one of the boxes to his contact and then said we were ready to continue on to Omaha. At that point I felt a little like a taxi driver, but this was war and also my job for the day. We started up engines, got ATC clearance for a flight direct to Omaha, taxied out to the runway, and soon were in the air and leaving the greater Washington area far behind.

We had been up about twelve hours at this point and I realized I was a little tired. Flying west into the sun reminded me of an earlier trip and I was determined not to get sleepy so I turned the plane over to my copilot and headed to the back to take a lap around the cargo bay and get a cup of coffee. I do not usually drink coffee, but I didn't have a coke and I needed caffeine. We motored on for another three hours and Kansas City Center gave us vectors and descent for the military runway outside of Omaha. The runway there is fairly short for heavy jets at just over nine thousand feet long and the parallel taxiway only extends toward the north end as far as the middle of the runway. My copilot made a nice landing and we back taxied for parking just south of the runway. I was glad to shut down the engines and the courier's transportation was waiting for him at the parking space. The crew looked at each other with a sigh of relief and we began packing up our gear to head into the local billeting operation for the night. As we passed the last of our gear down through the entry hatch, a staff car pulled up and a colonel got out. He thanked us for a good job getting the courier there and said a fuel truck would be at the airplane shortly to get us ready to return to Alaska. I told him that we were near the end of our crew duty day and pretty beat to be taking another long flight leg. He said that was my call, but there were several aircraft out of commission at our Alaskan base and our plane was desperately needed. In addition, they had a passenger who needed to be transported there immediately. I should have said no, but after asking the crew if they thought they could continue, and making sure that the headquarters had approved an extended period of duty so we could complete this last mission, I agreed. We went into base operations to get a couple of cans of coke and some cold sandwiches for the flight, checked the weather and went back out to the airplane.

The ramp was pretty empty of activity when we got back to the airplane. It was, after all, late on a Sunday afternoon and my crew chief was wrestling the heavy start cart up to the airplane. We strapped into our seats and put our headsets on and everyone checked in on interphone. I looked out my window to see a security police vehicle pull up and wondered why the driver had come to our airplane. A policeman got out on the passenger side and opened the back door to let out a handcuffed prisoner in the back seat. This looked odd and I unbuckled my seat belt and climbed down the ladder to see what was going on. The policeman gave me a snappy salute and informed me that he and his prisoner were our passengers for the flight. He told me that the prisoner was being arraigned for rape at our Alaskan base and needed to be there tomorrow. I didn't like the situation and told him to standby for a minute. I climbed back up the ladder and radioed the local command post to find out what was going on. They confirmed that we were to transport the prisoner and that he was not dangerous. As opposed to the courier we had just dropped off, I noticed that the policeman did not have a weapon. I reluctantly waved the policeman and his passenger on board and told my boom operator to get them ready for takeoff. We closed the entry door, started up, and back taxied to the departure end of the runway. After a last-minute check of systems, I pushed up the throttles and we were off into the fading light of the western sky.

After I leveled off and the copilot checked in the air traffic control, I called for the boom operator to bring up some more coffee. We still had seven hours to go and I felt physically drained and not very alert. When he came forward, I asked him how the prisoner was doing and he said the prisoner was up and walking around. I asked what the cop was doing and the boom said he had taken off the prisoner's handcuffs and promptly gone to sleep. While it was obvious that the prisoner could not escape, I told the boom operator to keep him away from the cockpit and I told the navigator that if the prisoner stuck his face into the cockpit he should shoot him. I told the boom to wake up the cop and pass those words to him. And I didn't see either one of them again until we landed in Alaska. What I didn't say was that prior experience made me not trust the navigator to shoot anything, so when the navigator had a gun, I always made sure the copilot kept his bullets. We had worked that way for some months and I felt that was a lot safer than any of us getting shot by accident. I started operating that way after the first time the navigator lost his firearm, but that is a story for another time.

The flight back home was uneventful, although we were dead tired and landing at Eielson in the early morning hours was not an especially pretty thing. I do not remember much of what happened after we shut the

engines down on the parking ramp, but we all slept for most of the next day. We were assigned strip alert a couple of times over the few days we had left and then it was time for redeployment. My boom operator asked if we were going to pick up a load of crab legs to take back, but after my experience on the previous deployment, I decided that I was not a fish salesman and said "no". We flew back in formation with another crew that was redeploying to their home station in North Dakota and the contrails formed by the lead plane's exhaust made for some nice pictures as we cruised over the frozen landscape. As we approached American airspace, the other plane turned to the south and wished us well on the radio. In another couple of hours, we were making the descent to our home station in Michigan and waiting families.

I was pleased that we had done well as a crew during the deployment to Alaska, despite some serious inflight challenges. The navigator asked for a transfer to another crew within a couple of days after we arrived home and we were assigned a brand-new replacement. I heard later that our old navigator's new crew had some exciting flights of their own and soon he requested and received permission for reassignment for non-flying duty.

Within six months, I was assigned duties as a senior instructor pilot and rarely flew with newer crewmembers except to evaluate them. I have not been back to Alaska since that deployment, but sometimes, late at night in the dead of winter, I think about high adventure in the night skies up north with a very young and very inexperienced crew. When those memories demand attention, they seem like dreams that happened to someone else or a version of something I saw in a movie. And then I remind myself that I am secure in my own bed as I push the memories of those cold winter nights back into the dark recesses of my mind along with demons of other scary times.

Water Dog

It was another beautiful, but cold fall day as we made our way east on US 2. Tony and I had no luck fishing earlier that day and figured we would stop to hunt for grouse around the edge of a pair of small lakes about thirty miles west of our usual hunting area. We had not seen many birds at Rice Lakes during previous scouting expeditions, but the place offered a chance for a short hunt to stretch our legs. There were no other tire tracks visible as we drove down the sandy, tree lined lane and turned in to a small open area covered with pine needles. We stepped out of the car into the crisp, pine-scented air and began pulling on our insulated boots and hunting gear. Our cartridge belts held evenly distributed loads of # 6 and # 4 shot in readiness for grouse or ducks. We slipped the red Federal #6 shells into our magazines and headed through the trees to a faint trail through the brush that led to the perimeter of the nearest lake.

We had tried duck hunting a couple of other times at Rice Lakes with Bob, a fellow pilot. The lack of cover around the lakes and the difficulty of dragging a canoe several hundred yards through the marsh to the water's edge made it a difficult place to hunt. On our last trip to Rice lakes Bob had tried shooting from a camouflaged canoe, and he and a friend had almost turned over the canoe firing out of the same side at a passing duck. We decided the shore was much safer, if less effective. On that trip I ended up lying on the wet, mucky peat behind a small dead tree branch and wondering if any healthy duck would come within gun range of the nice man playing dead in the meager brush screen of the shoreline. After we spent an unproductive couple of hours lying in ambush, it took Bob an hour to recover his decoys with a hand line thrown from shore into the opaque blue-black water. None of us was brave enough to try to wade out into the mucky bottomed lake to get the decoys. A test of the depth with a branch revealed no apparent bottom.

But today Tony and I were out for a chance at grouse and I was enjoying the quiet hunt through the brushy woods. Rice Lakes are encircled by a twenty-yard wide matting of spongy peat and grasses that gives way to a thin screen of scrub pines. The peat matting provides fairly secure footing if you are not weighed down with a heavy load of gear. If you break through the peat you are sure to get wet and it is unclear how far down you will sink. Today we were in the cover of the trees, however, and the footing there was a little more solid. We spread out about ten yards apart and began moving through the trees to remain concealed from any ducks on the water and any grouse that might be in the scrub pine ahead. I could see Tony's yellow ball cap moving through the thick brush off to my right and his slow, steady pace reminded me that we were in no rush. The damp, cushioned effect of the soft ground let us ghost through the woods and listen for the muffled launch of an escaping grouse. We had not gone very far when I heard noises on the water, followed by the report of Tony's shotgun. I moved in that direction to see what luck he had and found him looking out into the lake and scratching his head. He had dropped a nice drake mallard, but it was about ten yards from shore, floating on the still water. There was not a breath of wind and it looked like the duck was not going to float towards shore anytime soon. The water looked deep and the late Fall temperatures did not encourage wading/ swimming as a viable option. This duck dinner wasn't going anywhere, and I had no idea how we were going to get it. Now Tony has great patience and he liked to carefully consider problems like the one we had before us. He sat down on a nearby log, pulled out a blue can of Sail tobacco, and filled his pipe. I waited patiently while he lit his pipe and took a couple of puffs. Suddenly, he sat up and announced, "Let's get the fish poles." I didn't have a better idea for duck retrieval, so back to the car we went, left the shotguns there, and returned to the lake with fishing equipment.

We decided the fishing lure of choice for duck retrieval would be a large three to four-inch spoon bearing huge trebles hooks. These lures had previously served no other purpose than casting for twenty-pound fish (imagined but never seen) and taking up space in our tackle boxes. About 200 casts (each) later, we finally had our prize and more than enough "fishing" for the day. It was a fat healthy duck and we were pleased not to leave it behind. In the past we had lost a few ducks that had fallen in deep cover, but this seemingly lost bird was secured. For the first few minutes as we drove towards home, Tony was quiet. Then he observed "we need to buy ourselves some hunting dogs. They can save us a lot of lost game and besides they make great family pets." I had not owned a dog since childhood, and I was not sure how a big hunting dog would work out in my small house, but Tony was an expert on hunting matters, so as far as I was concerned, those were details to be resolved later. We planned to get together during the coming weekend to discuss how to get some first-class hunting dogs.

Tony was in his living room pouring over a number of sporting magazines when I arrived at his house a couple of days later. He fixed me some hot chocolate and then warmed to the topic of dogs. When I first met Tony, he had an Irish Setter which he eventually had to put down for health issues. He now asked if I knew anything about different retriever breeds. I told him that I had a German shepherd when I was much younger. Old Sarge was famous for chasing poisonous snakes and skunks. He also had a nasty habit of picking the wrong places to relieve himself, which put him on my mother's blacklist. No, I didn't know anything about retrievers. Tony gave me the short course on sporting dogs, starting with English pointers and ending with Labrador retrievers. He thought the lab was a great dog, but if we were going to get the right dogs for hunting, we needed to carefully think through how the dogs would be used. We had been doing a lot of duck and grouse hunting. With the bitter fall and winter weather in the Forest Primeval and surrounding waters, Tony thought that the Chesapeake Bay retriever would be the best choice. I had never heard of the breed, but he was ready with a couple books that detailed what great dogs they were. He pointed out that they could survive almost any amount of cold and swam like a fish. Their oily, curly coat shed water like a duck. They had been known to make blind retrieves, whatever that was, of more than 200 yards. This all sounded pretty good. Besides, he said, "this kind of dog has a reputation for being loyal to their master to the point of death. They will guard your hunting gear and birds from anyone who tries to take them." Although I had never had to worry about any one taking my hunting gear or birds, a dog that could do expert guard duty seemed like a useful thing. I asked Tony how we should go about getting these dogs and he showed me an advertisement for a registered Chesapeake breeder in Iowa. It said that the dogs were guaranteed healthy and came from champion stock. And they were priced reasonably at only $150. At the time, that seemed like a lot of money for a dog. I was already thinking how I would explain to my wife what an important and needed purchase this would be.

The next day we put our checks for $150 each in the mail to Cedar Falls, Iowa and the deal was done. In just a few days, the breeder called to confirm our order. He said that he expected a new litter of pups soon and he would call us back about six weeks after they were born. While we waited anxiously for word from Iowa, we each bought a book that the breeder recommended, titled "Water Dog" by Tom Wolters. The book promised all kinds of exciting adventures with your new retriever and recommended several implements to get the most training value out of a dog. Canvas retrieving dummies and a device named the Retriever Trainer were recommended to get your dog properly trained. We ordered the stuff immediately. My wife was not happy with the cost of the training gear that added another $200 to the cost of the dog. But it seemed like a good idea to get this stuff so as to correctly train the dog. Almost eight weeks later the breeder called to say that he had picked two fine pups for us and that they would be flown to our local airport on the daily airline run from Cedar Falls, with two intermediate stops. He said he would put enough food and water in their traveling kennels to take care of the dogs for the day, but it was essential that we met the dogs at the appointed arrival time.

On the appointed day, we waited nervously at the airport as the plane unloaded its cargo and the baggage handlers walked away. The dogs were not on the airplane. We called the breeder and he said he had watched as the dogs were loaded prior to departure. It took several hours before the airlines finally located the dogs at a small Midwestern airport where they had mistakenly been offloaded. They would probably arrive the next day. When the dogs finally arrived two days later, they were in bad shape. They had had little water and no food for the preceding 36 hours. The little pups could hardly move. After getting them some water, I took one with a reddish coat and Tony took one that was a sandy grey color. We headed home with our dogs and our separate ideas about training and care. Tony had explained earlier that the Chesapeake Retriever has a noble history as the only native American breed of dog and that we should choose something nautical sounding for a name. The names we chose were Nordic Sailor, for Tony's dog and Yankee Clipper for mine. Tony called his dog Sailor. I could not think of a clever nickname for my dog, so he became Clipper.

The dogs recovered nicely. Tony built a fenced ten-foot concrete run for his

dog and began training almost immediately. Clipper decided he would be a house dog and I agreed. He was a hit with my family. Except for those times when he found a way to eat something which was normally non-edible or when he rejected the normal process of house training. The Wolter's book said formal dog training should begin at about six months, so I was in no rush. We held the first joint training session for our dogs at a nearby pond. I was nervous about how the Clipper would behave. He was pretty frisky while Sailor seemed focused on Tony's every move. We met at the pond and let the dogs run free. They seemed to enjoy a brotherly bit of play as they romped near the shoreline. Tony and I took turns restraining our dogs on a leash while the other responded to thrown canvas dummies. After a couple of throws on land, Tony threw a dummy about ten feet out into the water, and after a short hesitation, Sailor jumped in and brought it back. It looked so easy. It was my turn. I threw the dummy on land a couple of times. Clipper seemed interested in the throwing, but not the bringing. He would grab the dummy in his mouth and then shake his head like he was trying to tear it to pieces. Then I tried a throw into the water. There was no way he was going in. He whined and looked confused, but would not budge from shore. After a couple more attempts, I waded out to get the dummy with a branch and we were done for the day. The following weekend we took both dogs out to work on our duck blind and both dogs ended up in the water in the course of their play. When a dummy was thrown, they both went for it. So far so good! I was optimistic that both dogs would perform expertly with the real thing. We put the dogs in the back of my truck closed the cap door and headed home. As we drove, we were congratulating each other on our dogs' progress and speculating on what a fine hunting season it would be. The dogs were still young and this would be a learning season, but they were definitely going to be an asset. That was when all hell broke loose in the back of my pickup truck.

I was driving down the highway at 65 mph talking to Tony when I heard a

loud bang and commotion in the back. Through the back window I could see something flying around and the dogs were going nuts. Something sprayed across the window and my first thought was that the spray was blood and that the dogs were killing each other. I brought the truck to a hard stop in the roadside gravel and we both jumped out to save our dogs. As I raised the back hatch, both dogs came flying out of the truck. Tony grabbed Sailor and I got a tight hold on Clipper's choke collar. That's when we noticed the coats on both dogs had taken on a decidedly green shade. It took a few seconds before I remembered that I had left my boat painting materials in a box in the back of the truck. One of the dogs had bitten into a spray paint can, which instantly became a missile that coated the inside of the truck bed, the dogs and our gear a lovely shade of pea green. This dog handling was not going to be as easy as we had imagined.

Our key dog training device was called the Retriever Trainer. It was basically a straight hollow pipe with a bicycle handle grip on one end that could be opened to accept a .22 caliber blank load. A canvas bag with an enclosed, slightly larger metal pipe could be fitted over the open end of the retriever trainer. When discharged, the device would launch the dummy 50 to 200 yards, depending on the angle of launch and the size of the powder charge in the blank. A green marked cartridge was a low power load that would make considerable noise and launch the dummy about eighty to one hundred feet. A red marked change was more powerful. It would leave your ears ringing and make your hand numb for a few seconds as it blasted the dummy out of sight. The purpose of the retriever trainer was to get the dog accustomed to hearing a shot, and watching for where a downed bird might fall. Clipper made the connection between shot and bird right away. After only two shots, he would blast off running in the direction I was pointing the device, before I even launched. It required some ingenuity on my part so that he wouldn't catch the thing before it landed. When he would run off in an anticipated direction, I would point the thing in the opposite direction, call him to stop and then fire when he looked back at me. He would give me a dirty look as he ran back past me in the opposite direction, indicating I was somehow untrustworthy in holding up my end of the retrieving bargain.

On our next visit to the pond, it was time to work on the dogs' swimming strength. Both dogs swam easily out to the thrown dummies. With our best throws, we could get the dummies out about 25 yards. After a few such efforts, it was time for the big show. I made sure Clipper was ready and watching. He shivered with excitement as I put in a red cartridge and pointed the trainer out towards the center of the lake. I hated the pain of firing those big loads, but it was time for the big test. I fired. Clipper watched. And watched some more. He looked at me and looked at the water. No amount of urging could get him in the water. We could see the dummy clearly floating on the water about 100 yards out. An hour later, the dummy finally floated back to shore on a light breeze and after I disgustedly retrieved it, we put the dogs in the back of the truck and headed home.

Clipper was good at retrieving things, as long as it was his idea. He frequently wrestled a long, heavy branch from a lake bottom, blowing bubbles from his nose, and brought it to shore for my inspection. A friendly and playful dog, he sometimes attempted to retrieve my young sons, much to their displeasure, either on family outings or in a backyard snowdrift. He accompanied me on one ill-advised fishing trip where he decided to retrieve my cast from the middle of a river. It took me ten minutes to extract the treble hook from his upper lip. Like most dogs, if you were willing to throw something, he was willing to retrieve it. Eventually, he also got the hang of the Retriever Trainer. He just never liked to bring the canvas dummy directly back to me after he had retrieved it. The shore was about as close as he would get. As a result, he trained me to meet him at the shore and even tried to avoid me there as he trained me to take part in his keep away game. One early fall afternoon, I took him to East Lake to practice retrieving before the start of the season. After several launches and retrieves into the lake, two Fish and Game Department cruisers rolled up in a cloud of dust and the officers motioned me over. They said they had a report that I was hunting out of season and demanded to look in my truck and at my gun. The occupant of a nearby cabin had heard shots from my direction and had seen something fall into the water that was retrieved by my dog. After some fast talking and a demonstration of the Retriever Trainer, the officers relaxed and sat down to watch my training efforts. After watching Clipper's repeated deposits on the shoreline instead of to me, one officer said, "That's a neat gizmo, but

the dog is useless." I ignored him. That was my dog he was talking about.

Clipper was very focused when it came to retrieving. On one memorable hunting trip, I was racing across East Lake, heading to my duck hunting blind, with Clipper enjoying the breeze from the front of my 14-foot aluminum boat. East Lake is a circular lake about a half mile across. The blind I used was on the opposite shore from the launch ramp, but my 15 horse Evinrude motor made short work of the crossing. I could see several flights of ducks in motion around the lake, but Clipper seemed to be focused on something on the water ahead. I soon saw his attention was on a large group of ducks floating on the water and I adjusted the course of the boat to pass to their downwind side. As we got within twenty or thirty yards, Clipper's ears went up and before I could react, he launched. The action reminded me of the WWII torpedoes that are launched from the deck of a PT boat. He hit the water and planed underneath. When he came up his eyes were as big as saucers and his refined swimming stroke had turned into a panicked thrashing as he tried to levitate out of the water. He splashed back to the boat and I pulled him aboard where he slumped down in the front of the boat, eyeing me in the suspicion that I had somehow punished him for chasing ducks. That was a lesson well learned. He did not launch from a moving boat again.

The two hunting dogs were trained very differently. Tony's dog spent all his non-hunting hours in a dog run. He was not a very friendly dog and most people, including Tony's family seemed very nervous around him. Once an errant golfer hit a ball into Tony's back yard near Sailor's run and went to retrieve his ball. When Sailor attempted to eat his way through the wire fence to get at the golfer, the golfer left immediately and the ball became the start of a considerable collection. Sailor's menacing growl, and bared teeth even made me uncomfortable. He was like Stephen King's Cujo, except worse. In the field, however, he and Tony were a finely tuned team. Tony would order Sailor to sit and stay and the dog responded like a robot. I had no doubt that Tony could drop a steak in front of the dog and he wouldn't move until approval was pronounced. Tony demonstrated how he could give the dog a heading to follow by passing his hand near the dog's head in the direction the dog was supposed to go. When Tony gave him that line to follow, Sailor would head in that direction until a blast of Tony's whistle told the dog to stop and look back for further instructions. Tony would then gesture which direction the dog should go next. This directed maneuvering would continue until two blasts of the whistle directed the dog to return to his master. I was really impressed. Clipper, on the other hand, was rarely distracted by commands or signals and seemed to follow some inner guidelines. By this time, I had become very frustrated with the whole training deal, but then the tradeoff was I had a dog who was loved by all members of his family and who moonlighted as a hunting dog, rather than the other way around.

As the two dogs got bigger, the playful activity between two brothers began to turn more serious. After the first season they each quickly grew to around 100 pounds of lean, mean retrieving machine (well Clipper wasn't very mean except when around his brother and then I suspect it was in self-defense!). After separating the dogs a couple of times, with both bleeding from the muzzle, we decided to only take one dog at a time on our hunting trips. And then it was my turn to bring Clipper on the first grouse hunting trip of the second season. It was Tony's turn to drive so we were in his green International Scout. I was concerned about the dog getting mud on car's upholstery, but Tony threw an old blanket on the back seat and said to not worry about it. We headed off for the long drive to the Forest Primeval and grouse territory. We had been driving for about a half hour and talking about how the upcoming season might unfold, when I remembered Clipper was in the back seat and I was pleased how quiet and well behaved he was. As we talked, I turned to commend Clipper for being a good dog, only to observe with great horror that the dog had just finished chewing off the arm rest of the left rear door of Tony's car. The dog looked at me sheepishly and hung his head. After a few moments, I broke the news as gently as I could to Tony and he was very gracious in saying not to worry about it. That was the last time Clipper rode in the scout.

After the second season, I moved a couple of times in quick succession to jobs in different states and finally ended up in Nebraska where flat farmlands and plentiful game provide the perfect setting for a retriever. The first hunting season after we arrived, my dad visited and we went hunting at a small unnamed farm pond that I had previously scouted, about twenty miles south of my house. Although there was not much cover around the shallow little pond, someone had fashioned a reasonably camouflaged duck blind on the northern shore that could seat two or three hunters comfortably. It was the first time Clipper had been around my father and the dog was very excited as we arrived at the lake in the early morning gloom. I put on my hip boots and with flashlight in hand, I positioned a large spread of three dozen decoys about twenty yards in front of the blind. I could hear Clipper splashing in the dark and dragging sticks and logs about as I stepped on the lead weights on the decoy anchor lines to drive them into the soft lake bottom. This would prevent the decoys from floating away if the wind came up. Seating was on an eight foot, two by ten board in the blind, balanced on two plastic buckets. My dad and I got in the blind, loaded our guns, poured some coffee and settled in to wait for first light. Clipper lay down between us, under the board. He was still shivering with excitement. When the first duck flew over some minutes later, we got up to shoot, and Clipper immediately ran from the blind causing the duck quickly flare up out of range. I scolded him and we settled back in. My dad suggested that maybe we should tie him up until we had fired and were ready to have ducks retrieved. I agreed and tied Clipper to the board we were setting on with some rope I had in my pack. Another half hour went by and Clipper seemed to settle down at my feet. However, at the least noise outside the blind or one of us shifting our position, his eyes would roll from me to the blind entrance, hoping to get approval for a quick departure. He must have felt the pressure of the tethering rope, because his eyes were the only thing that moved. He got up once when we heard some nearby quacking from a circling flock, but he seemed to sense that he was still attached to the long board we were setting on so he lay back down.

An hour went by without any action and as the morning sun rose higher in the sky, it was looking like a very pleasant and "unducky" kind of day. We were thinking about calling it quits, when I heard some quacking above and behind the blind and the distinctive sound of primary feathers bending in the wind as approaching ducks maneuvered for landing. I peeked through the camouflage material in the back of the blind and alerted my dad that a flight of six mallards was heading into the decoys from behind us and to get ready. We snapped our safeties off and tensed for the right moment. The ducks came by wide of the blind and continued towards the center of the lake as we watched through small openings in the front blind material. Then they swung around into the wind and headed right for us. Then the ducks were flaring for landing and we were jumping up. I picked out a drake coming towards my side of the blind and I fired at almost same time as my dad. The duck I was targeting immediately folded up but I did not get an opportunity to see him hit the water because my dad and I immediately went flying as Clipper blasted out of the blind, taking the long seat board with him. When we were able to untangle and scramble to our feet, we looked over the blind front and saw Clipper heading out for one of the ducks we had shot, straight as an arrow. As he went through the decoy spread, the board he was dragging collected four or five decoys and their trailing anchor lines. Added weight reduced his forward progress by half, but he made it to the downed duck, grabbed it and turned for shore. By now we were both outside of the blind and watching from the shore in amazement. As he came back through the decoy spread, he collected another four or five decoys with the trailing board. By the time he was twenty feet from shore his forward motion had slowed to nothing. He was dog paddling as hard as he could, and I could hear him trying to cough out water around the duck in his mouth as he settled lower in the water. He obviously was not going to make it so I waded out and disconnected him from the board and decoys. He was then able to take the duck to shore where he promptly dropped it and went off to play in the water. My dad shook his head in wonder and we both had a good laugh about the intensity with which the dog had completed his retrieve. By then, the wind was dying down, there wasn't a cloud in the sky, and it seemed like the morning hunt was over. And besides, half the decoys were already on the shore. We packed up and headed for home.

Although Clipper was good in duck hunting situations, he was equally good with pheasant hunting. No matter how thick the cover, if he went into it he usually found the birds. Mind you, I sometimes had to throw a stick into the brush for him to retrieve, to get him to go in, but once he was there and got wind of a pheasant or quail, he was relentless. We went hunting almost every weekend during pheasant season. It took some time, for me to trust Clipper's instincts. He seemed to think pheasant were in the most unlikely places, including under cars, in abandoned buildings, and near grazing livestock. Once, when I was returning from a successful hunt with a friend, Clipper went ahead of us and started barking at the area under my truck. We ignored him and unloaded our guns as we walked, only to see a rooster erupt from underneath the vehicle as we approached it. On another hunt, a friend and I were walking in an extremely flat and barren field on the way to an area of good cover. Clipper ranged ahead of us forty or fifty yards and I saw no reason to rein him in until we got closer to the cover. Suddenly, he stopped and started sniffing at a small clump of grass in the open field that was barely a foot high and maybe a foot wide. There was clearly not enough cover to hold a mouse much less a pheasant. I stopped in curiosity as he poked his nose into the tuft and he then jumped back with his ears up. He did this twice and after the second time started barking at the grass. I yelled at him to settle down and we continued our leisurely stroll towards the heavier cover. The dog would not leave the clump and when I got within thirty feet of it a cock pheasant suddenly materialized out of that little bit of grass. We were not ready, and the bird was quickly out of range. We realized the bird had been holding tight and was pecking Clipper on the nose every time he stuck it in to check the scent. I suspect the dog thought we were the ones that needed the training. After that episode, I did not doubt his nose again.

Whenever I headed for the door with either shotgun or hunting gear in hand, Clipper would materialize next to me with a pleading look. Even if I didn't have anything in hand, he always seemed to know when I was headed out to hunt or fish. It was impossible to refuse that look. And there was such joy on his face when he got to go! A few weeks into one season, I got home from work early and figured I had time to hunt a brushy area a few hundred yards behind the house. I had heard pheasant cackling in that area several times during the previous week. Clipper was eager to go and we headed out to a very nice fall afternoon. I let Clipper run free as we walked up a dirt road that ran behind the house and we soon came to a huge brush-covered punchbowl area that looked pretty good. It was a natural shooting gallery and Clipper immediately jumped a rooster that I dropped in the deep brush. I had no sooner fired than a second bird went up and I also dropped that one. This was fairly unusual success and I was little miffed that my marksmanship had only been witnessed by a dog. Clipper headed off for the first bird and I waded through the brush towards the second one. No sooner had I entered the brush than a third bird erupted from cover and I dropped that one. I was pretty excited about three birds with three shots, but I reminded myself that if I couldn't recover them all, no one would believe me. I thought I had a good mark on the last bird and I found it right away. It took me ten or fifteen minutes before I found a second one. Meanwhile, Clipper had gone into the brush as soon as I shot at the first bird. I called him several times but he did not reappear and I could hear him crashing through the brush somewhere down in the middle of the brush pile. I sat down to wait and five or ten minutes later he appeared. Since he didn't return with anything, I decided that I had lost the first bird. But it was still a pretty good shoot. And then I remembered his habit of not bringing birds to hand. I walked the dirt road around the perimeter of the brush bowl and sure enough, about fifty yards further, was the dead bird. Clipper had brought it up to the road and left it for me to find. And I was too pleased with three birds to make a big deal out of it.

Our time in Nebraska only lasted two seasons and we next moved to Northern Virginia, within a couple of hour's drive of the Chesapeake Bay. Clipper became a house dog and occasionally I took him to a nearby pond on weekends so he could make some swimming retrieves and keep in shape. We frequently had an audience of city dwellers who were entertained by his retrieving skill. We were now in a huge city, with no obvious hunting nearby. However, Clipper was great to have around to scare off salesmen or unwanted houseguests. A knock on the front door would cause him to go momentarily berserk as he tried to claw and bark his way through the door to get at whoever was there. His barking was loud enough to give you a headache and I frequently opened the door to find that whoever had knocked had fled to safety. Unfortunately (or fortunately, depending on how you looked at it), once any visitor got inside, Clipper became a tail wagging lap dog and I was convinced if we were ever burgled, he would show the burglar exactly where everything was. The days went by and Clipper and I both missed our days in the field.

The following fall, I was talking with a friend from work about how much I missed hunting now that we were in "the big city". You would think that by owning a Chesapeake Bay Retriever, I would have known there had to be hunting near the Chesapeake Bay. He told me there was lots of good hunting with a couple of hours drive and that the Chesapeake Bay was one of the premier waterfowl hunting places in the world. He told me of a goose hunting club I could join and I did so the following week. Fall weekends each season were happy times as Clipper joined me on 200 acres of farmland located just northeast of the Bay Bridge. There were four goose hunting blinds on the bay side to the west and three duck hunting blinds on the Chester River to the east. In the middle of the property there were five field blinds for use by the club members. The first couple of weekends before each season were work detail days as members repaired blinds and decoys and constructed new blinds. Several hours were spent putting new paint on the several hundred decoys owned by the club. The days were warm and we could see waterfowl flying in all directions as the season approached. The farmer who owned the property let us use an old chicken coop as a storage and work area and he encouraged us to take as many apples from the four nearby apple trees as we could carry. Work details on late September and early October days were a treat with the easy camaraderie of fellow hunters and mild fall weather. The veteran hunters said to enjoy the nice weather, because winter hunting on the bay would be brutal.

I did not take Clipper on the first few hunts that fall because I was sharing blinds with people I had just met and I did not want to have problems with him staying put. About three weeks into the season, however, I had a chance to go out during the week with only one other guy who seemed happy to have any dog there to make retrieves on the bay side of the property. Although the water was only about three feet deep for about twenty yards from the shore, when the tide was out, it dropped off steeply thereafter. We had an old row boat to use for long retrieves, but it was barely seaworthy and in a strong wind could be difficult to handle. We arrived at the property two hours before dawn and made the long trek across the fields to the blind. Most of the property consisted of corn fields that had been harvested the month before and I could hear Clipper ranging out ahead in the dark through the corn stubble. The shore blinds were perched on a bank about 20 feet above the water line. At the bottom of the bank, the sand beach extended about 20 to 30 feet to the water, depending on the level of the tide. We put our gear in the blind, took out the decoys from a box attached to the back of the blind, and then I climbed down the bank to place the decoys. I waded out to hip deep in my chest waders and placed two dozen magnum sized goose decoys. The decoys were anchored with fifteen-foot lines and heavy lead weights to handle to tide, but I still stepped them into the sandy bottom, just in case. Meanwhile, my hunting partner placed about fifty or sixty half shell goose decoys in the field behind the blind. The hard work done, we climbed into the blind loaded up with number two shot and poured cups of boiling hot coffee from a thermos. The spacious goose blinds were designed to hold four hunters and their gear in relative comfort while being subjected to the worst winter storms. I say relative because although you were usually out of the direct wind, rain, and snow, late season wind chills were usually measured in minus degrees and the little portable heaters we used did not provide much comfort.

As we settled into the blind, I could hear flights of geese calling from all directions, and as the sun came up,

we could see several flights working back and forth far out in front of the blind. I watched through my binoculars as several flights started generally towards our position, but in each case the flight changed direction and headed off into the distance. Clipper, as usual, was vibrating with excitement when we entered the blind, but after an hour or two of boredom, closed his eyes and seemed dead to the world. The weather was mild for a late October day and as I watched the flights of waterfowl., I could also see oyster trawlers working their dredges a couple of miles off shore. I leaned against the back of the blind and soon was watching with my ears as my eyelids closed to make up for lost sleep. My partner nudged me about the same time I heard some geese honking substantially closer than earlier flights. As I leaned forward to peer over the front sill of the blind, I saw a flight of eight geese headed right at us from about 100yards out. As they reached about 40 to 50 yards from the blind we both stood and fired. One crippled goose dropped towards the water, and I felt motion by my side as Clipper launched himself over the front sill of the blind. I guess he expected to find ground there, rather than a twenty foot drop to the beach. I grabbed for him and missed and then watched him hit the sand with a thump and continue his charge. His rear legs kept churning and his nose plowed a furrow for a few feet before his front legs were able to support his forward half. He hit the water and began swimming, straight for the crippled goose which was rapidly swimming out of gun range. I put down my gun and got out the binoculars to watch the action.

As Clipper reached the bird and moved in to take it in his mouth, the goose turned towards him and pecked him soundly on the muzzle. I heard the dog yip and he tried to move to a different side of the goose. It pecked him again. He looked confused and after a couple of move attempts to get position on the bird, he paddled back into shore. My hunting partner advised me that this was a very bad thing and that I would probably not be able to get him to make a water retrieve in the future. He was aware of other dogs that had experienced a similar episode which led to the end of their usefulness for hunting. I didn't doubt his story and was very concerned. I was not sure what to do about the problem, and any books I could later find on the subject seemed to pronounce the situation hopeless.

The next weekend we went hunting again. I shot a goose right after sunup and went out to retrieve it, since Clipper made no effort. Once on shore, I teased him with the dead goose until he seemed ready to rip it to shreds. I finally had to hide that goose in the decoy box to keep him away from it. Later in the morning, a flight of geese came in and my partner knocked one down at long range. Unfortunately, it was only wounded. With some apprehension, I made sure Clipper saw the goose and sent him after it. By the time he hit the water it was about 80 yards out and moving further away. He swam strongly for the goose and it turned to face him. It tried to peck him and through the binoculars I saw him use his front leg to try to knock the goose's head down. The goose then dove underwater...followed by the dog. They came up about ten yards apart and the dog renewed his pursuit. They both dove again. The dog was getting so far out, I was concerned that I couldn't get to him in time and started down the cliff for the boat, while watching the action. I need not have worried. This time the dog surfaced with the goose in his mouth and headed for the shore. I met him and he very reluctantly gave up his prize. My pride in his success was overwhelming. We didn't get another shot that day, but the dog's ability as a retriever was confirmed.

After three seasons, our time on the bay ended and I moved to Oklahoma. The waterfowl hunting there was not as good as other places we had been and by this time Clipper was showing signs of significant aging after 11 seasons of hard hunting. He still gamely joined me on

expeditions, either for hunting or just getting out of the house. His last hunt was late in our second season in Oklahoma, along a section of flooded timber where I downed a cinnamon teal and he headed out to make the retrieve. On this particular day I was distracted and had forgotten to remove his collar before heading out to hunt. As a result, when he swam out to get the downed duck, he got hung up on a tree branch in the water and was unable to get loose. I watched for a couple of minutes hoping he could free himself but he soon had trouble keeping his nose above the water and it was apparent he was in serious trouble. It was bone-chilling cold but I emptied my pockets and waded out in chest high water to rescue him. By the time I got him to shore, he was so worn out that I had to help him into the front of the truck, where I turned the heater on high to help us both recover. We headed home and I didn't take him out again that season. A month or so later, as winter weather settled in, I noticed that he was having trouble jumping into the truck and that his back legs were not working very well. I took him to the vet for a check-up. The vet confirmed that there was a serious problem which could be cancer in his hips or something similar. After talking about whether surgery might help and the poor likelihood of success, I agreed that we should put him down. It was a sad day for the family and one of the harder decisions I have had to make. I have not had another dog since, but the memories of a good dog, in a fine field on a perfect day, linger.

The Carp

If there is a constant or touchstone for all my outdoor adventures, it is the Carp River. Located just north of Saint Ignace in Michigan's Upper Peninsula, it runs about forty miles from its origin at Trout Lake to its river mouth in Lake Huron's St. Martins Bay. Its width is a constant 30 to 40 feet and the depth in summer months is two or three feet with an occasional hole over your head. When the ice breaks up in early April, the river roars with excess flow and it is unfishable for two or three weeks. The Upper Carp contains a lot of still water with little current which is attractive to beavers and waterfowl. The best fishing starts about a mile above the Carp River campground and continues all the way to the river mouth. Schooling salmon and steelhead trout frequent the river mouth waiting for the right water temperature before they enter the river in May and October to either spawn or feast on salmon eggs and small minnows. A run of smelt in April draws many locals who use hand nets to catch bucket loads of the tasty sardine-sized fish. The Carp is a peaceful place to spend the day, lost in thought, with an occasional cast to attract a hungry fish.

We had heard about the Carp River from a local fishing guide. The action on the Lake Superior streams had become slow that first summer in Michigan so on a whim we drove down to towards St. Ignace to check out the Carp. First, we tried just below the Interstate highway bridge, but the water there was slow flowing and too deep to wade. We then drove down to the boat launch ramp near the river mouth. Several anglers were there, mostly older types, with a collection of fishing gear that looked barely serviceable. We asked one older woman if she had any luck and she pointed out what she said was a rainbow trout in the brush behind her that she said she had just caught. After checking this out we laughed and congratulated her on her catch. The fish in question was obviously a red horse sucker, commonly discarded by most fishermen. This fish as well as the more common white suckers were what gave the river its name. We left the carp to check other fishing streams.

That fall we again heard tales about large salmon being taken at the Carp River in a place called McDonalds rapids. We got directions to this location about five miles upstream from the river mouth. When we arrived, the small dirt parking area was crammed with vehicles. We left the truck to walk along the river bank and saw wading anglers up and down this section of the river, as well as many spawning salmon that could be seen splashing their way up the shallow section of stream. We decided to return in the middle of the week when the weekend sports were at work.

When we returned, there were still a number of fishermen around so we trekked about two miles upriver until we no longer saw anyone. The river there was so shallow and clear that we could spot the salmon either holding on a bed or slowing finning in the current at the bottom of a set of rapids. Rather than fish in deep, cloudy water where there was no way to tell if fish were present, we adopted a technique we called "see em catch em". We walked the banks until a fish was spotted and then waded in the river upstream and cast to the target fish. It worked very well. When no fish could be seen, it was time to either fish in deep pools and hope for a bite or give it up

for the day.

Over the next months we explored the lower carp river, trying different places each time we were there. Eventually we settled on shallow run of water about two hundred yards upstream from the river mouth. The first time there, my partner Tony and I both caught nice steelhead trout that weighed in at a hefty six pounds. I do not remember who first proposed the name, but ever after that run was known to us as Murphy's. We usually arrived at Murphy's in late afternoon after work and stayed until dark. My usual tactic was to work a small Cleo spoon across the end of the run, hoping to tempt a fish waiting in the fast water. While this was going on, Tony often would be perched on a log on the bank, smoke from his pipe protecting his face from mosquitos and taking notes in his journal about what fly hatch was going on and the current water conditions. Just below Murphy's was a pocket in the stream about a dozen feet across that we called the whirlpool as the water formed a circular eddy there. The whirlpool was about ten feet deep and we surmised that fish may hold there from time to time, but we rarely caught anything there.

One afternoon late in June I could not find a fishing partner and went down to the Carp alone. The salmon and steelhead run had ended a week or two earlier, but I walked the bank of a little island just above the whirlpool looking for fish. I was just about ready to leave when I saw a large fish about a foot from the bank, just below the surface, in the fast current. I dangled a silver Cleo in front of the fish and he took it immediately. I played him down into the whirlpool and soon had a nice four- pound steelhead on the bank. I went back upstream and saw a second fish in the same place. He soon joined the first fish on the bank. I was really excited and wished someone was with me to see my success. And I saw a third fish in the same place. I remembered the limit was five fish and I could imagine that soon I would have that limit. I dangled the Cleo again and the fish struck. At the same time, the handle of my reel flew off into the deep water. Now I had

a fish on with no way to play him. It was like fishing with a cane pole and I had to work my way around trees as I moved down stream to the whirlpool. Somehow, I was able hand line the fish onto the bank to join the other two. I did not have replacement reel parts with me and I was sad to be done for the day, but happy that I could take an almost limit home. After that, I always carried a second fishing reel with me.

As spring turns into summer, the carp water levels drop and the big fish move back into the bay. Now the action turns to fly fishing. My friend Tony explained that this was about 'matching the hatch' of the flies that emerged from the surface of the water. He would wave his large, wide brimmed hat through the air and examine the flies he caught. Comparing them with the flies in his small metal box, he would select one that closely matched the live version and tie it on to his fly line. More times than not, he was soon hooked up to a fish. At this time of year, we caught small rainbow or brown trout. The fish were rarely longer than six or seven inches and were carefully released. The game was to see who could catch and release the most fish. On a typical afternoon that could be a dozen or more fish each. If we caught a fish that was ten or twelve inches, we would release them into a small holding pool we constructed. When we were ready to go home, if we had three or four this size we would take them home for supper. Otherwise we released them back into the main stream.

Some days we would arrive at the river to find a sucker run in progress. At the tail end of the run above the whirlpool there would be a ferocious splashing of ten or twenty suckers making their way upstream to spawn. We were concerned that these fish would deposit fry that would compete with trout and salmon fry for food so we took it as a summer challenge to remove these fish from the river. Thus, sucker snagging became a summer diversion. We would cast into a pod of suckers and soon snag a fish which we reeled in and threw on the nearby bank to provide tasty snacks for the resident black bear population. We knew bears were around due to the many tracks on the bank, and the next time we went fishing all the banked suckers were gone, so either bears or seagulls appreciated our efforts. However, it seemed that we hardly put a dent in the sucker population, because their numbers remained large until the run was over each summer and then the suckers moved back into the bay.

Although I had never seen a bear at the carp, one evening Tony stopped by my house to tell of a bear adventure. That afternoon I was at work so he decided to take his wife fishing. Once at the carp, he installed her on the bank of a small island above the whirlpool and after some instruction on where to cast her line, he moved about a hundred yards upstream, where he could still watch her if she needed help, but could have some quite time on his own stretch of water. He periodically paused his casting to look downstream, but was satisfied she was engaged in her own casts. Then, he looked in time to see a large black bear emerge from the island, sniffing the air, about fifty feet below where his wife was fishing. She was concentrating so much on where she was casting she had not noticed the bear. Tony quickly and quietly moved down to his wife, took her by the arm, moved back upstream, and then on to their car. She had had enough fishing for the day and was glad to leave, but wondered what was the rush. He did not tell her about the bear until the end of that summer.

After we moved from Michigan, the Carp was often on my mind. Every year, I made the return to the Carp no matter where I was living at the time. Sometimes that made for a very long drive. I drove my truck to the Carp either in the spring or fall every year. I drove there from Oklahoma, Indiana, Virginia, and Nebraska, depending

on where I was currently living. Usually I drove alone, but a couple times people I knew had heard my carp stories and talked me into taking them along. Those were not my favorite trips and the few fish we caught left the people I brought along doubting my stories. I could have a great time at the Carp and not catch a single fish, but that did not work well for most people. Sometimes the weather would not be good for fishing when I arrived. One October I left the carp after two days of unusual snow that made the fishing poor in the bitter cold. Sometimes the spring fishing would be very rainy the whole time I was there. I had good rain gear for fishing, but the damp and cold took away much of the enjoyment. One such time, after fishing in the rain for two days I came down with a very bad cold. I spent the next two days in my sleeping bag in the back of my truck, drinking hot tea and soup I made on my Coleman stove. I probably should have gone to a local clinic for medicine, but I chose to tough it out. The rain finally stopped and I felt good enough to fish, but I had only one more day before it was time to head home.

On another spring trip as I drove to the gravel road that led into the back way to the Carp, I saw a man walking along a drainage ditch by the road. He seemed to be seeing something in the water there. I went about my fishing, but when I left for home I stopped by the drainage ditch to see what he was looking at. I got out of the truck and immediately heard splashing in the ditch. The ditch channel was overgrown with grass and weeds. It was about three feet across and maybe a foot deep. What I saw was two large steelhead heading up stream in the channel. I ran to get my fishing pole, not having an idea how I would catch them. They were moving fast. I followed them for about a hundred yards as the channel turned into the woods. I ended up at a shallow pool about twenty feet across and the stream continued to a large head-high culvert under the interstate. I had my waders on and headed into the dark, foot deep water. Splashes were happening all around me and large fish bumped my legs. There was not much room to cast but I did and was soon hooked up with a large fish who shot past me back out of the culvert, the drag on my reel screaming. I splashed my way back out of the tunnel to follow the fish that turned left up another very shallow channel that seemed to dead end. About that time the fish threw my lure and was off. This fish was not going to get away and I dove on top on it in the shallow water, scrambling to get a grip. My friend had told me years before that if you get a grip on a steelhead above the tail and hold on tight it cannot get away, unlike other fish whose tails will fold and your hand will slide off. I did just that and managed to throw the fish up on the bank. I had my fish but I was soaking wet in the 35-degree air. I headed back to my truck for a change of clothes and to clean the fish before I put it on ice.

The last time I visited the carp, I noticed large wire

mesh fish traps near the mouth of the river. These are used by fish and game researchers to catch sea lampreys which arrived via the St. Lawrence Seaway and have become a huge problem in the Great Lakes. The two or three feet long critters attach to fish by a suction mouth and bore a hole in the side of the fish. I have caught a few Salmon and Steelheads that had managed to dislodge the lampreys and had a large circular scar on their sides. Hopefully by trapping and removing lampreys, as well as other methods to reduce their numbers, the impact of these predators can be minimized. The Carp has survived many attacks over the years, either from sea lampreys, zebra mussels which deplete the food chain that fish depend upon, or unrestricted gill netting by native American tribes. The fish population in the carp has become much reduced over the years, but the river still inspires me to visit and absorb the quiet sounds of the water and drumming of grouse in the nearby woods.

Young Tiger

The crisp morning air and smell of jet fuel cut through lingering sleepiness as I stepped down from the crew bus and walked across the dimly lit aircraft parking ramp to the left main landing gear of my airplane where the crew chief was making his last entries in the maintenance log. While I was briefed on the status of the airplane, several other crew chiefs and maintenance technicians joined the rest of my crew to form a line and pass our baggage up the air stairs to be stowed along with other cargo. There was not much conversation. The only noise was the occasional grunt of extra effort as one of the heavier bags was accepted and sent up the line. A light frost coated the airplane surfaces and reflected the powerful overhead ramp lights, providing a reminder that winter was close. My crew, however, would not experience the discomfort of cold this year as we were about to deploy to the heat and humidity of Southeast Asia. It was 1973 and the Vietnam War had been consuming American assets and young men for almost eight years. Public protests over the war were in the news every day, and the appearance of protestors outside the gates of most military bases had become commonplace. We were deploying in support of bomber and fighter aircraft flying in the combat zone and we would be part of the Young Tiger Tanker Task Force.

Deployment like this one had become commonplace for Strategic Air Command bomber and tanker crews who, early in the war, had welcomed the change from a boring routine of living and working in an underground alert bunker one week out of every three. The tension on alert of being constantly ready to run to your aircraft at a moment's notice, and takeoff to execute a nuclear strike on the Soviet Union, was emotionally and physically debilitating. It did not help that the alert aircraft were loaded to such heavy weights with fuel or bombs that the resulting performance was barely sufficient to enable a safe takeoff. During alert duty, your family could periodically visit in the evening, but there was no chance to fly or to leave the base for relaxing activities such as fishing or personal travel. You just spent your time setting in an underground bunker and hoping time would pass so you could get back to some kind of normal routine. The thought that we could be part of a nuclear war that would end civilization, was never far from our minds while on alert.

When crews deployed overseas, they got away from the stresses of alert duty and flew frequently in a wide variety of mission roles. And when not flying, you could occasionally go into town to experience the foreign culture. The downside was that while deployed overseas, you were far away from friends and family for four to six months at a time. As the Vietnam War progressed, crews had begun to dread repeated deployments and the toll on families began to impact crewmember morale. By 1972, it was not unusual for a crew to return from a six-month deployment and a month later be deployed again. I had been deployed to Southeast Asia for four months the previous year, but this would be my first trip as crew commander so I was looking forward to it. For many crews, however, what had begun as a welcome change of pace had become a dreaded repetition of deployments with no end in sight.

Some B-52 crews were deployed from their bases in the

states to Anderson Air Force Base on the island of Guam. The round trip flight time from Guam for bombing missions over Vietnam was a dozen hours. Most deployed bomber and tanker crews, however, were assigned to Utapao Royal Thai Navy Base on the south Thailand coast where flight time to the combat zone in Vietnam was only a couple of hours. During the last years of the war, more than one hundred and fifty of the larger bomber and tanker aircraft filled every available section of ramp space at Utapao. My crew would be assigned to the Young Tiger Tanker Task force with responsibility for inflight refueling of bombers flying between Guam and Vietnam as well as for hundreds of fighter and reconnaissance aircraft operating from fixed bases in Southeast Asia or Navy carriers in the Gulf of Tonkin. We were to provide them with sufficient fuel to remain over their assigned targets and then return to their assigned bases.

• • •

After getting the final information on my aircraft status from the crew chief, I climbed up the crew entry chute and put my helmet and checklists within easy reach of the Captain's seat. A look aft through the cockpit door confirmed that all was in order in the rear of the airplane. There was more than six tons of cargo onboard, including an extra turbojet engine that was destined for one of our enroute stops. Our cargo filled the aircraft interior from the floor to within two feet of the ceiling and there was very little space between the sides of the cargo bins and the webbed passenger seats that lined both walls. The loadmaster had just finished checking that the heavy nylon cargo straps were securing baggage to the rings in the floor of the cargo bay and was starting his flight briefing for the 50 passengers who would travel with us.

Most of the passengers had flown in military transports before and were used to the bare bones flight briefing. Unlike our airline counterparts, there would be no flight attendants or special treatment on this trip. Back in the cockpit, the copilot and navigator were already completing their checklists and I climbed into my seat and secured my shoulder straps and seat belt. Outside the window, a maintenance person in a high-rise bucket was washing the forward airplane windows. He waved and gave me a 'thumbs up.' He probably wished he was going with us. The copilot passed me the flight plan and the takeoff performance data that he had finished calculating. Between the cargo, passengers and 120,000 pounds of fuel onboard, we were very heavy and takeoff performance would be marginal so I checked the numbers closely. They looked OK. We quickly completed the remaining checklist items. A crew chief checked in on interphone that he was ready for engine start, and about that time we got a call from the command post advising us to hold our engine start for six additional passengers that should arrive shortly. We waited. A half hour passed. Outside, I could see box vans and panel trucks moving among the other parked aircraft in support of planned flight operations for the day. On the ramp opposite our aircraft another flight crew was beginning to load equipment on their aircraft. I looked back through the cockpit entry door and I could see passengers standing in groups near the galley where our water and coffee were stored. Outside, the airmen who were to assist with engine start had taken off their headphones and were standing in a huddle to the left of the aircraft, smoking cigarettes. I called the command post for guidance and they said we should be patient as the additional passengers were urgently needed replacements for a redeploying bomber crew. The voice on the radio said the late arrivals should be arriving at any minute. I looked out the window towards the entry gate at the far end of the parking ramp and sure enough there was a six-passenger pickup truck just coming through the entry point. It turned our way and then, instead of following the marked access route, cut across the ramp towards us, passing through a line of aircraft. As the truck got closer, it seemed to be moving erratically and very fast for the parking area. As it got closer, it looked like it was going to ram our aircraft! About forty feet from the airplane, the driver braked hard enough to lock the brakes. As it came to a shuddering stop, all four doors flew open and bodies piled out, one man fell from the truck to lie prostrate on the pavement. Another staggered around to the back of the truck and began to unload baggage. A third man fell down twice on the way to help the one man who still lay on the ramp. Meanwhile, the truck had not fully stopped and was still slowly rolling towards the airplane. The driver, realizing this, ran back to the truck, stomped on the brakes and put the vehicle in park. This did not look good.

We had already closed the aft cargo hatch and removed the air stairs so the late arrivals had to pass their gear and themselves up the cockpit entry hatch ladder. My loadmaster knelt on the cockpit floor to help the first man up the ladder with his baggage and then got out of the way so the rest of the bomber crew could pass up their gear. With a lot of banging and cursing, the remainder of the late arrivals got onboard and headed aft. I advised the command post that we had our remaining passengers and would be starting engines shortly for taxi and takeoff. Then my loadmaster came forward to say there was a problem with the recent arrivals. In his words they were 'drunk as skunks.' He said that one man had grabbed another's head thinking it was baggage to pass up the ladder. I got up and went to the back to see the problem for myself. The men did indeed look and smell drunk. One of their crew was in the process of vomiting into a large paper bag. I went back forward and called the command post to say I would not be taking these individuals with me and someone should come get them. I was told to stand by for further instructions. About ten minutes later, a senior Colonel arrived and asked me what the problem was. I pointed to the back of the airplane and he headed that way. Shortly he came back forward and I could see that he was disgusted. He asked me to step outside the airplane to talk and we did so. He said the bomber crew was desperately needed in Thailand and although they were clearly drunk, he asked if I would consent to taking them anyway. I told him my concern was that they would vomit all over the airplane or try to exit through a hatch while we were in the air. He asked me to come back to the cargo area with him. There was an armed security policeman onboard and the Colonel had that person accompany us to where the bomber crew was setting. The men all looked very green and it was clear that their captain was trying hard to sober up. The colonel advised the crew that they would not leave their seats for the entire flight. If they did so, the security policeman was authorized to shoot them. And I believed him. Each man was given a large paper bag and told that any vomiting had better be done into the bag. The colonel then turned to me to ask if those conditions were satisfactory. I still had some reservations, but I agreed, more than anything to just get underway. We had no further trouble from the bomber crew and they deplaned at our first stop, so I don't know what became of them. Fifteen B-52 crews had been shot down over Hanoi the previous winter, including one from our base, so whether or not they would survive their current deployment was yet to be determined.

• • •

We started engines and taxied out to the east end of the

main runway. Looking out the window at the fall colors in the nearby woods, I couldn't help but regret that I would be missing the upcoming hunting season, but those thoughts quickly passed as we received takeoff clearance and I lined the big jet up with the runway centerline and advanced power. The takeoff was uneventful and we were on our way. We leveled off at our initial cruising altitude of 29,000 feet and the copilot tuned the navigation radios to the first way point of our flight plan while I adjusted the engines for optimum fuel conservation. The five-hour flight to the west coast passed quickly and soon we were letting down for our approach to March Air Force Base in Southern California. A replacement crew would continue on with our plane and cargo, while we would remain there overnight, awaiting the next arriving airplane. During the approach, the visibility was unusually clear for that time of year with no smog layer in sight, and I could see many familiar towns and points of interest on the ground. I had lived there during my teen years and it was hard to concentrate on flying the airplane as I pointed out local towns to the crew. To the left was the town I grew up in and straight ahead was the Mt. Palomar Observatory, and off to the west you could see Laguna Beach. With a little prompting from my copilot, however, I quickly got back to the business at hand and made a decent approach and landing. We taxied to parking, I shut down engines and we unloaded our personal baggage. A refueling truck and the replacement crew were standing by and I walked to the new crew commander to brief him about the maintenance status of the aircraft. Other than a minor electrical problem, the airplane was in good shape. We wished them well on their flight and then headed for the hotel.

The next day we reported three hours before our scheduled takeoff and were provided with a detailed flight plan and map for the next leg of our deployment.

We would be continuing our journey in an airplane from North Dakota and the flight time to our next stop, the Hawaiian Islands, was about six hours. After getting our flight information and weather, we camped out in the crew lounge for another hour until we heard that our plane had landed. A crew bus took us to that airplane where flight preparations went smoothly and soon we were on our way again. After takeoff, I leveled the airplane at 31,000 feet, quickly leaving the California coast behind and heading out over the ocean through a cloudless, bright blue sky. The copilot contacted Los Angeles Center on the HF radio to request flight monitoring for our flight. Until we reached Hawaiian airspace, we would rely on HF radio contact with Los Angeles Center to keep us clear of other transiting aircraft and for any weather advisories. Our navigator would take sextant readings on the sun through a porthole in the top of the aircraft to make sure we stayed on course. The prevailing westerly winds at altitude were steady, our heading to the islands was pretty much directly west, and the weather was forecast to be clear all the way. Other a problem with fluctuating cabin temperature, the trip was uneventful and five hours later we could see the first of the Hawaiian Islands on the horizon as we began a very gradual letdown to ten thousand feet. We could see surf breaking around the shore of the Big Island. Soon Maui came into view on the horizon and we could also see a number of cruise ships and large freighters moving between the islands. A half hour later, the island of Oahu came into view and we began our final descent into the traffic pattern for Honolulu International Airport. When we were still about forty miles out, the air traffic controller asked us if we could see the Boeing 747 about seven miles in front of us at our twelve o'clock position and that we should follow that aircraft. We could see a tiny speck ahead and the cockpit radar was painting something at about that distance, but I was reluctant to confirm we had the aircraft in sight because I knew that as soon as I did, the controller would quit providing us with directions and traffic spacing. I had not landed at that airport before and I wanted someone to give me directions until the airport was in clear view, right in front of me. However, when I said I could not see the aircraft clearly, the controller advised me I would have to take a southerly heading to a holding pattern and he would get back to me. That was a bad plan as we did not have a lot of extra fuel, so I reluctantly said I could see the airplane ahead and I pushed the throttles forward so I could get closer for a better view. The controller then advised me that I was aircraft number fifteen in the landing sequence, behind the 747. With all the crew looking intently ahead, we finally saw the distinctive outline of a big Boeing jet and began to configure our airplane for landing. We followed the 747 along the Oahu coastline and then through a turn inland, followed by another turn to line up with the runway about ten miles ahead. I slowed the airplane to approach speed while the crew ran their final checklists and the loadmaster collected the customs forms from the passengers. The weather for landing was absolutely gorgeous and upon touchdown we were directed to taxi to the end of the runway and then to parking on the military ramp where eight other tanker aircraft were parked along with several Hawaiian National Guard fighter aircraft. Busses came for the passengers and we boarded a panel truck for the ride into the operations desk to find out what we were supposed to do next. An officer gave us directions to hotel rooms and told us to report back to him in three days when we would continue with our next leg of the deployment. We were on our own for three days in Hawaii!

• • •

The next day we rented a car and decided to go to Hanama Bay which we were told was one of the premier snorkeling spots in the Hawaiian Islands. The traffic in downtown Honolulu was surprisingly heavy but soon we were on a less congested highway headed east towards Diamond Head. We followed signs north to Hanama Bay and arrived about an hour later, quickly renting snorkeling gear and changing into swims trunks. It was a weekday, and the beach was not very crowded. We headed down to the shore and passed a couple of open air showers where we got an eyeful of a tourist in a fishnet bikini. We stared and she glared. We moved on.

Hanama Bay is about a mile and a half wide at its mouth and the lagoon is separated from the ocean and surf by two coral reefs. The inner lagoon is very calm and that is where most of the snorkelers operate. The first reef barrier is about two hundred yards from shore and the water depth at that point only reaches ten or twelve feet. The inner lagoon waters are sheltered, and rarely entered by sharks, barracudas, or other large unfriendly fish. At least that is what we were told, but I nervously paddled along with my head on a swivel to observe the water in all directions. As I stroked along the surface near the reef, I was absolutely amazed by the view underwater that included all kinds bright yellow, deep blue, or iridescent green fish that sparkled and maneuvered around the coral formations that covered the sandy bottom. After an hour of investigating the nooks and crannies of the inner lagoon, my copilot and navigator decided they wanted to see more and headed out past the first barrier reef to the deeper waters of the outer lagoons. It seemed like a good idea. There would be fewer swimmers out there, clearer water, and correspondingly more fish to see. We quickly swam to the inner edge of the reef and looked for a place to climb out without getting cut up by the coral. My other crew members seemed to have no trouble getting up on the reef, but it took me some minutes to find a way out of the water. When I did get up on the reef, my crewmen were just getting into the deeper water on the far side, about forty feet ahead. Walking on the reef wearing swim fins, in about a foot of water, was very difficult. The alternative was to get your feet cut up on the sharp coral. I kept my fins on and lost my balance several times. It took me about fifteen minutes to traverse the reef and finally jump into the deeper water on the far side. By then, my companions were a hundred yards ahead, face down in the water, their snorkels occasionally visible in the light chop.

As soon as I entered the outer lagoon, the difference in conditions was immediately apparent. Here in the outer lagoon the bottom was forty or fifty feet below, and the water was crystal clear. The color of corals, vegetation, and aquatic life on the bottom was breath taking. I was only a short distance from the inner reef, and directly below me was a moving carpet of thousands of silvery fish, each one about a foot long. This was truly the place to be to see what most people only see on television. I was enjoying the view, but getting a little uncomfortable with the water depth at that location. I am a good swimmer, but not a strong swimmer. My companions were well out ahead of me. About that time, something very big shot past me. It moved so fast I could not get a good look at it, but it was definitely big. My 'mental playback' provided an impression of something about three or four feet long and silvery. My first thought was a tuna or a barracuda, but it happened so quickly, that I wasn't really sure what I saw. In any case, it had come very close and I was in its element. It took me about five seconds to decide I did not belong in the outer lagoon and I made a frantic, flailing return to the wall of the reef. My legs were so unsteady at that point that it took me a few minutes to get up out of the water and then all was good again. I splashed my way back across the reef to the inner lagoon and remained there for rest of the afternoon. When my companions returned from the outer lagoon, we all headed up the beach to our car and made the drive back to our hotel. That night we went to see a Hawaiian show complete with hula and fire dancers. We felt like we were on vacation and were in no hurry to continue our journey.

The next day two days went by quickly and soon we were back at the operations building ready for the next leg of the deployment which was an eight and one-half hour flight to the island of Guam in the Marianas Islands. We left late in the afternoon and the sun and stars would be used to update our navigation. We would not know if we had maintained an accurate course until about seven and a half hours into the flight when we could pick up the navigation beacon from the runway at the military base on Guam. A miscalculation of a few degrees in heading could result in missing the island and we would not get very far on the remaining fuel. The first part of the trip went smoothly and we were able to maintain radio contact with Honolulu Center until we were passed on to a traffic controller in the Philippine Islands who would maintain radio contact with us until landing. After about four hours into the flight we were flying between intermittent layers of clouds and having trouble updating our heading with sextant readings. Our HF radio contact advised us that a tropical cyclone had moved a little further north of track than anticipated and clouds would continue for the entire flight. There was little turbulence at our altitude and most of the thunderstorm cells associate with the cyclone were south of our track, but it was unsettling that we could not update our navigation with a star fix and then we began picking up St. Elmo's fire on the forward windows. These static discharges have little effect on the airplane but were precursors to an ice buildup that began to concern me. When about a quarter inch of ice began to show on the edges of the forward window, I began to deviate north of course to find better weather conditions. We were able to get approval from our radio contact to climb to a higher altitude, but soon were near our maximum operating altitude of 41,000 feet and still the ice buildup continued. The further north I deviated, the more concerned I became with the icing, our diminishing fuel reserves, and our ability to find our way to Guam. At 100 miles north of course, I told the navigator we would deviate no further and that he should plot a direct path from our current position directly to Guam. He gave me a new heading of about twenty degrees to the right. Eventually we moved out of icing conditions, but now we were well off from our original flight path. Time went by and after eight hours in the air there was no sign of any land on the radar. I tried calling on the radio in the blind to any station that would answer, hoping we were within radio range. No answer. Another half hour went by and I began to think about the possibility of surviving a ditching at sea. The odds were not good. I was considering how soon I would need to make a mayday call. I made one more call on the radio frequency for the controller on the island of Guam and although weak, I got a response! Shortly thereafter, we saw the island appear on our radar at about 200 miles ahead. The deviation for weather had extended our flight time, but the navigator had done a good job and we were right where we needed to be. We broke out of the clouds over water at about eight thousand feet and the radar controller directed us to a landing on a very long runway surrounded by a maze of taxiways and parking spaces. At the edge of this concrete layout was a very dense jungle. After taxiing to parking and shutting down the engines, we were once again met by busses for the crew and passengers. Some of our cargo was downloaded as Guam was its final destination and we were told that we would have several days to rest up for the next leg of our journey to southern Thailand.

It was very hot on Guam and everything smelled moldy in the rooms we were assigned…a byproduct of the high humidity which left us dripping sweat anytime we were outside. Although there were window air conditioners, they did not do much to improve the inside air. There was not much to do on the base to keep busy during the day and the only method of transportation was a military shuttle bus that infrequently made its rounds. There was a movie theater, but most of the features were very dated and it was only open three days a week in the early evening. There was a recreation center where you could play basketball or pool, but that was it. There was also a dining hall where we could eat, but it was some distance from our rooms and had restricted operating hours, so you made sure you were waiting when it opened or you might be out of luck for that meal. The main entertainment on Guam was to take the bus off base to Torregi Beach at the bottom of the thousand-foot cliff that marked the end of the main runway. Torregi had a small lagoon for swimming and snorkeling. The well-groomed sandy beach was backed by dense jungle. This area had been the refuge for Japanese holdouts from the WWII Pacific Campaign and a few of those soldiers had held out for almost twenty years after the war ended, living in caves that lined the nearby cliff face. A sign at the beach advised visitors to stay within the marked beach and lagoon area as areas outside of the perimeter were littered with the rusted hulks of ships and landing craft as well as unexploded ordinance. If that was not enough incentive to not wander off, we were told that a small marine resident called the stonefish could be found in the shallows around the island. There had been deaths caused by stepping on the poisonous spines of this fish. Yes, staying on the nice safe base beach would do for us. And there was a snack cart available during the day where you could buy a cold beer and a hot dog so in any case there was no reason to leave. We passed the time each afternoon on the beach and worked on our tans. Time went by very slowly.

The third morning I got a call from a pilot I had worked with when I first started flying in the military. He had heard I was passing through Guam and wanted to know if I wanted to go on a flight to the outer islands with him that afternoon. I was tired of setting around and was eager for the adventure. I took my crew and met him at the flight line a couple of hours later. He explained we would be flying out to the island of Tinian to pick up fresh fruits and vegetables for the base commissary. Although he had a desk job on Guam, he also volunteered as pilot for the weekly commissary run to keep his flying skills sharp. We received a weather briefing and then he filed a flight plan from the base to Tinian and back. Then we walked out to the airplane which turned out to be a Korean War vintage C-54 airplane, the military version of the DC-6 airliner. In addition to the two pilots and a crew chief, the only other people onboard were me and my three crewmen. The old propeller driven airplane started easily and soon we taxied out to the runway and took off over the ocean into a hot, clear, sky. The flight to Tinian was planned for an hour and twenty minutes, and on the way, we passed over Rota and Saipan, two other prominent islands in the Marianas chain. Over Saipan, the pilot dropped down to a thousand feet altitude and he pointed out a herd of wild goats that stampeded upon hearing the noise from our engines. He indicated he frequently liked to chase goats up and down the island to break up the boredom. His flight engineer looked at me and shook his head smiling. I guessed that fun came in many forms for these guys. Soon we were approaching our destination island and my friend explained that this was the island from where the B-29s flew to bomb Japan during WWII. We circled the island and he pointed out four runways that stood out from the dense jungle. Most were overgrown and had an occasional palm tree sprouting up through the steel PSP runway matting. The pilot circled the island a couple of times so that the indigenous farmers, most émigrés from Europe, would know to meet us at the landing strip. Sure enough, after the third circuit, I could see a convoy of six small pickup trucks moving through the jungle towards the only runway that appeared to be completely clear of vegetation. Then we descended and lined up on the impossibly small runway. I was watching the landing from behind the captain's seat as he expertly worked the flight controls to drop in over a dense palm grove and touchdown just past the start of the runway. It looked like the jungle zipped by only forty or fifty feet on either side of the airplane as my friend stood on the brakes and slipped the propellers into reverse. We came to a screeching stop barely two hundred yards from the end of the runway where there was a small metal building and waiting farmers who lounged by their vehicles.

We had an hour to explore the nearby jungle and shore while the farmers and crew loaded the cargo bay of the airplane with boxes of fruits and vegetables as well as a wide variety of melons. As on the shores of Guam, there were rusted hulks of tanks, landing craft, and pillboxes all along the beach. The jungle had overgrown most of what appeared to be shore batteries and other military installations. As we wandered along the beach, my young boom operator talked about how exciting it was to be so near to so much history and said we should search the jungle for military souvenirs or even some dead Japanese soldiers. That idea was very creepy for me and besides it was time to go, so despite some grumbling, we headed back to the airplane. When we arrived, my friend was handing one of the farmers a receipt for delivered goods and then we climbed back on board the airplane. The pilot started the engines and turned the airplane around in a dirt area near the tin shack that was designed for that purpose and then gunned the engines for takeoff. We somehow got airborne, just clearing the palm trees at the end of the runway and headed back to Guam. After landing I thanked my friend for the flight experience and we headed to base operations to find out if we would ever get to continue our trip to Southeast Asia. As it turned out, another airplane was expected soon and we were to report for flight planning and departure early the next day.

• • •

The next leg of our journey would be a five-hour flight to Clark Air Force Base in the Philippine Islands and after a quick stop for offloading cargo and refueling we would continue another four hours to our final destination. We were glad to leave Guam behind as we were getting really bored. With the naïve anticipation of youth, we were ready for some 'real action' in the combat zone. Our takeoff was delayed while we waited for a last couple of cargo pallets and then finally we had our engines started and were rolling down the runway on takeoff. We passed over the departure end of the runway and symbolically waved goodbye to crewmen on the beach at the bottom of the cliff. Our journey was almost over. Once we were leveled off at our cruising altitude, everyone was ready for their box lunch. Since it was Thanksgiving, we were told that we would get a special inflight meal. Sure enough, inside each box was a turkey sandwich and a little container of cranberry sauce as well as a boiled egg, a piece of pumpkin pie and some condiments. I put the airplane on autopilot, leaned my seat back and dug into the goodies, as did my other crewmembers. This was probably the most unique Thanksgiving I had experienced and I was reveling in my six-mile high view of the ocean below. I finished my sandwich and picked up the boiled egg for the next course. I cracked it on the flight controls to find that it was a raw egg, much to the amusement of my copilot. What a mess. Still, that was a small setback in an otherwise fine day for flying.

After arriving at Clark, we went into the air-conditioned terminal building to check the weather for the last leg of the flight and to pick up some sodas and snacks while the cargo was being downloaded and the plane refueled. Then it was a quick engine start and takeoff. We were looking forward to the end of the trip and finally getting into some kind of daily routine that included our first up close look at the Vietnam War…as close as you can look from 35,000 feet anyway. Soon we were completing our approach and landing checklists and starting our descent into the base on the southern shore of Thailand. As we taxied to parking after landing, we could see camouflaged aircraft everywhere we looked as well as refueling trucks, trucks towing racks of 500 and 1,000-pound bombs, and all manner of other support vehicles scurrying between the aircraft and the nearby buildings. A pickup truck with a flashing 'follow me' sign came out from the main ramp and turned in front of our airplane to lead us to our parking spot. Ground crewmen with marshalling batons waived us into the designated spot and I signaled for them to place chocks around our landing gear. As soon as I shut down the engines, a vehicle pulled up and two officers came aboard to give us instructions on where we needed to go and what we needed to bring with us. Our first stop was the maintenance building where we gave the formal aircraft maintenance log to an officer and explained what minor problems needed fixing on the aircraft. Then we were taken to our housing. The three officers were to share a

modular trailer. I had the room on one end and my copilot and navigator shared the room on the other end. A restroom and shower were in between. It was a convenient arrangement since it was near the flight operations building and the flight line. Our trailer was one of about 200 similar structures and as we were taken through the trailer complex we could see lots of activity by either crewmembers or Thai support personnel. The boom operator was billeted in a dormitory on the other side of the base. After dropping off the boom operator and leaving our baggage at the trailer, we were taken to the dining hall for the evening meal and then left on our own until a scheduled orientation briefing the next day.

• • •

After a quick breakfast we arrived for the morning briefing. We were reminded that although we were located in Southern Thailand, our flight operations areas were on the border of a combat zone and we were given briefings about evading capture should we be shot down.

We would be flying with survival vests and handguns although it didn't seem to me that they would be much use against any hostile force or environment. Next, was a briefing on our planned refueling missions. We would be flying about every other day in support of bomber, fighter, and reconnaissance aircraft operating over Vietnam. The main refueling orbits or anchors were situated over northern Thailand, on the border with North Vietnam, and were named for fruit. There were orange, lemon, and cherry anchors as well as three or four others. There were also a couple of orbits located near South Vietnam and a couple over the Gulf of Tonkin. The flight time to each orbit was a little over an hour and we would remain on station until we delivered our available offload, either to scheduled receivers or any aircraft that were diverted to our position. To have the most fuel available for offload, our takeoff weight was as heavy as possible. As a result, the takeoff roll frequently took up most of the runway, meaning that any aircraft malfunction would probably

lead to a flaming death upon impact off the departure end of the runway. There had been two such crashes the previous month with no survivors. We were very attentive to any potential malfunction with our assigned aircraft each day and particularly during the first part of the takeoff roll. There were about 100 tanker aircraft assigned to the base and when the word got around that a particular aircraft number was temperamental, crews frequently found something wrong with that aircraft so that they could move to a different aircraft and thereby avoid bad luck. One aircraft, tail number 59-0003 or 'balls three' to the pilots, had a particular bad record of engine failures and electrical systems problems. Whenever we flew, we always looked to make sure that was not our assigned aircraft for the day.

On the days we did not fly, we usually had refresher training on aircraft procedures or survival equipment. If we were not flying at night, we went to the officers' club for dinner and then hung out at the bar to listen to music of the time…Santana, CCR, or even the Beetles. Frequently, there was a band of musicians from the Philippines who knew not a word of English but could do a decent imitation of the words if you were properly fogged by two or three drinks. The heavily amplified refrains of 'Jellow Liver' (Yellow River) stayed with you long after you went to bed for the night. Sometimes, after dinner we would move outside to at a table on the patio. The humid evening air, barely lit by hanging lanterns, would be periodically punctuated by the roar of a departing tanker or bomber aircraft. Pilots would share stories of that day's flight or talk about what they would do when they got back home. One evening as we set nursing our beers, a Thai barmaid on the far side of the patio screamed loudly and ran off. The men at the table she was attending also quickly pushed back their chairs and backed off looking at something on the ground. Soon the barmaid returned with a man carrying a big stick with which he began to flail away at something under the table. As it turned out, an extremely deadly pit viper had found its way into the patio area. Soon, the offending reptile, somewhat worse for wear, was removed, people returned to their seats, and conversation resumed. For some time after that, I noticed people always looked under their tables at the patio. And I was no exception.

• • •

A few days later we were scheduled to fly in the afternoon, but received a call in the morning to report to the flight line early. A fighter aircraft had been shot down south of Hanoi and all available tanker forces were needed to provide refueling support for the effort. We received a quick briefing and joined several other crews to be taken to our assigned airplanes. I quickly started engines, taxied out, and soon we were in the air. Our assigned air refueling area was Orange Anchor and before we arrived, the ground controller at NKP, a military base in northern Thailand, was vectoring aircraft to our position for refueling. We refueled four F-4 aircraft on the way up and a dozen more were waiting when we got there. It took very little time to offload our available 20,000 gallons of fuel and the remaining receiver aircraft were diverted to another inbound tanker. We turned for home base and were back on the ground within three hours from takeoff. As we got ready to leave the airplane, I received a call on the radio to head to another airplane further down the ramp to fly a second mission. We normally flew once every two or three days, so this was highly unusual, but we quickly grabbed our gear and moved to the second airplane. Again, thirsty aircraft, this time F-105 fighter/bombers were waiting for us almost as soon as we were in the air. The lead fighter closed on our refueling boom while the other fighters took up positions near our wing tips to wait their turn. We could hear radio calls from many other aircraft who were heading north in support of the rescue operation. For the second time, we quickly offloaded our available fuel, leaving just enough for us to return to home base. As we taxied in after landing, the command post again directed us to another airplane for a third flight of the day. It was now early evening, and we were told that our receivers would be a flight of post-Korean War vintage RB-66 bombers that had been converted to an electronic warfare capability. Since these aircraft could only be refueled with a special drogue basket, and that basket could not be changed in flight for different kinds of aircraft, they were to be our only receivers. We moved close to the border of North Vietnam and awaited the receivers. As we circled high in the sky, my boom operator, from his position in the rear of the aircraft, reminded me not to go too far north and thereby end up in North Vietnamese airspace. We had been briefed that there were 100mm anti-aircraft guns on the border than could reach our altitude. The border was marked by the Mekong River, that during the day could be easily seen in the jungle far below the boom operator's observation window. And he continually reminded me that he thought we were getting awfully close to the border. Soon the receivers checked in on the radio and were vectored towards our position. We turned to meet them with a combined closure rate of almost 800 knots. We rocketed towards the closing aircraft, only able to track their position on radar. The navigator called 30 miles separation, then 25, 24, 23, 22 and when the blip on our radar reached twenty-one miles, we began a turn so as to roll out two miles in front of them. Halfway through the turn I picked up the navigation lights on the approaching flight and on intercom advised the boom operator that he should see the receivers soon. The two RB-66s quickly

closed on our position and the boom operator reported he had their flashing navigation lights in sight, about a half mile behind us. The lead RB-66 came in for his fuel and when he was full, he moved off to the side and his wingman moved into position to receive fuel. Then they called to confirm how much gas they had received and headed off into the night. We turned for home after notifying the NKP controller that we were bingo fuel (no more gas to offload). After the short flight back to base and landing we were very happy that there was not a fourth flight assignment with our name on it. We were tired. We did not hear until several days later that the rescue effort had been successful, but that two additional airplanes involved in the rescue had been shot down.

• • •

We changed clothes at our trailer and headed to the patio for a round of drinks. As we sat on the patio talking about an upcoming flight, I saw the door to the women's restroom fly open and a woman ran off apparently agitated about something. I wondered if another snake had been found. Soon she came back with a bartender and was gesturing wildly at the restroom door. The bartender remained by the door and the woman went off into the interior of the club. About ten minutes later she returned with two military policemen. Most of the patrons setting in the patio area had stopped talking and were watching to see what would happen next. The policemen listened to the woman and then one went into the women's restroom. He soon came out and then they opened a door next to the restroom door which revealed a small maintenance storage closet with ceiling access to the attic area over the entire club. Soon a ladder was brought to the maintenance closet and both policemen climbed the ladder and disappeared into the attic area. Several minutes went by and conversation on the patio area returned to normal. Then there was a muffled bang followed by running footsteps. Soon six men burst into the patio area from the direction of a card playing room down a nearby hallway. The men ran through the patio and disappeared into the night. Things were getting very interesting. About ten minutes later, one of the policemen came down the ladder, followed by another man in civilian clothes and then the second policeman. The policemen put handcuffs on the man and then they all left the area. We sat there for another several minutes and finally one of the guys at our table went into the main club area to found out what was going on. As it turned out, when one of the barmaids was in the restroom, she noticed a set of eyes staring at her from a crack in the ceiling where a tile had been moved. She ran outside and called the police. The police responded and were not sure what they would encounter when they went into the dark attic which extended for 100 feet over the club complex. As a result, after climbing into the attic, they spread out with guns at the ready. Just about the time that one of the policemen spotted a man hiding in the far corner of the attic, the policeman's foot broke through the ceiling causing him to discharge his weapon which sent a bullet through the ceiling and into the table below where several pilots were in the middle of a poker game and discussing whether the base was safe from attack by guerrilla forces or terrorists. The result was several minutes of pandemonium by all involved. But now, the pervert was in custody, the poker game had resumed, and we toasted another boring evening in the war zone.

• • •

Two days later we were scheduled for a day off and decided to investigate the local culture. A fishing trip could be scheduled with local Thai fishermen by contacting the Thai military liaison office. The person we met at that office said we were to show up at the beach near the end of the runway at first light and a local fisherman would meet us there. The base beach, like the one in Guam, was a place where crew members could hang out during the day and get a tan and a beer. Unlike Guam, however, you swam in the water at your own risk as raw sewage from nearby villages frequently ended up along the shoreline. But we were not getting into the water and hopefully our Thai guide would take us far away from the beach and to cleaner water. We arrived at the beach just after sunup and the guide was already there in his beached boat. The guide was dressed in a sarong and apparently only knew a few words of English but by gestures indicated we were to climb aboard, so we did. No gesture from us could adequately describe the poor condition of the boat and it would have been in bad form anyway. The wooden-hulled boat was about 20 to 25 feet long with a wooden awning that covered the middle third of the boat and was painted in several brightly colored patches of red, blue, and yellow. The deck of the boat was very weather beaten and littered with ropes, buckets of various colors which were covered with Thai lettering, and wooden spars and canvas that might serve as a makeshift sail if the occupants were absolutely desperate. The boat was powered by an ancient car engine that sputtered and puffed clouds of exhaust as he fired it up and backed the boat away from the shore. The guide steered with a wooden tiller from the rear of the boat and we headed out to sea. We took off our shirts and shoes and settled in at the bow to catch some rays on the way to the fishing grounds. We headed southwest into the Gulf of Siam and were soon heading south along a chain of islands that were just in sight to the west. We tried talking to the boatman, but it was clear that his English vocabulary was limited to about a dozen words and a lot of smiling. He didn't have many teeth and it was hard to guess his age. Our ability to converse in Thai was limited to *sawatdee kahp*, the local greeting, *tee lai baht* (how much does it cost), and *kahp cuhn mak* (go fast). If we needed a bathroom break or something to eat, we were going to have to be pretty inventive with gestures. We hoped the guide knew enough to take us fishing and then return us to the base beach before it got dark. It would also be good if he had not just captured some foolish Americans that he was about to sell into slavery on some pirate vessel.

We motored along offshore for about an hour and a half and then he turned inland towards a narrow passage between two small islands. The gentle swells of the open water mellowed to calm as we chugged up a muddy channel with thick jungle right up to the shore edge on both sides. Brightly colored birds called from nearby trees as we motored along and soon a crude village and a dilapidated dock came into view. Small fishing boats were beached along the nearby shore and a woman was washing clothes in the channel with a baby on her back. A number of weather beaten dwellings on stilts and connected by elevated walkways masked the interior of the island from view. A heavy smell of fish and cooking smoke hung in the air. Children peered at us from windows while the few adults in sight busied themselves with fishing nets, and preparation of the day's catch. Our boat was evidently expected, and as soon as we were tied up at the dock, an elderly toothless man in a multicolored shirt and worn khaki shorts appeared with a wicker basket and began a spirited conversation with our guide. Soon the apparent haggling was completed, and the guide indicated we were to provide money. We counted out a stack of notes and when we reached thirty baht, it seemed we had enough. The basket exchanged hands and was brought aboard. We left the dock and headed back down the channel to the ocean. I moved to look into the basket which contained several dozen translucent squid. I hoped this was our fishing bait and not lunch. The boatman remained silent and expressionless as he steered towards some destination further out in the sea.

After another hour of peaceful motoring, we arrived at a location about a half mile off another small island. The guide killed the boat motor and went below into a small cabin in the center of the boat. He soon returned with five or six ancient looking fishing poles. The poles were very short and thicker than a man's thumb. There were three or four hooks and a large lead weight at the end of heavy braided fishing line on each pole. While we watched, he demonstrated how to cut the squid into pieces which were placed on each hook. Then he motioned that we should do the same and to begin fishing. With hand motions he encouraged us to play out line until he was satisfied that our hooks were at the correct depth. Judging by how much line I let out, I guessed we were in at least a hundred feet of water. I had no idea what we were trying to catch, however in a very short time there was a tug on my navigator's line and he reeled in a very strange looking greenish fish with spines all over its body. He was not interested in touching the ugly fish. The guide quickly moved to remove the fish and threw it overboard exclaiming 'dog fish…bad". Hmmm. So, we were not fishing for dog fish. That was good to know. We continued to fish and drifted with the current past the island and further into the sea. We caught a wide variety of fish, most in the twelve to eighteen-inch range. Some were 'dog fish' and others were "number one eat' according to the guide. After an hour or two we grew tired of fishing and we all getting pretty sun burnt. We moved under the boat awning and relaxed in the warm afternoon air. The boatman soon figured we had had enough and started the engine to turn back to the north. A couple of hours later we arrived back at the base beach and gave the guide a forty-baht tip for the day's adventure…a nice tip in Thailand, but only a dollar or two in US money.

• • •

A couple of days later we were called into the operations building to be briefed on a special mission. We would be flying a special 'razorback' aircraft, so named because of the forest of antennas protruding from the top and bottom of the fuselage. The flight would be responsible for relaying radio communications between US Navy carriers in the gulf and aircraft flying over North

Vietnam. The aircraft was very similar to the tanker aircraft we had been previously flying, but the cargo area was filled with several communications stations manned by radio operators. In addition, there were a few extra switches and gages in the cockpit to monitor the required extra radio and electronic equipment. After arriving over the Gulf of Tonkin we were to fly orbits at that location. Shallow aircraft bank angles were required during turns so as to prevent the radio antennas from being masked by the aircraft fuselage and thereby disrupting the communications link. That meant our turns would be very wide and that the resulting orbit would be forty miles long with legs ten or fifteen miles apart. Our relieving aircraft would not arrive until about eight hours later and we were not to leave the orbit except for a very dire emergency. The flight across South Vietnam to the Gulf took less than two hours. Soon we were in radio contact with the departing radio relay aircraft and began slowing to endurance airspeed to conserve fuel. Below, on the dark blue ocean, we could see a few large ships far off shore. The visibility at altitude was amazing and we could see sixty or seventy miles in all directions. To the west was the shoreline of Vietnam and just North of our orbit was Hainan Island. We knew there were enemy airfields on that island, and I wondered why no one thought they posed a threat to naval vessels or aircraft in the area. We were told we would be warned by Red Crown, the designation for the nearest aircraft carrier, if any enemy aircraft were seen on radar as converging on our position, but I didn't like the odds of trying to outrun enemy fighters in our relatively slow-moving transport aircraft. Just days before, we had heard of a radio relay crew that had to leave their assigned orbit to avoid enemy aircraft. Like us, they were monitoring radio transmissions and heard a call advising all aircraft that 'blue bandits' were heading south from 'Squid'. Blue bandits were MIG 21s and Squid was the designation for Hainan Island. As the radio relay crew monitored the changing position of the threat, they realized they were right in the path of the enemy aircraft. The crew radioed that they were under attack and executed the designated evasion maneuver. That meant lowering the nose of the aircraft until reaching maximum airspeed and diving for the ocean while heading inland towards friendly territory. The crew was told that navy fighters were on the way, but would not arrive until after the enemy aircraft reached their position. The crew dove sharply towards the water, the aircraft shuddering under the buffeting caused by nearing the maximum airspeed. If they exceeded that speed, the airplane would begin to come apart. The crew leveled their airplane at a thousand feet over the ocean and continued towards the coast of Vietnam and the relative safety of Tan Son Nhut Air Base. About that time, the radio relay aircraft pilot was informed that the 'threatening aircraft' was in fact a civilian airliner that had wandered into combat zone airspace. By that time, however, their aircraft had received structural damage from the airframe stresses caused by the emergency descent and had to land at the nearest airfield. The aircraft was later determined to be so damaged that it was stripped and abandoned after landing. As for us, our eight hours on radio relay duty went by in sheer boredom and I even got in a couple of naps while the copilot flew the airplane.

The days went by and we soon became veterans of flight operations over northern Thailand. Some flights were routine, and others filled with stress. Fighter aircraft loaded with bombs and missiles would rendezvous with us for fuel and an hour or two later they or their comrades would return, some with battle damage and fuel streaming from holes in the fuselage. We would provide all the gas we could and then turn for home base, leaving the job to other arriving tankers. Evenings were spent at the bar, listening to music from the jukebox or some third-rate band. Occasionally, we would go to a movie at the outdoor theater near the beach end of the runway. The setup was much like a drive-in theater in the states, only instead of parking slots and speakers, there were hundreds of wooden benches for seats and a couple of huge speakers on tripods placed near the screen. The patrons were a broad cross section of American and Thai military men, many arriving with a six-pack beer or a bottle of something more substantial. Periodically, the feature would be interrupted by the earsplitting rumble of a departing bomber or tanker aircraft, followed by a wave of jet exhaust that would roll through the theater area. We weren't there to watch the movies, as much as to get away from the boredom and have some contact with 'home'. With the constant rumble of departing and arriving aircraft, however, you were repeatedly reminded you were far from home and that there was a war going on.

• • •

Enlisted personnel lived in dormitories on the far side of the base from where our trailers were located. That meant we had to take a detour to pick up our boom operator whenever we went to fly. Dwain was a 19-year old Cajun from the bayou country in Louisiana and had never been far from home. All the new sights, sounds, and experiences of this foreign country and his job must have been overwhelming, but, on the surface, he seemed to take everything in stride. To Dwain, we probably seemed like a bunch of college boys from the city who did not have much sense when it came to things that go on in the outside world. He advised us to be careful walking around the base at night because there were all kinds of wild animals about, including crocodiles. We listened with patronizing smiles, allowing his vivid imagination to run its course, until he pointed out a twelve-foot caiman, the local version of the crocodile, in the drainage ditch a block from his dormitory. Dwayne knew his critters. There were also several kinds of poisonous snake in that part of Thailand and three to four-inch long rice bugs that were a local delicacy. At night we were entertained by the chirping of geckoes that scurried across the walls and ceilings of every building in search of tasty insects. Lights attracted all sorts of flying bugs including moths the size of birds. Our navigator was the frequent target of bug-related pranks since early in the trip he expressed an inordinate fear of all reptiles and bugs. It was the usual practice to leave a bug or dead lizard on his hat or boots to see how loud a shriek he would produce. Whenever he found one of these critters, after the initial reaction of terror, he would look at each of us in turn to identify the culprit and it was a challenge to keep a straight face after his initial reaction. One evening we had placed a six-inch dead moth on his pillow and were discussing the day's activities while he got ready for bed. When he pulled back the bedspread and saw the moth, we got the expected response and it was impossible to keep from falling down laughing. He cussed us out for an hour and after that he checked his hat, his boots, his bedding, and all of his other belongings several times before he would be satisfied that everything was in order. I think he was convinced that at some point we would put a live snake in his bed. That, however, would have been a little too much fun at his expense and we agreed to end the bug planting. He did not however, quit looking for the remainder of the deployment.

Although the officers were paid a considerable sum for meals, the enlisted personnel were expected to eat in the military dining hall and their meal allowance was paltry. As a result, we sometimes took Dwain, our enlisted boom operator, with us to the club to eat and paid his way. On one particular weekend, I mentioned to him that an all-you-can-eat spaghetti special was scheduled at the club that evening and would he be interested in joining us. Would he ever! He told us he could probably eat a dozen plates of spaghetti and had done so many times before. Although Dwain looked like he could put away a plate or two of food, we guessed anything more than that was an exaggeration, but we looked forward to his company and enthusiasm for the meal. And so, after landing from an afternoon flight, the three of us took Dwain to the club for dinner. That particular meal was very popular and the club was still two thirds full of eager diners although meal time had started an hour before we arrived. We were seated at a table near the middle of the dining room and soon were served plates piled high with spaghetti as well as garlic bread and a complimentary bottle of cheap red wine.

We talked about the day's flight and how things were going back in the states while we ate. All asked for a second plate as we were very hungry, and the nearby waiter was quick to respond. After finishing the second plate we were full but Dwain was just getting warmed up. Plate two then plate three went by. The number of dining room patrons dwindled as we watched Dwain eat. Plate four went down a little slower. Soon we were the only ones left in the dining room and all of the other waiters had come to stand near our table and watch the action. Waiters soon began making bets on how many plates Dwain would eat and when he called for plate number five, a cheer went up from a couple of watching winners. We had nothing better to do that evening and the excitement of the kitchen staff was catching. As plate number five arrived and was emptied, the waiter stood by expectantly and Dwain, after a short pause, looked at the waiter and said he believed he would have another. I looked at my copilot who, with a big grin on his face, slowly shook his head. Dwain's progress was much slower with plate six and upon finishing it pushed his plate away, seemed to ponder continuing, and then announced that he believed that would be enough. A cheer went up from the waiters and the kitchen staff who had come into the dining room to watch. A new record had been set and we had "ring side seats" to the event.

• • •

One evening a week later, I was at the bar with some friends when an older officer who was assigned to the staff, asked if anyone at the table wanted to go off base for some fun. It was late and everyone said they were too tired to join this grandfatherly type for an evening on the town. I was not sure what the man meant by fun, but I was uncomfortable going off base during the day much less at night. A few days earlier I had gone into town with my crew to do some shopping at a local bazaar. On the way home the driver of our baht bus, local Toyota pickup version of the taxi cab, nearly got into a wreck with his kamikaze driving style and then we were chased by a group of Thai hoodlums demanding money as we walked towards the main gate. No, I had no interest in going out for fun, especially after dark. I headed back to my trailer and bed. The next morning, we went to the club for breakfast and there was a buzz of conversation about some recent development. Apparently, the older man had gone into town by himself to one of the local nightclubs. It was commonly known that when he went into town he would spread out several of his business cards on the counter, with a reverse side that looked like folded fifty-dollar bills, to impress the locals. Apparently, someone had seen him do this and attempted to rob him as he left the night club. He resisted and was shot. His body was found outside the base gate that morning. Although the local Thai police arrested and executed three men who they believed were the culprits, I didn't go off base again.

Life in the trailer village was very repetitious. Unless we had an early flight, we slept in until eight or nine in the morning, showered, and went to breakfast. Then we were off to the day's activities. While we were gone our clothes would be washed, boots would be shined, and the trailer would be cleaned. It was the crew's responsibility to contact a local Thai woman who would be hired to complete these activities for the duration of the deployment. The woman who took care of us had contracted for cleaning services with the previous tenants of our trailer and probably many tenants before that. I am not sure how our clothes were washed, whether on a rock in a drainage canal or in some kind of washing machine, but after several months in Thailand most clothes assumed a dirty lemonade hue that could not be removed once we returned to the states. Like many Thai employees on base, the 'mama-san' who cared for us and our trailer did not speak much English. It was hard to tell how old the woman was. She had wrinkled, sun baked skin, and her age could have been from mid-fifties to early eighties. Every morning she showed up around first light in native dress and whenever we were around, she seemed very industrious. When we came home each day, everything was in order with shoes/boots lined up by the door and clothes neatly folded on the bed of each owner.

The heat and humidity, plus the daily regimen of huge anti-malarial pills, left us feeling very dehydrated and beaten down at the end of most days. One Saturday after an especially long work day, I had dinner and went to bed early. For us, early was anything before midnight. The room air conditioner had cooled the air a couple of degrees below the outside temperature, but did nothing to lower the humidity. I went right to bed after a cold shower, with only a sheet for a cover. I slept soundly through the night, until at some point something woke me up. I sat up in bed and realized that the overhead light was on. I reached for my watch and saw that it was 4am. I was groggy and I was sure that I had turned the light off. Then a figure rose up at the foot of my bed. It was a young Thai woman, in maybe her late teens or early twenties. In a knee jerk move of modesty I yanked the bed sheet up to just under my chin and asked her what the heck she was doing in my room. She turned her eyes to the floor and in a very soft voice asked "you no like Oolai?" I still didn't know what was going on and I yelled at her to leave my room. She shuffled off and quietly closed the door behind her. I jumped out of bed and made sure the door was locked. I lay there in bed for a long time wondering if I had just woken from a bad dream or if I was still asleep. Then my alarm went off and it was seven am.

I got up remembering the dream about a nighttime visitor. I stepped into a hot shower and quickly shifted my thoughts to the day's work schedule. I toweled off, got dressed, and knocked on the interconnecting door to my crewmember's room to make sure they were up. They were ready to go and we exited the trailer through the outside door to their room. Outside, we were approached by the mama-san who was just arriving for work. She came up to me and began shaking her fist and jabbering away in a very loud voice. It seemed she was angry about something, and I wondered if we had forgotten to pay her for the month's cleaning or if we had not paid her enough. I raised my hands in a gesture of puzzlement and she was still firing words at me as we left. We walked to the two blocks to the dining hall for breakfast and as we sat down at the table with our trays of food, I noticed that the other two officers were grinning broadly at each other and seemed to be sharing some secret. Finally, the navigator asked me if I had slept well. I told him I had a dream about being woken up by an unexpected visitor. He laughed and asked what I thought of the girl. He was pleased with himself as he told me that he and the copilot had made arrangements to 'fix me up' for the night. They had approached the mama-san to send a girl to my room. What they didn't know and I didn't find out until later was that the girl was the mama-san's daughter. Now I understood why the mama-san was upset. After chewing out my two crewmembers and ordering them never to do such a thing again, I assigned them the job of getting back in the mama-san's good graces. I worried that she might either damage our belongings, or worse, leave a snake, hand grenade, or some other bad thing in one of our rooms. In the end, the present of a few large bath towels and a bottle of cheap perfume from the Base Exchange (BX) made the whole misunderstanding go away. For the remainder of the deployment, however, the mama-san glared at me every time I was in her presence. I guess I had failed her good etiquette test.

The days went by slowly and we tried our best to keep busy when we weren't flying. Some days we played racquetball or tennis before the heat of the day made the outdoor court unbearable. There was a daily trip to the Base Exchange to see if any new goods had arrived. Between purchases at the BX and in the local village over a several-week period, we had collected a substantial pile of souvenirs and goods to take back to the states. New items arrived daily from Japan, India, and Koreas and were dirt cheap at the BX. Things purchased in town were even cheaper since we were able to haggle with the merchants to arrive at a fair price. In the end, the merchants probably got more than things were worth, but we paid much less than equivalent merchandise would have cost in the states. We went to the BX for cameras, binoculars, watches, and similar items, as well as an occasional clothing item to replace those that had been 'colored' by the maid's washing practices. In addition to those purchases, most of us were fascinated with the wide variety of unique items for sale in the nearby village. There were bowls and figurines (some very explicit) carved from monkey pod wood, all kinds of wicker containers and furniture, cheap jewelry with every kind of metal and stone, brass creations of all kinds including five-foot high candlesticks, leather goods, and any number of specialty items that you could have made to your exact specifications. You could also have the local Indian or Pakistani tailor make a very nice civilian suit that would be tailored to your exact measurements in a couple of days. Some of the cloth patterns used to make the suits might have been more appropriate for rock stars of the day, but heck it was a real suit. The tailors could also make you a Sawatdee (party) suit. These short sleeved, one-piece, brightly colored flight suits could be worn at unofficial party functions and the louder the color the better. They came in powder blue, red, pink, orange, lime green, and any number of other colors complete with patches that indicated the name and rank of the wearer, pilot wings, and maybe a patch or two to indicate some imagined or actual accomplishment while deployed in Thailand. It was always interesting to see who would show up with the most outrageous party suit at functions held for that purpose. At least it was interesting if one was sober enough to register such things.

Somehow the days passed, we survived our last flights up to 'the fence' as the Mekong River border was called, and were assigned a departure date. Although we flew a different airplane every day during the deployment, we were to take an airplane from our own base all the way home. Layovers at intermediate stops would only be overnight so the trip should take four or five days if the airplane and weather cooperated. On the day of departure, we had to requisition a 2 ½ ton stake bed truck to get our purchases, as well as those of our passengers, to the airplane. There were several large high-backed wicker chairs, several sets of brass candlesticks, plaster elephant and temple dog statues, and many boxes of all sizes. I had purchased a set of Noritake China at the BX and gave special attention to making sure that those cartons were carefully placed on board and securely tied down. Soon the cargo bay looked much fuller than it had when we arrived and although my loadmaster assured me that we had not exceeded our allowed takeoff weight, it certainly looked like a lot of stuff. We called on the radio to have our passengers brought out from the terminal. It was time to go home.

The trip home was uneventful and when we landed at home base we were greeted by a spring snow shower and temperatures near freezing. We must have looked like people from another world to those who greeted us as we stepped down from the airplane. We had grown mustaches and let our hair grow long in the civilian style of the time. We were deeply tanned and moved with the assurance of those who had 'gone to war' and were now experienced in all things. I am sure we looked and smelled of the moldy, sweaty environment from which we were returning. We looked forward to family time and days off when we would catch up with fishing and evenings of parties at friend's houses where we could tell of our great adventures. As the last of our baggage and purchases were offloaded from the airplanes and family members left to bring vehicles to be loaded, the colonel I worked for motioned me over near the airplane wingtip, away from the rest of the crew members. He said 'Welcome Home' and that I should report to him the day after next so he could brief me on our upcoming deployment to Alaska in ten days. 'And by the way', he said, 'you and your crew will want to get a shave and haircut before you report to my office.' The crew greeted me with big smiles when I rejoined them at the crew bus, and the navigator asked me what the colonel wanted. After a short pause, I told him it would keep until tomorrow and eased into to my seat as the bus pulled away from the airplane heading off the flight line.

Midnight Missiles

This was the last stop in a whirlwind visit to European locations that housed personnel for whom I was responsible as the new commander of the USAF Air Combat Camera Service. Since I knew little of the daily work completed by the more than 800 men and women who worked for me as still and motion photographers, it seemed a little time "in the trenches" would get me up to speed. Earlier in the week I had visited a site just outside of London, England, and then another near Stuttgart, Germany where I visited with local officials and was briefed on their daily operations. Now it was late in the evening and I was in an aircrew briefing room in Northern Italy. The local director of operations had asked if I would like to go along on one of their flights and I said I would. The air wing's current mission was airdrop of supplies to the civilian population of Bosnia. I was directed to a seat in the front row and as I scanned the room I saw a couple of flight crewmembers talking with a captain in air force blues up front. In the back of the room several other crewmembers were huddled around a large map spread out on a metal table. An aerial photographer who was assigned to the local combat camera detachment was to fly on the mission and he now approached me with a very welcome can of diet Pepsi. As he sat down beside me, someone called the room to attention and the local wing commander, a brigadier general, entered the room and quickly moved to the podium.

After everyone in the room took their seats, the general welcomed me to their operations and began the briefing. He announced that the mission for that night was a C-130 airdrop of food and medical supplies over a designated friendly area near the town of Gorazde in southern Bosnia. He introduced the weather officer who gave a short briefing on flight conditions enroute and said that weather over the drop zone should be basically clear although there were occasional snow showers in the area. The tactical officer briefed next and he stepped to a map of our routing that was displayed on a wall behind him. He pointed out suspected 37 and 57-millimeter antiaircraft positions near our route and advised us that no gunfire from these positions had been observed on the previous mission earlier in the week. Although there was some concern with shoulder fired surface-to-air-missiles in the region, no missile launches had been observed to date on any flights in the southern half of the country. I had been advised earlier in the day that this was to be an airdrop mission, but no one had said anything about anti-aircraft fire or missiles. My uneasiness advanced another notch when we were advised to pick up weapons and survival gear on our way to the crew bus. The aircrew commander next gave the flight briefing for his crew, announced the takeoff time, time over the drop zone, and his expectations for each of the crewmembers under his command. Then the briefing was over and crewmembers gathered up their gear and headed down the hall to the survival equipment section. I had brought my own flight helmet on this trip and now checked my helmet oxygen mask operation with a nearby test console. Each crewmember picked up a webbed survival vest that contained emergency rations, signaling devices, and a small medical kit. A sergeant issued me a spare vest to use during the flight. We then headed down to the armory to pick up weapons.

At a screened cage that separated access to armory weapons from the armory lobby, crewmembers displayed their weapons qualification cards to the airman behind the cage. She passed each crewmember a shoulder holster that contained a Browning automatic pistol. Each person was also issued two clips of nine-millimeter ammunition. I had annually qualified expert with this weapon for the last several years and was very familiar with its operation. After our aerial photographer picked up his weapon, I presented my weapons card to the armory airman who seemed to scrutinize it more carefully than she had for the other crewmembers. After a few moments, she told me she was unable to issue me a weapon since my card was not locally validated. My efforts to convince her that validation at one USAF location should be good for all others fell on deaf ears. One of the crew loadmasters was standing nearby, a senior master sergeant, told me that if we had to bail out, I should stay close to him. In case anyone needed any shooting, he said he would take care of it and everything would be fine. Since there was not enough time before takeoff to take the issue to a high level, and the loadmaster assured me that no C-130 aircraft had ever been shot down over Bosnia, I decided, somewhat uncomfortably, that I could do without a weapon.

On the way to the airplane, the crew stopped by the cargo staging hangar to show me some of the different loads they carried. In the huge building were dozens of pallets loaded with boxes and containers of every description and covered with shrink wrap for protection from the elements. The crew chief proudly showed me one pallet that was loaded with four large cardboard boxes, each large enough to hold a couple of refrigerators. He had recently been commended for designing what he called the "MRE Delivery System". He pointed out several cuts that had been made in the side of the boxes and explained that when the boxes were airdropped, they came apart in the slip stream, showering the countryside with their contents. Each box was packed with hundreds of Meals-ready-to-eat (MREs), the freeze-dried fare that were currently being produced with new menus to meet the needs of the predominantly Muslim civilian population we were attempting to supply. As we moved on to other pallets, I noticed that thick wads of paper were visible in some of the loads. Closer inspection revealed that the wads were hundreds of six by three-inch leaflets covered with foreign writing and pictures of C-130 aircraft dropping boxes marked with a red cross. The chief explained that the leaflets informed the population of our humanitarian mission in Cyrillic writing on one side and Serbian on the other. I was told that an earlier version of the leaflet advised the reader not to shoot at the aircraft dropping supplies or the friendly aircraft would not return. Those leaflets worked only too well. When the local civilians heard C-130 engines, they ran outside and when they saw the descending parachutes with their load of supplies, hurried to be the first ones at the drop site. Unfortunately, in their eagerness, many people were crushed by the descending pallets which weighed several tons each. Accordingly, the latest leaflet version advised people that descending pallets weighed several tons and if they did not stay well clear until the pallets landed, they would become a permanent part of the landscape. At least with the "MRE Delivery System", the worst to happen would be to get beaned by a small plastic pouch of food. Then again, I had eaten the cheese and potato MRE during the Gulf War and maybe getting hit in the head with that was the lesser of two evils.

As the crew bus transported us across the darkened flight line, I could make out dozens of C-130 aircraft. Soon we arrived at one that was illuminated by ramp floodlights. As we left the bus and carried our personal gear onto the airplane, the loadmasters finished putting the last pallets on board, the cargo tugs pulled away, and the huge rear loading ramp was raised and locked into place. I was directed to a cockpit seat just behind the aircraft commander and strapped myself in. As soon as I put my headphones on, I heard each crewmember check in on interphone and the next half hour went by in a blur as each crewmember completed required checklists. Soon, the engine start was called for and the vibration from the turboprops coming up to idle was felt through the entire airframe. I had flown on C-130s a couple of times before, and each time I had been issued bubblegum-like earplugs to protect my ears from the roar of the engines. Although the plugs were satisfactory, you still were stuck with the constant vibration from the engines. However, I felt that the engine noise and vibration was a comfort. Especially when you consider the alternative! Soon we were ready to taxi and in the glow of cockpit lighting, I saw the copilot give the visual signal to remove chocks, the pilot advanced the throttles, and we began to move.

The taxi and takeoff were uneventful and I found myself critically watching the pilots for adherence to airspeed, altitude and heading during the climb out. I guess all pilots are back seat drivers when it comes to watching someone else maneuver the aircraft. Shortly after takeoff, I heard the navigator announce that we were approaching the Italian coastline and then we were droning off into the night over the Adriatic Sea. It felt good to be back in the cockpit and I sensed everyone was settling into their duties as we climbed to our assigned flight altitude for the route towards the drop zone. Our mission photographer came forward from the cargo hold as we leveled off and asked me if I wanted a cup of coffee. Although I don't normally drink the stuff, it seemed impolite to refuse and besides it was a little chilly in the airplane. I was wearing long johns under my flight suit and had a Nomex flight jacket on over my survival vest, but air outside the airplane was around minus fifteen degrees, and that temperature in the cargo hold for the drop would be substantially lower than that in the cockpit. As I accepted a cup of coffee, I heard the navigator announce that we were approaching the Bosnian coastline and soon he was radioing back to our base to announce "feet dry" over the Bosnian countryside.

It was well past midnight when the navigator announced thirty minutes from the drop zone. We had turned all external lighting off as we headed inland and all radios were turned off until we would return to the coast. It was critical not to give away our position to observers on the ground. The flight engineer had been standing behind the navigator discussing our position, but now he resumed his seat behind the throttle console and picked up a couple of large red handles laying on the floor near his jump seat that seemed to be connected by cable to the back of the throttle console. I asked what the handles were for and was told that they were the manual flare ejectors. Although the C-130 has an automatic flare and chaff ejector system to foil missile threats, the manual system is available as a backup. No sooner had the flight engineer taken his position than the copilot, in a voice that was two or three octaves above normal, announced over the interphone that he saw anti-aircraft fire about five miles away at about two o'clock. Up to this point in the flight, I was only mildly interested in the details of crew activity, but now the copilot had my full attention. I removed my seat belt and stood behind him to see what he saw. Sure enough, I saw a dashed stream of what looked like tracers off to the right of the aircraft. I was not sure if the five-mile estimate was accurate, but more importantly, someone seemed to be shooting at our general location. After several more streams of fire appeared at two other positions off to the front and side of our aircraft, the aircraft commander said it looked like 57-millimeter fire. I had no interest in the size, just whether it was going to get closer. The pilot announced confidently that they were just shooting up in the sky at our sound, and that they could only hit us with a lucky shot. A bigger concern was if they shot missiles and then it was up to the automatic system and the flight engineer to keep us out of trouble. That did not do much for my confidence level, but about that time the navigator tapped me on the back and said I should go to the cargo hold if I wanted to watch the drop. I looked to see that the flight engineer had a death grip on the manual flare ejector triggers as he peered over the copilot's shoulder. There was nothing I could do to help in the cockpit, so I opened the cockpit door and moved into the cargo hold.

It was significantly colder in the cargo bay. I could see the photographer getting his cameras ready and connecting himself with a snap connector to the internal aircraft framework, as he moved into position to photograph the drop. The loadmaster helped me into a parachute. Evidently crewmen have accidentally gotten tangled up in the network of drop cables and pulled out with the load, leading to the requirement for a parachute and helmet for anyone in the hold during a drop. I tightened the crotch straps on my parachute which made it impossible to stand erect. However, I could certainly put up with a little discomfort for a few minutes while the drop was completed. I pulled my grey flight helmet from its bag and put it on. I reached under the bottom of the helmet to "unfold" my ears, adjust the helmet fit, and snap the chin strap. At the front of the cargo bag was an oxygen panel and a spare oxygen bottle. I removed the bottle from its resting place and connected it to my helmet oxygen system. I pulled on my heavy winter flying gloves and then found a place where I could hold on to part of the aircraft structure to brace myself for unexpected aircraft

maneuvering. I looked to make sure there were no cables or load portions that were anywhere near my feet. About that time the lights in the cargo bay were turned from white to red and the loadmaster was advised over the intercom that we were ten minutes from the drop. He announced that the airplane was about to be depressurized and that everyone should go on oxygen. I hooked up my oxygen mask and turned on my oxygen supply as I felt the pressure begin to change in the cargo bay and then the loadmaster pushed a handle on the left side of the airplane. The top of the rear hatch began to descend into the slip stream of the aircraft. The temperature in cargo hold dropped immediately and I was glad I had decided to wear long johns on the flight. When the hatch was fully opened the loadmaster put his hands on another handle and stared intently at the small indicator lights on a nearby panel that would turn green when it was time for him to release the load. As I looked around the bay, the photographer was making his camera ready, the assistant loadmaster was watching the drop light indicator with his boss, and a stream of swirling snow was now apparent in the gaping dark hole where the rear ramp had been lowered. We must have been at a relatively low altitude by this time, because I could make out widely scattered ground lights of nearby towns. I could tell that the pilot was working the flight controls hard to stay on course for an exact drop as the airplane lurched from side to side and I increased my grip on the nearby aircraft beams to keep from losing my balance. As I stood in the front of the cargo bay looking over the top of the pallets, watching the ground lights go by in the swirling dark snowstorm, one light caught my eye. It was brighter than the surrounding ground lights and seemed to have a more reddish hue. More importantly, it seemed to be getting larger as it corkscrewed up towards us. I looked to see if anyone else in the cargo bay was seeing this. The photographer was twenty feet away, adjusting his camera lens, and the loadmasters were intently watching the drop lights. I was not connected to anyone on the airplane by interphone and by the time I could get to the cockpit to alert the crew, it would be too late. My impression was that the missile was going to come right into the cargo bay and I could not see anything to duck behind. It seemed like an eternity passed, but probably more like a few seconds when I realized that the light had not gotten any closer. About then I realized that I was seeing a ground light source that seemed to move due to the erratic aircraft movement. The relief was immediate and intense as I released my held breath and went back to watching the loadmasters. Then the green drop light came on and the loadmaster moved to release the load. Eight heavy pallets began to move down the rollers to the ramp. The first six pallets were connected to parachutes and as they passed the end of the ramp, dropped quickly out of view into the dark. The last two were MRE containers and the boxes exploded as soon as they hit the air stream, as advertised. Then the loadmasters were raising the ramp, pressurizing the cargo bay and storing the excess cables and straps. The photographer stowed his gear and I removed my parachute and helmet. My breath was clearly visible in the frosty night air and I was glad to return to the cockpit. As I strapped back into my seat up front, the pilot began to climb to a higher altitude for the return flight. The copilot continued to call out sporadic ground fire sightings and finally we approached the coast. The navigator turned on the radios and gave a report to our headquarters of a successful drop, along with a "feet wet" status as we once again flew over the east coast of the Adriatic. We were less than an hour from landing and the crew was finishing checklists and radioing for landing weather. The flight engineer was massaging his hands which had severely cramped after holding the manual flare triggers for a couple of hours. I was on interphone but alone with my thoughts. I thought what a great rush of adrenaline the mission had provided and how good it would be to experience it again...and then maybe not. The lights of the Italian coastline ahead looked good and I would be glad to get my feet back on the ground.

It's All About Looking Good

I firmly believe that fly fishermen come in two groups, those who have observed fly fishing on TV and actually believe that many large fish are caught in that manner and those who don't have anything else to do in the dog days of summer and just want to look good while whipping tiny feather-covered hooks through the air in some scenic locale. I was thinking that very thought as I was trying to maintain my balance in the middle of the Madison River in about three feet of fast moving, crystal clear water, while on vacation from my Michigan home. The bottom of the river was covered with gravel and softball-sized mossy rocks and I had just finished doing my version of break dancing, having made the mistake of turning my back to the flow of the river, which usually results in a thorough dunking.

It was mid-morning and I had arrived at what I thought was a good fishing spot in the northern part of Yellowstone Park. It was a good spot because it was the first place I found to park my truck where there were no other fishermen in sight. I had not used my fly rod in a couple of years, and I had no interest in embarrassing myself in front of fishermen who actually knew what they were doing. From past experience, I remembered that it was very easy to end up thoroughly ensnared in fly line or lose your balance in the fast current. The river was about

80 feet wide where I entered, but the water looked shallow enough for hip waders. I am not sure what possessed me to wade to the center of the thigh-deep river, since there were many good spots near the shore and you could even fish from the bank. But somehow, by shuffling my feet carefully over the rough bottom and with my arms widespread for balance, I had arrived at what I thought was a strategic location to cover the entire area with effective casts. And now after a momentary loss of balance, I turned to face up river and survey my surroundings. Spring comes late in Yellowstone and the patchy grass that covered both banks was still a deep emerald green. Although fir trees lined the road through most of this part of the park, the bank on the side where I had parked was fairly open and patches of yellow or blue wildflowers were in evidence all along the edge of the road. On the far bank the terrain rose steeply in a loose gray shale field to a craggy, rock face. I could see what looked like a small cave halfway up the incline and imagined that it was periodically occupied by a mountain lion or a wolf, even though that was unlikely this close to the highway. Most of the trees I could see on both banks were white pine or cedar and one about 100 yards upriver looked like it had been struck by lightning. Most of its top branches were dead and I noticed a Kingfisher, with his distinctive large blue head and relatively small body, setting about ten feet below the top of the tree. As I watched, the bird dove from his perch, landed with a splash in mid-stream and took off again with what looked like a five or six-inch fish in his large black beak. He disappeared upstream with his catch and I was thinking that the river must be loaded with fish if a bird could get one that easily. I waded up a little closer to where the bird had hit the water and began stripping off pale green fly line to false cast towards the spot. Just then, the peaceful sounds of nature were interrupted by the

noise of a vehicle turning off the nearby highway. I looked over towards the road to see a silver SUV pulling into the parking area. Car doors flew open and a group of elderly tourists with cameras soon assembled and began pointing towards the river in my general vicinity. I had purposefully wanted to avoid an audience and this did not look good. A short, heavy woman waved at me and held up her camera. I was not sure if she wanted some kind of pose, but I obliged by stripping out about as much line as I thought I could cast and begin working the line back and forth in the air. The heft of the fly rod felt comfortable and the line cooperated nicely as I concentrated on a place near the opposite bank where I thought a trout might be lurking. I imagined how good I looked in my blue tartan shirt, tan fly vest and straw cowboy hat. The pictures would probably end up in some fishing magazine or be displayed in home slide shows as depicting an expert western fisherman in his element. The fly line floated through the air and the gray dun fly dropped gently to the exact spot for which I had aimed. I was clearly showing off a mastery of my art and thought I might try a roll cast to move the fly another few feet towards the far shore. Always an impressive fly casting form, the roll cast takes several years to perfect. I stripped off some extra line and flipped the rod to send a two-foot standing loop down the length of floating fly line. I was feeling pretty pleased with my skills and was thinking about which pose to strike next when my reverie was broken by the slam of a car door. The photographers had gotten what they wanted and were leaving. Silence returned to the river.

I worked the tip of the leader line back to hand and as I did so I noticed that the wrapping on one of the line guides was getting frayed. I needed to buy a bottle of fingernail polish to secure the loose wrapping, but hopefully that repair work could wait until after the fishing trip. I used the nail clippers hanging from my vest loop to trim off the excess wrapping and returned my attention to the leader line. The Berkeley fly rod was starting to show its age. I had received it as a present from my wife back in the1960s when I was living in Pennsylvania. The clear limestone streams in the central part of that state held large trout and fly fishing was very popular there. The first weekend I went out with my new fly rod, I had great difficulty mastering the timing needed to lay the line out in a cast. To make things worse, the streams there were lined with trees and brush and almost every cast ended up tangled in one or the other. I could clearly make out large trout swimming casually up and down the stream, but I could not find a way to cast a fly to them. And when I tried dropping the line from the end of the rod directly above the place they swam, they ignored the offering. They could feel the vibrations of my footfalls on the bank and were not about to be fooled. After a few hours I gave up. I put the fly rod in a closet and it remained there collecting dust for several years. Six or seven years later, I was fishing in Michigan waters for large steelhead trout with spin casting equipment and not having much luck. A friend said he thought the water was too low and clear for that kind of gear and said he thought we needed to fish with fly rods. When I got home that day, I looked in my garage and found the fly rod and vest. The next weekend we used fly fishing equipment and did indeed catch fish. At least we had them on the line. They were easily fooled by the spider web-like leader line and the tiny feather covered hooks. Unfortunately, when you pair a ten-pound surging steelhead trout with a tiny leader line, something has to give. After a short battle, the fish usually won out over the fragile line. The fly equipment went back in the closet. The weeks of the early season went by, fish were caught with "regular" fishing poles, the days got warmer, water levels receded, and bugs became thick.

But now I was on the Madison River, where fish are supposed to be a more reasonable size and can be easily fooled into taking almost any kind of fly. At least that is what the park ranger who handed me the fishing guidebook said about fishing areas in Yellowstone. The ranger also said I should be careful to return to the water any fish I caught that were larger than eighteen inches and served as brood stock. At the time, that was the least of my worries since I had yet to catch a fish of any size. I reached in my vest and pulled out one of my metal folding fly boxes. Inside were two or three dozen flies of various types and sizes. Some were homemade, but most had been purchased at shops near fishing places around the country. Many had seen significant abuse by hard striking fish and were barely recognizable from what I remembered of their original appearance. Of course, even when new, anything I had tied didn't actually resemble a fly you might buy in a fishing supply store. For some reason, despite my careful attention to detail, the flies I tied always seemed to look like a gob of yarn and feathers that were trying to hide a hook, rather than like something that might be tasty for your average trout.

There are lots of books to help you determine what kind of fly to use for a particular fishing location or condition. The advice that experts always seem to use in their books is to "match the hatch" by using a fly that resembles some bug or food item that fish normally eat. You can look at what is in a fish's stomach to get an idea, but first you have to have a fish! An alternative is to examine bugs floating on the water or hovering about a stream. If you are lucky, you will see a fish jump to catch a flying bug or you will see a little eddy in the water where a fish has quietly taken a bug from the surface. I remember one fall afternoon watching my fishing partner Tony swinging his cap through the air trying to catch a representative bug from a hatch in progress over the surface of the stream. He would periodically examine what he had caught and compare that with his assortment of flies to determine which fly to use next. I had tried the same thing, lost my balance on a slippery rock, and got rewarded with a thorough soaking for my efforts. When I did catch a bug, it didn't look like anything in my fly box. Tony advised that a Royal Coachman dry fly serves as a good all-around fly if I couldn't find anything that matched the actual bugs seen in the area. He had given me several that he had tied and they got a lot of good use since everything else in my fly box looked like junk.

On the Madison, I couldn't see any bugs in the air or on the surface of the river. As I worked my way through my third and last fly box I did find one slightly worn Royal Coachman and tied it onto the tippet at the end of my leader line. I once again worked a length of fly line off my reel and began false casting. As I cast my line to different spots that looked "fishy," I worked my way further upriver from the parking area and around a bend in the river. Solitude set in and other than the sound of rushing water, everything was quiet. I liked the quiet, but began thinking about wild animals. The park ranger had said there had been problems the previous week with tourists that had gotten too close to buffalo or elk or bears or other critters they were trying to photograph. Although most of the larger animals headed to the more remote parts of the park during tourist season, a chance encounter was always possible. I was thinking my pocket knife would not be of much use if I had an encounter. I once split my finger down to the bone with it while giving a demonstration on knife safety to a group of young boy scouts. That was probably not a very good endorsement for my defensive skills with a knife. Maybe dangerous critters would not wade into the stream to get me and if they did I could poke them with my nine-foot long fly rod.

I was not sure that would be a sufficient deterrent for a determined bear. And bears can really be a distraction while fishing!

• • •

The last time I had worried about bears while fishing was during a late summer road trip to visit my new in-laws. On that occasion, I was nervous about the trip well before bears came into the equation. I had been married for about five years and Wildy, my father-in-law, had yet to speak to me. The in-laws lived in the mountains of eastern Idaho and I brought my fly fishing equipment along. I figured I could stay out of the way and avoid any unpleasant interaction by checking out some scenic mountain streams while my wife visited with her parents. The drive west to Jackson Hole was very scenic and the town was full of cowboy wannabe tourists who filled every sidewalk and gathering place. In the town square, tourists were taking pictures of huge arches made from hundreds of elk antlers, a tribute to the huge native elk herds that come down from the mountains in the winter to graze in the pastures on the north side of town. We quickly left the town behind and headed further west towards the Teton Mountains. The highway eventually began a winding climb of several thousand feet from the Wyoming meadows to the Utah border, high in the mountains. My in-laws lived in a small mining community of about thirty families near the town of Driggs, Utah. The area was very picturesque with stately pines and severe rock outcroppings in every direction. Nearer the town were meadows overgrown with wildflowers and grasses two to three feet high. Cold, clear mountain streams lined the highway and surged down the mountainside, sustained by snowmelt from the higher elevations. About an hour after crossing the Idaho border a few signs of civilization began to appear, including a sign that announced our entry to the community of Victor, population 120. There were not many houses or buildings in sight as we followed directions to the parent's house and pulled into a worn gravel area in front of a small double wide trailer home surrounded by well-kept white picket fence. As we pulled into the drive the front door opened and the in-laws came out to greet my wife. I hung back a bit and was introduced. Then the father-in-law said "come with me" and without waiting for an answer headed towards the back of the house. Not sure of what was up, I reluctantly followed. In the back, he approached a dog, a boxer, of about 100 pounds. The boxer seemed very agitated and it was soon obvious why. It had forty or fifty porcupine quills embedded in all aspects of its muzzle. I was instructed to get a tight grip on the dog's collar and the father-in-law began to pull out the quills with pliers. It took about 20 minutes and the dog fought my grip and quivered with pain at every pull. When the job was complete, the man said we could go in the house now. This was not the start to the visit that I expected.

Inside, lunch was being made and we soon sat down to eat. Over lunch, my wife mentioned that I would be interested in fishing in the area and would like some directions. Her mother said I could fish in a little pond that we had passed on the way into the village or that Wildy, who operated a nearby limestone quarry, could take me to a fishing place up in the mountains. I said I had fly fishing equipment and a flowing stream might be better. Wildy didn't comment and I was thinking maybe the village pond would be OK after all. After lunch and a little more conversation between the women, Wildy asked me if I was ready to go and it seemed like he had already decided what my choice of fishing places would be. He headed out the door and I quickly followed to get my fly rod, fishing vest, and waders from the car. We set off in his

Jeep and were soon headed east, back down the highway past where we had entered the town. I was thinking about saying that any place along the highway would be good but was reluctant to break the ominous silence in the car. About ten miles outside of town he turned off the highway and onto a gravel road that headed steeply up the mountainside. There wasn't much conversation and I didn't want to say anything that might make a bad impression. After several miles, the road ended near an open gravel quarry and we got out. Near the edge of the dig site was a rusty, metal-walled shack that Wildy said was a combination office and tool shed. There was also a shallow pool of water with a deep green chemical looking tint. It was only about forty feet across and I could not see any vegetation in it or near it. I imagined that the pond was some kind of collection point for poisonous runoff from the nearby mining operation. Across the road from where we stood, I could see a small stream that didn't look big enough to hold fish of any size, but I was a visitor here and willing to try anything the locals might recommend. Wildy took a couple of minutes to describe the local mining operation in very brief terms and seemed to be reluctantly trying to make conversation. I was only half paying attention because I was captivated by the beauty of the setting and the clean, pine-scented air, when I suddenly realized that he had just said that the place was so remote that elk and bear frequent the place. Uh oh. I looked around and didn't see any tracks in the dirt other than human footprints. I was hoping he viewed me as a city slicker and was just trying to impress me with the wildness of the place. After an awkward pause, and with me unsure of how to make an appropriate comment, he said he didn't fish and would be back in a couple of hours if that would be OK. Although I was nervous about being left way up the side of a mountain, I told him it would be OK. I watched as he walked over to the jeep, opened the door and fumbled under the front seat. He retrieved a bundle wrapped in an old towel and upon opening it, produced a huge handgun. Things were definitely taking a turn for the worse and although he had definitely not been very friendly towards me, I could not believe he would actually want to shoot me. And how would he explain that to his daughter! My pulse slowed as he said I could use the handgun in case any bear or elk came around. He reached back under the seat and came up with a worn leather holster and a box of .41 caliber bullets. He gave me these things and without further word or explanation, climbed back into the jeep, started the engine, and let me standing there in a cloud of dust as he drove off back down the mountain. Soon the noise of the departing car faded and the only sound was the gurgling stream and the call of a hawk that was circling high above me on the mountainside air currents. At least I hoped it was a hawk and not a buzzard.

I didn't think there would actually be any dangerous animals nearby, but it didn't hurt to see how the gun worked. Just in case. It was a black .41 caliber single action Ruger with wooden handgrips and a six-inch barrel. It looked like something out of a cowboy movie and it was very heavy. The ammunition in the box of cartridges looked ancient and the brass was a little oxidized, but I loaded five of the bullets into the gun and left the cylinder under the hammer empty. I remembered that lesson from an old sergeant who ran the military firing range where I was trained in the use of a .38 caliber handgun. He said many a man had a toe blown off or worse by leaving a round under the hammer. I put the gun into the holster and sat it on the ground nearby. Then I put on my hip waders and threaded the belt on my jeans through the wader loops and then through the handgun holster. I felt like some sort of comic gunslinger that had been required to wear fishing waders for a duel at noon in the middle of the river. Equipped in this manner, I was sure to lose any gunfight. At every step, the combination of tension on the rubber wader straps and the weight of the heavy handgun threatened to pull my pants down. With one hand on my sagging pants and the other on my fly rod, I waddled towards the nearby beckoning stream.

It took a little while to find a place where the stream was wide and deep enough to hold a fish of any size. In addition, there was a heavy growth of brush and pine trees along the edge of the stream that left almost no room to make a cast of any distance. I was also wondering if all the cover could hide a bear that would get to me well before I ever could draw my handgun. Assuming the handgun was powerful enough to stop a bear. And assuming the gun worked. I considered firing a round at a nearby rock face to make sure it worked and to judge how powerful the kick of the gun was. I decided not to do that because I might not be able to satisfactorily explain why I had fired the gun or unnecessarily wasted bullets. I worked my way down the road a short distance and found a place where I had a little better view of the area surrounding the stream. As I started to enter the stream, I noticed some tracks in the dirt. They looked a little like dog tracks. Or they could be wolf or bear tracks. They looked big. I never was very good in animal track identification in boy scouts. I worked my way back up the road to the place where I had been dropped off. Above the green pool, I found a large rock outcropping that had an unobstructed view in all directions and that hopefully a bear would not want to climb. I scrambled up the rocky slope, sending showers of loose gravel down into the pond. I sat there for a long time, taking in the mountain air and carefully observing the countryside. After a long period of inspecting the nearby terrain for any approaching critters, examining all the odds and ends in the pockets of my fly vest, and investigating mineral deposits on the outcropping, I finally heard the sound of an approaching vehicle and quickly scrambled down from my perch and waded into the emerald pool to get my waders wet. When the jeep came into sight, I put on my best casual expression and gave a little wave, hoping I looked like I had been diligently fishing for the last couple of hours.

Wildy climbed out of the jeep and asked was I ready to go back to town. I got out of my waders, unloaded the pistol and handed it back to him. He wrapped it back in the towel and returned it to its hiding place under the front seat, along with the cartridges and the holster. As we got back into the car, he said there was just one thing he wanted to say. He said his wife did not know about the pistol and he didn't want her to be alarmed so we should not mention it when we got back to the house. I eagerly nodded my agreement as he started the engine. He never said another word as we drove back to their house. The rest of the day was uneventful.

The next day after breakfast I thought I would try my own fishing expedition to the village pond. The pond didn't look like much on the way into town, but the mother assured me that there were fish there. I drove the short distance to the edge of town and parked in an unmarked gravel area within a few yards of the water. The pond was only about sixty or seventy yards across and there was a lot of brush and trees around the edge. I was not sure how I would be able to cast without tangling my line. On the south side of the pond, however, there was a ten or twelve-foot high mound of dirt that was only a few feet from the edge of the water. I climbed up to examine the water from a higher perspective. Despite its small size, the pond was fairly deep and clear with substantial growths of vegetation covering most of the bottom. As I continued to scan the surface, I realized I could actually see a few fish swimming just above the vegetation and about five or six feet below the surface of the water. The fish didn't look very big, but they were fish and I was a fish catcher! I rummaged around in one of my aluminum fly boxes and came up with a likely looking candidate for catching what I hoped were trout. The fly was one of my poorer homemade attempts, but it was colorful and might just attract the attention of a starving trout. I tied the fly on the leader and began to false cast from the top of the mound. I had a good twenty feet of fly line working and stripped another ten feet off the reel to extend the release. I couldn't cast very far out into the pond, but it looked like I could at least drop a fly on top of where I could see fish swimming. And with the downward vector from high on the dirt mound, my back cast was well above the surrounding brush. Things were looking up as I let the line fly forward and the fat glob of yarn and feathers floated gently to the surface of the pond. I waited a few seconds, expecting a strong reaction from the fish, but nothing happened. The fish were still swimming in slow irregular tracks, deep in the pond, and seemed oblivious to my tasty offering. I tried gently jerking the fly line to give the fly some action. No reaction from the fish. I reeled in the line and tried a different fly. Same results. After going through most of my fly collection I still had not raised a fish. Were the fish not hungry? Maybe they were too deep to see the fly. I searched through the pockets of my fly vest for additional boxes of flies, but all that remained were two or three plastic film canisters of interesting looking nymphs that I had bought at various specialty fishing stores. Supposedly these "wet" flies were really great, but I rarely used them, because as they sank beneath the surface of the water, it was difficult to see a strike and you had to depend on your sense of touch to be able to sense a subtle tug on the line. I was never very good at that technique. But now, I opened the film tube and poured the contents into my palm. There were six or seven nymphs there and one looked a bit like some of the black ants I had seen on the ground at the top of the mound. I tied one on, made a cast and let it sink. I immediately lost visual contact with the fly, but I noticed one of the swimming trout reversed course and darted to about the area where the fly sank. I figured I had nothing to lose and raised the rod tip to hopefully set the hook if the fish had taken the fly. To my amazement, I immediately felt a return tug and had a fish on. I climbed down from the mound and stepped to the shore to bring the fish to hand. Soon, I had a beautiful cutthroat trout of about 14 inches on the bank. I had brought a five-gallon bucket with me in case I caught anything and now I filled it with water and added the trout. In the next hour I caught four more trout in the same way, two cutthroat and two rainbows. Although I continued to see a few fishing swimming down deep, eventually they refused further offerings. And it had gotten very warm as the sun beat down through the thin, high altitude air. I took the fish back to the parent's house, cleaned them, and was praised by the assembly who had apparently doubted my skills.

• • •

Back on the Madison, I wondered if I still had any black ants in my film canisters. Fishing through my pockets, I could not find any but did find a few wet flies to try. Some were so small that I could barely find the hook eye to thread the tippet line. These flies were left from an expedition to the San Juan River in northern New Mexico. At that time, I was working with a group of military scientists at Los Alamos and was introduced to a friend of one of my coworkers. The friend, John, offered to take us on a fly fishing trip during second weekend of our stay. We met him at his house early on a Saturday afternoon.

Since we were on a business trip, we had no gear, but John, an accomplished outfitter, had everything we needed. Fly rods, vests, and waders were provided. He had already purchased food for the trip, and his popup camper trailer was attached to his jeep and ready to go. The trip north took about five hours and I was relegated to the back seat of the open-air jeep. The roads were mostly dirt or gravel and a couple hours after leaving Los Alamos, we took a road into the San Juan Mountains that crossed the top at an elevation of about eleven thousand feet in a shortcut to the four corners area of New Mexico. The sky was a brilliant blue with only a few cumulous clouds in sight. We left clouds of dust behind us as we bumped along the rough dirt road. Somewhere near the top, we ran into a rain shower and with no top for the back half of the jeep, I tried to lean in between the front seat riders while covering myself with a plastic tarp. I was not very successful and was soon soaked, but the air was warm and dry and a short time after the shower ended I was dry again. Soon we were heading down the northern slopes and entering water gouged canyons of sheeted slate and scrub cedar. We arrived at the river and set up camp about four miles below the damn on Navajo Lake. The view of the river in the gathering dusk was spectacular and while our new friend John set up the popup trailer, my friend Marty and I geared up and waded into the river to try our luck. We didn't catch anything that evening and soon the smell of food cooking on a Coleman stove and the cedar log campfire brought us out of the water, reminded us that we needed to do our share of the preparation in respect for our wonderful guide. The night noises of the nearby rushing stream and calling birds made sleep come very soon after we turned in.

We were up early the next morning and after a quick breakfast we packed up and headed up river to just below the dam on Navajo Lake. On the way, John handed me a small bag of pinion pine nuts. He said he had found that the seeds did much to quench your thirst on the river and helped extend your water supply. The expensive little bags of seeds were collected from pinion pine cones and sold by local Native American tribes at roadside stands. As we got closer to the dam, John told us that since this part of the river was catch and release, we could expect to catch some really huge fish. We turned into a parking place below the dam that already held four other vehicles. We dismounted and looked towards the distant river where we could see small specks that were the other fisherman. The walk from the jeep to the fishing area was a real challenge. It was already very warm and we were wearing waders. We clambered down a steep forty-foot embankment covered with loose shale and cactus. After that we hiked about a quarter of a mile over mudflats and through brush to the river. Well-worn paths between the thick screens of tall brush let us know that many fishermen had made this trek. Once there, the fun began. I could see several huge fish of maybe four to eight pounds moving in the shallow water. Occasionally, the large dorsal fin of a feeding trout would break the surface. John had told us that the clear, shallow water and heavy fishing pressure caused the trout to spook at the least disturbance. The fish were wary of all but the subtlest of fly offerings. He gave us each a dozen of the tiniest flies I have ever seen. They resembled midge flies and looked smaller than most gnats. John said the flies were tied on #23 hooks. I could not imagine how this tiny hook could be durable enough to take a trout. It was almost impossible to thread one of these flies on the line, but once in place they worked perfectly. I soon had a strike from a large trout of maybe 24 inches in length and it was all I could do to maintain contact without breaking the leader. Most of the fish we hooked did in fact break the line. I landed two very nice rainbow trout which I reluctantly

released. That day I lost most of the midge flies I had been given, but here on the Madison, I could see that there were still a couple left in the film canister.

• • •

The memory of the San Juan River fishing trip brought a smile to my face. I wondered if in the intervening years, John and my friend had returned to that beautiful spot with other friends to tangle with big fish. There probably weren't any fish that big here on the Madison, but I tied on the tiny midge just in case. I had by now worked my way upriver some distance from the truck. At least it seemed that way. When fly fishing on the Madison, somehow time seems to get away from you. It seemed like only minutes before I had seen the Kingfisher in the dead tree back near the truck and now, after a long straight stretch of river, I had turned another bend and there was a little area of rapids ahead of me. I carefully slid my feet over the mossy river bottom and climbed out on the far bank. Then I ducked through low hanging tree branches and worked my way around some thorny brush to move upriver from the rapids. My past experience has been that many trout hang just below a rocky stretch of rapids. Whether it is for the more oxygenated water or because bugs get funneled through in kind of a traveling buffet, I do not know. And my goal was to offer some bugs on the buffet table and hope for takers. I worked my way back into the stream above the rapids and scanned the water. There actually seemed to be some kind of fly hatch going on in this stretch of the river, and although the flies looked tiny, I had one in a fly box that sort of looked the same. I tied it on, shuffled my feet to move the larger rocks aside and got into a comfortable position with my feet anchored in sandy river bottom, turned sideways against the current. After a couple of false casts toward the shore above a likely spot, I let the line settle into the current and stripped off a bunch of line to lengthen the drift of the fly. I could barely maintain visual contact with the tiny fly on the surface about thirty feet away, but as the line straightened out and began to swing with the current there was a yank that moved the knot at the end of the fly line about a foot. I lifted the rod tip and had a fish on. It only took a few minutes to land a small but nice rainbow trout. I looked at the struggling, silvery fish beneath the surface and I stripped in line to bring him to hand. I wet my hand so as not to damage the fish and reached under the water to remove the fly. In a flash the fish was gone, headed back down the rapids. And probably so spooked as to not take another bug the rest of the day.

I thought about taking a few more casts, but it seemed like a good note on which to end the morning. I splashed my way across the river to the bank near the road. Although I was no longer concerned with scaring any nearby fish, I had enough common sense left to not splash my way into a cold bath. As I climbed the nearby bank, I cranked the fly line back into the reel, loosened the straps on my waders, and headed down the road towards the truck. It turned out to be nearly a quarter mile away, but the walk allowed me some additional time to consider the day and commend myself on a fine morning and a fish well caught. As I neared the truck a car full of tourists passed, with all eyes except the driver on me, the master fisherman. I touched the brim of my straw hat in a jaunty salute, seeing myself through their eyes, and thinking that fishing is all about looking good.

Pendills

There are days when the same old favored fishing places don't hold my attention. Although the drive to the Carp River is short and the fishing is good there in early spring, the water level is too low during summer and brief thunderstorms that add to the flow only cloud up the water. We didn't even get a bite on our last trip to the Carp. A change is needed and we may have to put an hour or more of highway behind us to get to something better. We need to head west towards Pendills Creek. The water there is always clear and maybe a few fish have come in from the big lake.

Most of Upper Michigan consists of old growth scrub pine and cedar swamps that frame the dark pavement as we head west. The ground cover by the road is thick, and you can travel for miles without seeing any sign of human construction. The short growing seasons and bitter winter weather restrict the height of most trees and the forest canopy rises no more than 15 to 25 feet. Should you choose to leave the paved surface, the poorly defined forest thoroughfares quickly give way to well worn, water filled ruts that provide no traction and force you to continue your journey on foot. In the forest, any sign of human traffic soon fades, and is replaced by sandy ground, covered in pine needles, that deadens footfalls and allows the careful traveler to encounter any number of woodland critters which might otherwise fade into the deeper woods. It is a place where woodcock forage in the boggy soil with their long beaks for earthworms and, should you come across one, it may burst forth from cover in a soaring vertical climb that quickly takes it to safety and out of sight. Further along, browsing deer may scamper sideways with a snort at our sudden presence. It takes a few moments for our heart rate to settle back down and only then can we resume our thoughtful pace through the darkened forest trails. The gloomy quiet of the woods is periodically interrupted by the drumming of a ruffled grouse on some hollow log or the questioning call of a nearby songbird. Unexpected surprises await us on the forest trails should we choose to wander that way.

Our destination, however, lies much further ahead and we elect to stay on the well maintained two-way highway that flows to the western horizon. The scenery lies unchanging for mile after mile. In the distance, the highway shrinks to a pinpoint as it climbs to meet the mottled gray overcast of a late fall sky. Our objective does not lie that way and we soon slow to make the turn north off the highway onto Dollar Settlement Road. After crossing a set of seldom used railroad tracks, we pass the old Civilian Conservation Corps forestry camp that was a beehive of activity, half a century ago. Its weather stained buildings now stand abandoned, windows permanently shuttered, rusty metal roofs covered in pine needles and loose branches that have fallen unnoticed from nearby aging fir trees. The camp fades behind us as we continue north and the roadside view changes from a thick screen of pine to rising terrain and sections of old growth hardwood trees. In early fall the brilliant foliage here overwhelms the eyes and raises the spirit, but now, with the approach of winter, those colors are gone and newly barren branches create a sense of bleakness and despair for those who come this way.

The paved road continues straight north for several miles in a shallow climb before leveling out and then beginning a steep descent towards the cold waters of Lake Superior. A wide vista of forest opens up ahead. In the distance, Lake Superior spreads to the north, dark and brooding. We can be content to prowl along its shore, but the fleeting thought of nearing that cold place causes a momentary shiver. The local native fishermen know the lake through legends and scary tales told late at night over a sheltering campfire. When they choose to go out on its surface, they pick their times carefully, and drop beads and other offerings to spirits that inhabit the lake. They do not venture far from shore. The big lake freighters seem free to test those waters, but it is less certain if others are welcome.

A few scattered houses come into view as we drive through a small Chippewa settlement where generations of men have sustained their families through commercial fishing for trout and salmon. Scattered toys and rusty swing sets in the yards provide scant evidence of family members who remain behind while the men are at work. Today, however, no one is in sight since we turned onto Dollar road. On the right side of the road are several telephone pole sized tree trunks stuck into the ground in a large circle, near a poorly maintained basketball court and the blackened remains of a huge council fire pit. Soon the ice will begin to form on the lake and members of the community will go out in boats to retrieve their gills nets one last time. They will hang the nets on these poles to dry and then store them inside for the long winter.

The village falls behind and we come to a three way stop. Ahead, white capped waves move into the shore which lies only a few yards from the intersection. The wind is up on the lake today and the intensity of the shore break tells us that wind gusts of 15 to 25 knots are likely. On the left is a rusty railroad dining car that once served passengers who gazed in wonder through its soot stained windows at the passing frontier. It is very much out of place. The nearest railway is more than five miles away and we can only wonder how the car came to be here. On my first trip up this way, I found the railroad car occupied by two elderly women who had turned it into a rural café. We stopped for lunch and the women seemed very pleased that we had done so. One woman introduced herself as Lucille and the other as her sister. I don't know if we ever knew the sister's name, but she was very quiet. The food was good and Lucille had some helpful information on the best places to fish. Her sister never said a word and busied herself cleaning and rearranging things on countertops and shelves. We finished our meal, paid the tab, and took our leave. I stopped there for lunch from time to time over that summer and fall, but never saw another customer. When we returned the following spring, the railroad car had been abandoned and seemed to have aged many years in that short stretch of time. I never learned the fate of the two women and there was no one around to ask. Like the occupants of the conservation camp, their time had come and gone and only faint memories were left for those who cared to remember.

We ponder a turn to the right but that way follows the shore line to the Point Iroquois Lighthouse and the main Chippewa reservation just beyond. To the left, across the road from the abandoned dining car, is a poorly constructed outbuilding, connected to an ancient trailer home. A faded wooden sign hanging near a half open door identifies the place as a general store. In years past, the store was maintained by a middle-aged woman with three children whose husband never seemed to be around. She was somewhat overweight and usually dressed in drab hand me down clothes. She was a heavy smoker and we could smell her presence well before we entered the building. A meager selection of junk food, along with some canned goods, would be scattered over pine board shelves that filled the walls on either side of the entry. A well-worn refrigerator stood near the back wall, with prices for soda and fishing bait posted on its door. The woman waited with her cashbox at a small desk near the entrance for us to make our selections. It was hard to imagine she did much business in this small community populated by families whose principal wage earners were mostly unemployed. A sign on the wall behind the desk announced "No Cheks Excepted". Such substitutes for money were creations of the wealthy and had no value here.

Our infrequent arrival always seemed to brighten the day for this woman and her small children, one or more of who played on scoured wooden floor nearby with weather beaten toys that held their attention and made them blind to the limitations of their meager existence. Like the sisters in the railroad car, this woman also had news of local fishing luck and we were eager to have it, along with a pile of potato chips, cookies and soda pop that was destined for quick consumption as we made our way through the forest byways, enroute to hallowed fishing spots. The woman's eyes always seemed to plead with us to stay and talk a bit longer, but after trading information with her, we said our goodbyes and left with a final bang of the screened entry. The woman and her children were quickly abandoned to the scraps of life they had been accorded and we were just two more people who had betrayed her trust by taking what little she had to offer and then departing for places and things that we held in higher esteem. One spring we came this way for snacks and information, but like the women in the railroad car, the family was gone, abandoning the store, the trailer and this bleak landscape for parts unknown.

Thoughts of these people quickly pass and we make a turn to the left, between the abandoned railroad car and similarly empty store. As our truck picks up speed the forest quickly returns to scrub pine and boggy lowlands. The woods seem to move closer to the road as if to remind us that we do not belong here and we hurry along, watching the roadside for any opening that will reveal the open water we know to be lurking only a hundred yards or so to the north. After a mile or two, we round a bend and pass a parking lot with a new metal sign that announces "Big Pine Picnic Area, No Camping Allowed." There is less ground cover here beneath the dense pine canopy and we catch glimpses of the water through the trees. A couple of picnic tables are barely visible behind the parking lot and a new outhouse can be seen on a cement pad, just inside the tree line. There are no vehicles in the lot and like other places we have passed, this does not seem to be a welcoming place for either families or happy couples. The only likely tenants are ghostly apparitions of past native American warriors or ancient seafarers. We hurry on.

A few miles further we cross a small bridge and slow to pull off the pavement into a sandy parking area that will accommodate perhaps four or five cars. We have arrived at Pendills Creek and are the only ones here. Across the street, the buildings of a small fish hatchery can be seen, but it is late in the season and the trout and salmon fingerlings it once contained have already been distributed to waters across the region. The shallow cement runs that held the tiny fish have been drained and the employees have left for the season. Exiting the truck, we breathe deeply of the fresh, clean air and can hear the sound of wave action on the nearby shore.

The headwaters of this small creek are a spring fed lake which lies a short distance inland. Pendills Lake stretches parallel to the Lake Superior shoreline and is located in the low hills above the fish hatchery. A relatively small body of water, it is only a mile long and a few hundred yards wide. It's uniform shallow depth and impenetrable black waters give no clue to the bottomless muck that lies beneath its surface. At Pendills Lake, one steps very cautiously from the shore and tests the bottom before transferring weight on the forward foot. To do otherwise is to invite a thorough dunking...or worse. Other than waterfowl and an occasional hawk, there are no other signs of life there.

A manmade access channel flows north from the western end of the lake for several hundred yards. Water from the channel continues on through a couple of retention pools before entering a rocky, winding section that is Pendills Creek. Very little light penetrates to illuminate the inky waters that are shielded by a thick screen of brush and pine trees on both banks. There is no room to cast a fishing line should you choose to do so and any fish who have ventured this far up the creek have earned a measure of safety. A dank and earthy smell hangs in the air and in the endless shade, the water stays very cold. A nearby drainage channel diverts some of the heavily oxygenated flow through the fish hatchery before it eventually passes through a culvert under the road, just west of the bridge, to rejoin the main creek by the parking lot where we now stand. The remaining short section of creek from the parking lot to the big lake is barren of vegetation and fish that swim through this section can be clearly seen gliding over the sandy bottom. It is a prime location for predators, be they man or beast, and not a place you will find fish of any size during the daylight hours. After dark it is a different story. Then, big trout enter the stream to feed on minnows, crayfish, and bugs that fall to the creek's surface. We sometimes arrive in the evening to see if we can intercept these fish. In the moonlight, large trout can sometimes be spotted from shore and we have even resorted to splashing after them in the shallow with long handle nets (an illegal practice!).

Even that technique has proven unsuccessful and proof of the advantage accorded our finny friends.

One fall weekend, a couple of hours after dark, my friend Tony and I drove to Pendills to fish for lake trout off the mouth of the creek. As we pulled into the parking lot, we could see light from a small campfire on the far bank, glowing embers floating up into the sky at each pop and crackle of the flames. We put on our waders, gathered our fishing gear, and walked from the lot, across the bridge, and down the opposite bank towards the flickering light. There was an elder from the nearby Chippewa reservation setting on a log by the campfire, whittling on a piece of wood. Our poor attempt at stealth was defeated by the clumping sound of loose boots on solid ground and the steady whisper of our nylon wader tops as we walked in his direction. As we drew closer he stopped his whittling and stared at us. He was simply dressed in worn jeans and a long-sleeved plaid shirt. His long gray hair was tied back in a ponytail. By the light from the campfire, his face looked extremely angular and aged. We offered a friendly greeting and after a short hesitation he gestured that we should join him by his campfire. Tony pulled out his pipe and charged it with some tobacco. He offered his pouch to the elder, but the man declined. We began talking about what a beautiful evening it was and whether the weather would hold for the remainder of the week. A few feet away, we could plainly see a fishing pole propped up on a forked stick, the line angling away toward the center of the creek. We asked him if he had had any success and he walked over to a stringer we had failed to notice, tied to the trunk of a tree by the water's edge. He lifted three fat trout out of the water to show us. Nearby on the bank was a slab of pine board topped with a skein of fresh fish eggs he had taken from one of the fish. He said he had started the evening using crawfish for bait, but fresh fish eggs were better. He gave us a small portion of the skein and we thanked him before moving on. We left the glow of his campfire and rustled through a last section of brush before crossing the stream near the west side of the creek mouth. Here we waded into the big lake, almost to the tops of our waders, and rigged up our poles, fishing in absolute silence for the next couple of hours. We used silver spoons and then tried the fish eggs. Periodically, one or the other of us would wade back to stand on the sandy shore to get some feeling back into our legs. Although our waders were insulated, and we were wearing thermal underwear, they did not provide much of a barrier against the 38-degree water. We managed to catch two nice lake trout on the fish eggs and lose a couple more as they broke off after huge, line ripping runs in the dark. Almost without perception time passed and then I glanced at my luminous watch dial to see that it was approaching midnight. It was time to go. I picked up the stringer with our fish and we trudged down the beach and up the trail through the trees to the parking lot, our way dimly lit by the small Maglite we carried. As we loaded our equipment and catch into the truck I looked across the creek, but there was no evidence of the campfire or its tender. Apparently, the humans had "left the building" and Pendills once again belonged to the regular nighttime inhabitants.

Pendills looks very different in winter. Ice builds to great thickness on the big lake and the only roads open to traffic are those that receive regular attention from the big state-owned snowplows. Along the road, snow can easily reach a depth of more than ten feet and the plows rely on twelve-foot high branches stuck into the roadside to guide them on their rounds. We do not often venture this way in the winter. There was easier access and a more likely chance of ice fishing success at the big inland bays on the St Mary's river. One February, however, we had heard reports of ice fishing success off the mouth of Pendills and other streams that emptied into Lake Superior so we decided to investigate. There had been a heavy snowfall the day before, but the plows had already made their morning runs and the roads were clear. We trudged out to Tony's Scout, frozen breath streaming from our noses in the subzero air and cleared the windows of about five inches of fresh snow. It took a few minutes for the car heater to become effective but finally we were able to shrug off jackets and gloves for the long ride to Pendills. Avoiding the unplowed secondary roads, we carefully negotiated the freshly plowed highway, noting several disabled vehicles half buried in snowdrifts by the side of the road. Although the road was still icy we soon arrived at the bridge by the fish hatchery. The parking lot was snowed in, but there were four or five vehicles parked by the edge of the road, barely leaving room for passing cars. They, like us did not expect much traffic in this weather and this place.

We got out and exchanged our coats and boots for snowmobile suits and mukluks. Mukluks are military issue footwear, adapted from an Eskimo design for severely cold climates, and walking in them feels like traveling in loose house slippers with a light blanket thrown around your lower legs for additional warmth. Although not suited for agile maneuvering, they do keep your feet warm, even though the rest of your body may be frozen solid. After donning knit head coverings, gloves, and sunglasses, we headed out through the snow to investigate the action on the big lake. It was difficult to force our way through the deep snow in the parking lot and it was hard to tell where the parking lot ended and the frozen creek began. The creek obviously lay somewhere in the opening between the trees that lined both banks. There were footprints in the snow from others who had come this way, skirting the creek, and continuing through the trees towards the shore and ice beyond. As we passed through the last few trees, the ice-covered surface of Lake

Superior came into view, stretching to the northern horizon, and marred only by the presence of a few fishermen and improvised shelters that were arrayed in an arc within a couple hundred yards of shore. About a half mile offshore I could see a pair of snowmobiles speeding across the ice. The operators had to be crazy to be that far out, and in whiteout conditions, distance is hard to judge but they probably were minimally alert to the potential for danger. I had been ice fishing on the surface of shallow lakes many times before, but there is something different about walking or riding on ice where the depth quickly drops off to several hundred feet. That probably explained why the most of the fishermen we could see were so close to shore. There was something reassuring about being able to maintain visual contact with the bottom, which they could do, even if it was 20 or 30 feet deep where they had drilled their fishing holes. We passed a fisherman walking in from the ice, carrying an armload of gear and a bucket that he had been using for a seat. He said he had been out there for a couple of hours fishing in the open and found the steady wind to be unbearable with a wind chill approaching minus 20 degrees. He had not had a bite all morning.

We walked out on the lake and could see many holes that had been drilled by fishermen who had since departed. The surface of most holes was newly opaque with a thin skim of ice. We headed for one of the more distant fisherman to see how he was doing. As we neared we could see that his face was scoured raw by the wind. He didn't have gloves or a coat on but he seemed to be having a great time. A half dozen nice sized perch lay beside him on the ice, frozen so solid they could be used to pound a nail. He told us that he was getting cold and it was almost time for him to head to his car to warm up and eat lunch. As we talked, a few yards away the entry flap on a small orange tent opened and an old gent we knew as

"Henry" emerged. Henry was a local character who we would see two or three times a year during our expeditions to the Pendills area. He was a short, wiry, clean shaven man who always wore a hat of the type I associated with Gilligan of the old TV series, no matter the weather. His age was impossible to discern and we had decided on our first meeting that he could be anywhere from forty to seventy years old. Sometimes we would meet him hiking out from fishing at a distant beaver dam. Another time he would be on his hands and knees in low lying bog, filling his hat with cranberries. Today, he recognized us right away and said he was headed in for lunch. He offered us the use of his setup if we were so inclined. Since we had not brought any equipment with us this sounded like a great idea. We followed him into the tent on our hands and knees to find that it did not have a floor. He had used a chain saw to cut a four by four feet hole in the two-foot thick ice and the clarity of the water gave us an unrestricted view of the bottom some fifteen or twenty feet below. At hand was a five-foot long weighted metal spear with four barbed points on the business end. There was about thirty feet of light rope tied to the spear so it could be retrieved once thrown. Henry said he had seen schools of herring passing through the area as well as a few salmon but he had not had any luck yet. I didn't know whether Henry was suggesting we go after salmon, but it was illegal to take salmon with a spear in any case. He wished us luck and pushed his way out through the tent entry, announcing that he would be back in about an hour.

The bright winter sunlight passed easily through the surface of the ice outside of the tent and lit up the lake bottom in great detail. I could see small rocks, a couple of sunken logs and a beer bottle on the sandy bottom. We sat there for maybe fifteen minutes before we saw a sizeable fish quickly dart past the hole, halfway between the bottom and where we sat. I think we had become mesmerized just looking through the hole, but now we were fully alert. I stretched out on the ice in a prone position to get a better look at more of the lake further off to the side to spot approaching fish, but my field of vision was limited by the size of the hole. By moving around the hole, I could see an area of about twenty feet by twenty feet. Then a formation of medium-sized herring suddenly appeared going from right to left. Tony slowly dipped the tip of the spear into the water and then threw it towards the fish with great force, line trailing out behind to the loop he held in his other hand. The fish moved on, seemingly unaware of the descending spear which stuck in the bottom a good six feet behind them. He tried two more times with the same results before he realized the refraction of the water led him to miscalculate his aim point. A few minutes later two more fish appeared and finally, by leading his target by five or six feet, he pinned a nice herring of about two pounds to the bottom. The fish was held securely by the barbs and was easily retrieved through the hole in the ice. By the time Henry got back, we had four good-sized herring on the ice outside the tent. The cold, however, had begun to seep into our insulated snowsuits and gloves and it was time head for the truck and warmth. We thanked Henry for the use of his equipment and offered him our catch to show our appreciation. He seemed ready to resist, but not having had any luck himself, agreed to accept the fish. We wished him well and headed toward the shore as he climbed back into his tent.

We had walked halfway back to shore when I heard Tony fall behind me and start swearing. I turned to see that he had fallen through a partly frozen over hole, up to his thigh. As I moved to his side, I could see several other holes in the area that had been masked by drifting snow. He strained with effort to pull his leg out but was having no success. He said he thought his leg was swelling up and that it was getting very cold. I was concerned that we would both break through the ice in this area that was riddled with holes, but I seeing no one hurrying to our aide, I grabbed one of his arms and began pulling while he used his other arm to try and gain leverage against the ice surface. The combined effort was enough and his leg came free with a slosh of lake water that quickly froze into a clear film on the icy surface. With me providing support, Tony limped to the car where he took off his snowsuit, mukluks, and jeans while I started the car and waited for the heater to warm up. There was a little swelling in his leg but otherwise, no damage was done. As I pulled onto the road and turned for home, we both laughed about the close call and then quickly moved the discussion to when we might return for more ice spearing action. As luck would have it, we did not get back to Pendills that winter.

We rarely visited Pendills during early spring. There were so many other bodies of water where there was more room to cast and where the fishing action seemed better. The one exception, however, was when the ice began to break up on Lake Superior each year in late March or early April. At that time, large schools of hungry jack salmon would congregate just off the creek mouth to feed. These second-year fish were a uniform one to two pounds in weight and the perfect size for great action on light tackle. They would school near the shore during the night and remain in the area until a few hours after first light when the sun rose high enough that they felt exposed. Then the fish would return to deeper water and safety. Although some fishermen cast their lines from the shore, we found we could have better luck if we went out a short distance in a canoe. In fifteen or twenty feet of perfectly clear water, there was enough bottom structure to hold the fish in the dim morning light while we worked hard to transfer some of their number to the stringer that dangled from the side of our canoe.

Just before sunup, we would unload the canoe from the top of my truck and slide it down the sandy bank into Pendills creek. The water would be so shallow, that I could wade along towing the canoe with the painter until we neared the creek mouth and then it was deep enough for us to get in and paddle out into the big lake. There was rarely any wind or wave action at this time of day, so very little rowing was required to hold or change position over the bottom structure. Occasionally, a few strokes of a paddle were needed to move us back to a prime spot where we had previously hooked fish. The air temperature nearly matched the chilly 38-degree water, but there was enough action that personal comfort was quickly forgotten. We could count on catching eight or ten nice fish during a couple of hours of fishing, while watching the two or three jealous fishermen on shore who wished they had brought some kind of boat. The fish would remain in this general area each morning, for a week or two after the ice began to break up. Then they would move to deeper water for good and it was time for us to leave Pendills in search of better fishing.

During our summer expeditions, we always stopped at Pendills for a few minutes to stretch our legs. The walk from the parking lot down to the shore often led to a young couple or family group who were picking up the odds and ends that had been deposited by wave action. In addition to small stones, shells, and pieces of drift wood, there would be sections of gill net, bottles, pieces of Styrofoam and any number of things that fall or are dumped from ships at sea. A freshening breeze might riffle the water near shore and produce white caps further out in Whitefish Bay. The clean air blowing in from the north would be refreshing and at the same time provide a reminder to move on to wherever our destination lay for that day.

Pendills would be forgotten as the summer wore on and we became distracted by work, family obligations, and other expeditions. Life would settle into a holding pattern of sameness that endured until the first frost arrived and local trees began to take on their fall hues. Travel through the area held great wonder as we drank in shades of red and orange that clothed oak, maple, beech, and other hardwood trees; the passing color show periodically interrupted by peeling white trunks in scattered stands of birch trees with their vibrant yellow leaves. At the same time the sky would fill with vast flocks of waterfowl making their way south across Lake Superior, on their way to winter refuge. As the flocks approached the southern shoreline, the safety and plentiful food supply of Pendills and other small lakes nearby would offer a welcome shelter that drew them in like desperate travelers to the last motel with a vacancy sign. The normally quiet waters would then become home to a symphony of wildlife sounds where floating pods of ducks and geese called a throaty welcome to arriving numbers of their kin. The sound of wind whistling through bended primary feathers, cupped for the steep descent, sounded like jet aircraft in the still air and would be terminated with the staccato splashes of each arriving flight. Distant members of their clan from all across northern Canada were now gathering in one excited, congested location.

We too were excited about the arrival of fall. We found an abandoned duck blind at Pendills Lake during one of our fishing expeditions early that spring. We had spotted the lake in the distance, from high up on the Dollar Settlement Road, but there did not seem to be any access route or signs indicating how to get there. We followed several sand-based forestry roads on the north side of the little lake, but all either dead ended or curved back to the paved road. Finally, we found an overgrown road that led to a section with deep ruts that had been filled with cut branches to permit the escape of a previous adventurer. Although we had no assurance that this road led to the lake, we had an axe and saw in the scout so we chopped up pieces of a nearby downed tree and added them to the existing base. Our goal was to create a semi-submerged platform with enough support to get our vehicle across the bog. It took the better part of an hour to accomplish the task and by then we were both drenched with sweat. I waded across our platform and watched Tony carefully maneuver the scout onto the makeshift bridge in four-wheel drive. Once across, I climbed back aboard and we proceeded up the narrow, rutted road. We bounced over tree roots and deep ruts for a half mile until the road ended at a small clearing with enough space to turn the scout around. Ahead, there was a small opening in the brush and we could see a narrow channel that led to open water. Since we had not brought waders or any kind of boat with us, our investigation of the lake that day was minimal, but we could hear all kinds of splashing and quacking from unseen waterfowl on the other side of the screen of brush and trees. We would be back.

The following weekend we returned with Tony's eighteen-foot fiberglass canoe secured to the roof of the scout. He had a little one-horsepower motor that attached to the stern of the canoe and could be tilted up out of the water when we chose to paddle. We turned off the paved road and headed into the forest on the road near the Pendills fish hatchery to find that our makeshift bridge was still in place. Although we were concerned that travel over the rough road would shake the canoe from the roof of the jeep, we made the passage without mishap. It was a beautiful morning for exploring the lake, and after we unloaded the canoe and slid it into the access channel, we climbed in and poled our way through a screen of reeds towards the main lake. As we made our way over the water, we found ourselves in a series of reed beds that prevented us from seeing very far ahead. After passing through several sections of reeds, a pair of mallards took off ahead of us with a splash and quacking that disrupted the still of the morning. With the hen in the lead, the ducks turned to follow the shoreline and were soon lost to view. We continued to work our way through the reeds toward open water, roughly paralleling where we thought the north shoreline lay. After paddling for twenty minutes we could see tall pines trees on a small island just off our bow to the right. We steered towards it and spotted what appeared to be a manmade construction on the shore. As we drew near, our paddles struck the lake bottom in about a foot of water. We climbed out and pulled the canoe up on shore near the remains of an old hunting blind, anchored between two large pine trees. The plywood and two by four boards that made up three sides of the structure were very weathered and warped. We found a few rusted shotgun shells on the ground inside and what appeared to be a crude gun rack and storage box. It looked like the setup had not been used in several seasons. The open area of shallow water right in front of the blind spread out in a 180-degree arc that would permit a field of fire extending from the left side of the blind through directly in front to the right side. And the shallow water would make it easy to set out our duck decoys. We were already imagining perfect shooting days and filling our limits of ducks and geese. We got back in the canoe and continued on to explore the rest of the lake. Patchy sections of reeds continued to the west for another quarter of a mile until we broke out into a wide expanse of open water and another island, also home to the remains of a duck blind. However, the water at the western island was fairly deep and presented a difficult problem both for getting ashore and for setting out decoys. Our exploratory run was over and Tony tilted the little outboard motor

down into the water and with a couple of pulls on the starter cord and a puff of exhaust smoke, we headed back towards our starting point and the channel that led to the scout. As we slowly motored east, large and small groups of waterfowl periodically lifted off the water and soon the sky above the lake was crisscrossed with flights of birds that were carefully monitoring our progress away from their desired resting areas. We finally arrived at the entry channel and reluctantly steered the canoe in towards shore. It was time to head home, but we had made a great find for the upcoming hunting season.

Early that fall, we returned with half a dozen boards and a couple of sheets of plywood to do some repair work. After delivery me to the blind, it took Tony two more trips to ferry the lumber and tools to the island. While I began removing old boards and replacing them with new ones, he set off in the canoe, motor purring, to the southern shore where he had seen huge stands of cattails that would provide camouflage for the front of the blind. He made several trips, returning from each with a tall mound of reeds in the front of the canoe that shielded from view all but his black, wide-brim Indian hat and clouds of smoke from his pipe. After we unloaded the last of the reeds, we tied a mesh of twine around the front of the blind and wove the reeds in to completely mask our presence from feathered visitors. With the last of the repair job complete, we waded out in the shallow water and looked back towards the blind to evaluate our efforts. There was some hint of a human hand in the final work, but we thought the blind looked natural enough to fool the average duck. It was already late afternoon when we paddled back to the truck and began the long ride home.

The opening weekend of hunting season at Pendills provided everything we had hoped for. To the uninitiated, it is hard to imagine a sane person getting out of a warm bed in the hours before sunrise, to stand for hours in a cold rain, exposed to the elements. However, that is when the best duck hunting can be expected and we eagerly loaded up the canoe at the launch point, smiles faintly framed in the falling rain by the truck headlights. We secured the truck and headed out through the entry channel for the lake with the rain increasing in intensity and our searching flashlights unable to penetrate the gloom more than a few feet. We paddled with a steady rain washing over us and quickly accumulating in the canoe bottom as we searched for the opening that would signal the island's proximity. Finally, from my position in the front of the canoe, I could see the dark outline of the island ahead and we paddled that way with strong, steady strokes. After we pulled the canoe ashore and up behind the blind, Tony unloaded the burlap sacks of decoys and splashed out through the shallows to place a dozen or so that would hopefully make our little section of water more appealing to discriminating flights of ducks. I stowed our cased shotguns, ammunition, sandwiches, and a thermos of hot coffee inside the blind and covered all with a small tarp that we had brought along for that purpose. There was not much protection from the elements, save for a few pine branches high overhead that served to filter large rain drops into many smaller ones. As we took our places in the blind and loaded our guns, the gusty wind blew the rain in all directions to help it penetrate our cold weather gear in the most uncomfortable places. After a short time, there was a steady trickle of water that started somewhere near my shoulder blades and ended up as a puddle in the vicinity of my wallet. We tilted out faces down towards the floor of the blind and let the hoods on our wet weather gear ward off the rain, but every few minutes we just had to look to see if any ducks were arriving over the decoys. We would be rewarded with another blast of water in the eyes and return our eyes to the ground. Periodically, Tony would sound off with his duck call and an answer would come from a circling flight that would draw our eyes to peer through the reeds woven into the front of the blind. The action was intermittent but steady and by nine in the morning we had taken our limit of mallards. We put our shotguns back in their cases and sat in the blind another hour, watching flight after flight of ducks bore in towards our position and splash into our decoys. We took turns jumping up to yell "bang" and watch the started ducks take off again, escaping into the sheeting rain. Finally, the discomfort of the weather overcame the pleasure of watching arriving waterfowl. It was a relief to exercise stiff muscles as we loaded up the canoe and rowed back to the truck. After stowing our equipment and shedding our wet outer gear, we climbed into the truck and our breathing quickly fogged up the inside windows so as to require a steady measure of window wiping with my shirt sleeve as we bumped the truck over the trail out to the

main road. On the way home, the heater did its work while the windshield wipers beat a steady tattoo and cold, damp clothes became warm damp clothes. It was a grand day.

After a couple of weeks, I decided others of our friends should have an opportunity to enjoy our great new hunting location. Two additions were people we knew from other hunting and fishing expeditions. Two others were guys we had not hunted with before. It was obvious to me that Tony was not happy to have new hunters along, and he was uncharacteristically quiet as we headed off to the lake in a two-vehicle convoy. It had rained hard the day before and when we turned off the paved road into the woods, we found the boggy crossing deep in mud and water. The second vehicle initially got stuck there. However, after we added more branches to the crossing and with considerable tire spin and pushing, flying mud thoroughly coating the pushers, the vehicle slid across the obstacle. Further along, in one very rutted area, the second vehicle slid into and took a huge chunk out of a pine tree, but the damage to the old army jeep was minimal. Both vehicles finally arrived at the launching point and unloaded canoes. I announced that we would be going to "our island" while the others should head to the far end of the lake where a blind was located on another island. With our departure delayed by the need to pick up other hunters and the further delay at the boggy crossing, we had arrived at the lake a little later than we had hoped and the sun was already coming up without a cloud in the sky. I could read the recriminations in Tony's eyes. We would miss the best shooting time of the day and the novice hunters were the reason.

We still had to get everything to the island. A third hunter, along with the decoys and gear, would severely task the capacity of our canoe, so we would ferry gear to the island and then come back for our remaining hunter. The other canoe was even smaller than ours and I was not sure how they would make the trip of almost a mile with only a couple of inches of freeboard above the cold waters. But that was not our problem.

A few hundred yards from the launch, we turned right, towards the island, and the other canoe headed off in the dark. When Tony returned with our extra hunter he glided in to shore and after pulling our canoe up behind the blind, he told the new guy to set in the blind while we waded out to set up our decoys. Each decoy was secured to its position on the water with a six-foot line attached to a lead anchor. We waded ashore and unpacked binoculars, duck calls, guns and other necessities to be "open for business." Then we hunkered down inside the blind to wait for the action to start. As soon as we loaded our guns, the new guy began asking questions about when we would know to shoot and how much lead should he take for his shots, and who should shoot first. He was not very quick to take the hint from Tony's lack of response. I provided a couple of short answers to his questions and then indicated that we should be silent so as not to spook any incoming ducks. The sun came up over the trees and highlighted a disturbingly clear day with not a duck in sight. However, a flight of four pintails soon appeared from the west and headed into our decoys. As they neared, Tony signaled we should shoot and all three of us jumped up to fire. We moved too soon and the ducks quickly flared out of range as we fired, the newbie emptying his gun at the retreating birds, spraying shot across the center of the decoy spread. At the start of the season, we had lovingly repainted and repaired our spread of Styrofoam duck decoys. Although not bulletproof, they could absorb a little shot without significant damage, but we tried to avoid firing directly at them. Our companion seemed unaware of this concern, and in any case his aim was so wild that the decoys were definitely in harm's way. We sat back down and reloaded. I glanced at Tony and he was shaking his head in silent disgust. I knew it was not for the missed ducks, but at the probable damage to the decoys. Time passed and the morning continued its development into a really nice day…for fishing. Tony tried calling ducks using every type friendly invitation I had ever heard. We tried repositioning the decoys, using the activity to stretch legs stiffened by setting motionless for long intervals on a two by six board. I tried leaning against the back of the blind and pretended to be just closing my eyes for a short interval, although the loud snoring put the lie to my charade. I was awakened out of a dream…I was fluffing up the pillow in my warm bed… by a loud blast of Tony's duck call and answering quacks from across the lake. My two companions had their faces pressed against the front of the blind, peering through the reeds to watch a flight of mallards that was circling the lake to our front. The ducks headed downwind and appeared to be leaving but another blast on the duck call turned them in our direction and they set their wings to land among their counterfeit kin. Tony called for us to shoot as they were about thirty yards out and we arose and began firing. Out of the corner of my eye I saw Tony drop the lead drake just before I folded a hen about halfway back in the formation. At the same time, a blast from the new guy took the head clean off a decoy on the edge of our spread. The smell of gunpowder punctuated the last echoes of the shots as confetti-like pieces of Styrofoam slowly settled to the water. The new guy gave a nervous laugh and announced that he was sure he had shot the hen. Tony gave a resigned sigh and sat down as the new guy and I went out to retrieve the downed ducks.

No more ducks arrived and binoculars did not reveal any other flights headed our way from further down the lake. The morning was almost gone and it looked like the hunting was over. To get Tony away from the new guy and thereby prevent an accidental homicide, I suggested that he and I go see how our friends were doing at the other island. We had heard one or two shots from that end of the lake earlier. We put the canoe back in the water and headed out after Tony reminded the new guy that he should be careful not to shoot his foot off. I think it is safe to say there was a fair amount of sarcasm in his words. As we left, he thankfully made no further comment about our companion, but I knew what he was thinking...don't do this to me again!

We disturbed a couple of small groups of ducks during our row, but they quickly climbed to altitude and flew away over the trees, heading south. Soon we came to the big open area and could see the other island to the west. It immediately became apparent that something was up as we could see odd patches of color spread over the trees and brush where the blind was located. As we got closer, the patches of color resolved into various articles of clothing, spread over every branch and bush within a few yards of the blind. Then three figures appeared from the woods and came to the shore to meet us. They looked woefully underdressed for the freezing weather and one hunter seemed to be wearing not much more than a white T-shirt and a pair of thermal underwear bottoms. Our friend Bob explained that when they arrived, their new guy offered to hold the canoe steady while they got out. He did not do a very good job and managed to overturn the canoe, soaking occupants, guns, gear, and lunches. He was very apologetic and did not offer much resistance when they demanded his extra layers of dry clothes, leaving him with a t-shirt and jeans. They had shot one gadwall shortly afterwards and when the action slowed, they spread their clothes in the trees in a feeble attempt to dry them out. The current temperature did little to promote drying and they had started a fire, cannibalizing most of their blind in an attempt to keep warm. They had just decided to call it a day when we arrived. I did not tell them about our adventures, and besides, it looked like our experience paled in comparison to theirs.

We helped them pack up and took some of their gear in our canoe to lighten their load. No one spoke during the row back to the vehicles. The stillness on the water seemed to drain off any ill will that resulted from the misadventures and the rising sun brought the air temperature up a few degrees to complement the warmth generated by paddling. As we floated down the lake, our passing was momentarily marked by the twin wakes of our canoes and then all returned to as it was before we arrived. On the way back, I picked up Tony and some of our gear and left our third hunter at our blind. After making sure our friends were safely loaded up at the vehicle and on their way, I thought to remind Tony that we needed to pick up the hunter we left in the blind. He seemed to be considering abandonment as a fate for our new guy, but then he decided to head back to our blind to pick up our decoys and spare gear. The concern on our third hunter's face as they returned confirmed that he too thought he would be left to the elements. We loaded up in silence, tied down the canoe, and made ready to head down the forest trail back to civilization. I made one last look around before we left. Our adventure this day was far from perfect, but it was still Pendills and I hated to leave.

I did not invite any other hunters for the remaining hunts of that season. Special times should be shared with special friends. Some of those days on Pendills were wonderfully blustery and others were bluebird days with little action. In late November we went out one more time and the weather was too stormy even for duck hunting. It was the last weekend of the season and a thin coating of ice covered parts of the surface of Pendills. Gale warnings were out and we had great difficulty getting from the launch point to the island in the driving wind. Even the little outboard motor struggled to maintain headway. Any deviation from the westerly wind would result in the canoe turning broadside with a corresponding adventure in maintaining stability. We finally arrived at the blind and set up our decoys, but the few ducks that were moving over the lake were leaving for safer havens to the south. The decoy anchors were unable to contend with the strong wind and most of the decoys began to blow out of position, dragging their anchors over the muddy bottom until they became tangled in the reed beds located just out of shooting range. After several trips to recover decoys that the wind blew down the lake, we pulled in the spread and took up positions well below the front wall of the blind for protection. Pine trees overhead were swinging back and forth causing a loud creaking of the blind boards to which they were attached, leaving us wondering at the wisdom of staying in this temporary refuge. A drake mallard came by our blind flying down the lake, but unable to gain ground in the gusting wind, quickly turned downwind and disappeared into the rain. We hung on that way for an hour or two and finally decided to call it a season and head home. The passage downwind from the blind felt like we were flying over the water and we were relieved to be back on land and loading up for departure. As we bounced along the forest trail towards the main road, we turned on the truck heater and then the radio to learn that the steamer Edmund Fitzgerald had just been reported lost a few miles north of our position on the Lake Superior shore. It was a somber end to a season of memories and time to spend winter days by the fire, telling stories of adventures past at Pendills and other north woods places.

The Desert

A few years later, it was a bitter cold November day on the northern plains of Montana and, as the lead accident investigator, I had just finished giving a briefing on the crash of two C-141 aircraft that had collided in flight, scattering wreckage across the countryside. A half dozen microphones and cameras were stuck in my face, transmitting my words to CNN and other worldwide news media. The reporters all wanted to know what caused the accident, but there was little to pass on as we had just arrived at the crash site the previous day and were focused on securing the site. As I turned to return to the warmth of my staff car, one of the communications officers on the accident team came up and said that my boss, the wing commander, wanted me to return to base immediately and my replacement was already headed to the accident site. After giving assignments to the members of my team I headed out on the three-hour drive home, wondering what the boss wanted.

I checked in at the headquarters building and after some small talk about the progress of the accident investigation, my boss said I was being assigned as the commander of the 1900th Provisional Strategic Wing in Riyahd, Saudi Arabia. The commander position had responsibility for all aerial refueling operations in the region, oversight of EC/RC135 reconnaissance aircraft, and a U-2 detachment in southern Saudi Arabia.

Oversight of the latter two groups was merely to provide any needed support as each detachment operated independently with their own detachment commanders. This was not as shocking as the news that I needed to be there in three days. I left for home to tell my family that I would be gone for the holidays on this 90-day assignment and would be leaving the following day.

Duty in 'the sand box' as the region was known had changed dramatically in the preceding weeks. Operation Desert Storm was concluding and a political decision had been made to not invade Iraq, even though Iraqi air and ground forces had for the most part been neutralized. The military role was now one of containment and watching for any further aggressive activity by the Iraqi military. I had watched the news of Scud missile firings, some of which had landed in Saudi territory killing US troops, for the preceding months and was not really sure how safe I would be in my new assignment. I did not pass those concerns on to my family or troops.

The flight line was very busy the next day and supplies and aircraft spare parts were loaded on our aircraft. In addition to the crew scheduled to fly that day, there was a spare crew, my operations staff and a chief of maintenance who would be traveling with us. Soon all were aboard, engines were started, and we taxied for takeoff. The short flight to Griffiss AFB in New York was uneventful and there was little small talk among passengers as all onboard contemplated what we would experience when we arrived in the middle east. The stopover at Griffiss was to process all onboard for duty in the combat zone. Dog tags were checked, desert camouflage uniforms were issued, last will and testaments were updated, and briefings were given on special rules that applied to duty in Saudi Arabia. Alcohol was not allowed in the Kingdom. No outward displays of Christianity were permitted. Dangerous snakes and insects were discussed.

Interactions with Saudi nationals was very limited and Saudi women were to be avoided in any context. We were to be very careful on the duties assigned to our female military, especially regarding their ability to operate vehicles. Such duties were considered offensive to Saudis. Our female staff were expected to were veils and abayas if they went off our military installations. Some of these rules were repugnant, especially to our female officers, but the US government was very sensitive about offending our Saudi hosts.

We checked into quarters for a night of rest, and the next day we took off on a six-hour flight across the Atlantic to RAF Mildenhall Air Base outside of London. Upon landing we were directed to a special parking area in a remote part of the base where our aircraft and onboard stores received extra sentry protection. Passengers and crew checked in billeting. The officers were billeted in the Mildenhall Officers Club which boasted some very fancy rooms as well as a bar with extensive memorabilia from World War II. There were a few slot machines in the club for evening play. There were several different levers and buttons on each machine and there were no instructions what purpose any of them served. The machines were unlike any I had seen before and payouts were in several coin denominations from fat, quarter-sized pound coins to very large 2 pence coins. With all the different coins spewing from the payout slot, it was hard to tell if you had won big or just received a little bit of loose change.

The next day we assembled all our passengers and crew, as well as a few last-minute arrivals, for the long flight to Riyadh. After takeoff, we crossed the English Channel and southern Spain. Our flight plan skirted the northern coast of the Mediterranean Sea and from my position in the aircraft commander chair I marveled at the passing geography. One of the boom operators brought

our inflight lunches to the flight deck as we made a turn to the southeast to overfly Egypt. At 35,000 feet we could see pyramids on the Giza Plateau below and soon were over the Red Sea. Soon the shoreline of Saudi Arabia came into view and we flew over endless sands for another two hours before we were able to contact approach control for our descent in Riyahd. As we approached touchdown, we could see skyscrapers of this city with ten million inhabitants, just past the far end of the runway. The runway itself was covered with the aircraft tire markings from heavy use by both military and commercial aircraft. After turning off the runway, it was a long taxi back to our parking space, and we passed a separate ramp that held an EC-135 AWACS aircraft and an RC-135 reconnaissance aircraft. Soon we turned into the tanker ramp and were guided to parking and shut down the engines. Maintenance troops quickly put covers on the engines and windshield to protect them from blowing sand.

The commander I was replacing, Colonel Ondrejko, met us as we deplaned and maintenance personnel began to unload the aircraft and make it ready for a mission the next day. Colonel O introduced me to several of his staff and gave me a tour of the operation which consisted four airconditioned Quonset huts, one each for operations, meal preparation, dining hall seating, and a storage hut for uniforms and administrative supplies. There was also a large building for heavy maintenance work and storage for aircraft spare engines and parts. After our tour, he had me bring my bags to a new Ford Crown Victoria car which was to be my personal transport. He explained that the Japanese government did not want to provide military forces for the Operation Desert Storm effort but felt their contribution could be civilian vehicles for the US operating locations in Saudi Arabia. We drove through the military compound adjacent to the taxiway and I saw a large tent city which I was told housed US marines and army personnel. I expected to be in a tent, hopefully air conditioned, but we exited the area through a gate manned by Saudi military guards. Soon we were on a modern four lane highway headed out into the desert.

On the highway, the traffic was civilian vehicles, most driven by civilians who wore the distinctive headgear and white robes of Saudi nationals. I saw green roadside signs

with information in Arabic and English, and we passed small Japanese pickups with a seated camel or two filling the back. We also passed parked pickups and a driver could be seen heading off across the sands on the back of his recently unloaded camel. Colonel O explained we were headed a half hour into the desert to a guarded compound the Saudi's had built for our air force personnel. Soon we came to a gate and were waived through by US military policemen. Eskan village consisted of about one hundred stucco houses as well as dining facilities, a recreation building, a gymnasium, more storage facilities, and a building that served as a clubhouse for after-hours entertainment and relaxation. I would be spending the night in a house shared with two of my senior staff officers. Separate houses were provided for each crew and the houses were very spacious with a modern kitchen, a living room with satellite TV, and separate bedrooms for three officers. There was little vegetation in the village save for an occasional desiccated tree. The daytime temp was around 110 degrees at this time of year and there was no humidity, leaving your skin paper dry. I can only imagine what the army and marine officers would have made off our accommodations. We could choose to eat in the dining hall near the runway, or drive into the outskirts of Riyahd where a US embassy compound had a store with all the typical things you would find in an American grocery store. This was a sweet deal! After stowing my gear in the house, I took a walking tour of the village. One of the three-bedroom houses had been converted to a video game building to entertain the troops when they were not on duty. There was an all ranks club complete with a bar that served non-alcoholic beer like Moussy or O'Doules. As I walked through I saw several card games going on and everyone seemed very relaxed although several seemed interested in why a colonel would be walking through.

Outside, courts had been set up for tennis and racket ball. I learned that they were only in use after dark when the temperatures cooled down to around ninety degrees. I did not see many troops outside other than a few who seemed to be making their way to their houses and the safety of air conditioning. It was time for me to do the same after a short stop at the dining hall for dinner. The evening meal had ended, but the cooks were happy to dig me up something to eat.

Early the next morning after breakfast, I headed in to base with the departing commander. I dropped him off by his redeploying aircraft and headed into the operation hut to survey the day's scheduled flights. One was planned for the coast near Kuwait to refuel navy fighters from a carrier in the Persian Gulf. A second was a practice refueling for F-117 jets over central Saudi Arabia. My operations staff had taken over for the departing staff and seemed to be on top of the action so I sat down at a computer to prepare my arrival and assessment report for transmittal back to headquarters in the US. My second in command advised me that I would be presiding over the base flag lowering ceremony that evening. Usually the

flag was raised and lowered by a detail of security policemen, but on Friday evenings the ceremony was a bit more formal. As I had been involved in similar events over the years, this was not a big deal.

The next day I was briefed as part of the crew to take an aircraft and some supplies to Dhahran Air Base about two hours to the north. This was the headquarters of the US general who was in charge of all US Air forces in the region. He greeted me and after introducing me to his staff at his headquarters in Khobar Towers which doubled as housing for military personnel of all services. He made sure I knew that he expected me to run things in a manner in Riyahd so as to not cause him any concern. He had bigger issues to manage in his operation. After the staff meeting and lunch I returned to the aircraft to find ground crew loading about a ton of cases on board. This was a load of various candies that had been sent for the troops from the US. Dhahran was being buried in the continuing shipments from the US and wanted to disperse the stuff to other locations. Unfortunately, after setting in hot warehouses for weeks, not much of this was barely edible. That did not faze the young enlisted troops who quickly carted off cases to their rooms after we arrived back in

Riyahd. A week later during inspection of personnel rooms I found one your troop with about fifty cases of candy in his room. He said no one else wanted it so he thought to take it. As far as I was concerned, it was inedible so he could have as much as he wanted.

The days passed in endless fashion and there was plenty to do except in the evening. Most missions were scheduled during the daytime and active hostilities were at a standstill. The exception was occasional F-117 training missions since practice for their combat activities occurred late at night. Since F-117s were tactical assets, I had no oversight of their activities other than to provide air refueling. One day I stopped by to visit the operations building for reconnaissance and AWACS assets near their flight line. After a quick tour with the Lieutenant Colonel in charge, it was clear they did not need me micromanaging their operations and I did not visit them again during my time in Riyahd. At the end of the month, I flew one of our aircraft down to Taef Air Base to visit with U-2 operations. Since they were considered strategic assets they were also under my control, albeit loosely since they received their orders direct from their base in the US. Since Taef is near Mecca, the most sacred place in the Muslim world, our arrival there was carefully scripted. It was not good to have American military seen by the local population. After landing, we quickly taxied to a remote location on the base where the sole U-2 aircraft was kept in a closed hangar. The whole operation consisted of two pilots and a small maintenance and administrative staff. The pilots showed me around the facilities and also gave me a look into the very small U-2 cockpit. After confirming they did not need anything from me, we said our goodbyes and I flew back to Riyahd. It had been clear that my work in the desert would be solely focused on the refueling mission and assets.

My second in command did a good job of scheduling

me to fly almost every day. I am sure the aircrew commanders were less than happy to be replaced in the left seat. As a result, for most flights I tried to spend most of the inflight time in the jump seat behind the pilots. On some days I flew with my second in command as copilot and my staff navigator and boom operator. I think regular crews were happy to get a day off, but on the other hand, most were eager to build flight time and there was not a lot to do if setting around the base or their quarters while I flew.

On Thanksgiving, we had an early morning flight supporting a formation of Saudi F-15s. After takeoff we climbed to our refueling altitude of 31,000 feet and headed north towards the Iraq border. Four F-15s took off after us and quickly joined on our wing during the climb. There had been reports of Iraqi MIG31 aircraft operating in the area south of Bagdad, although most had flown to Iran to escape US forces during Desert Storm action. The F-15s were to patrol near the border to engage any hostiles. Since I was setting in the jump seat during the refueling, I decided to go to the boom pod to watch. As we approached the refueling point, the first fighter dropped back from a position near our wing and moved into position so that that the boomer could plug into the refueling receptacle on the fighter's wing. I noted sidewinder missiles hanging under both wings and I could see the pilot clearly. I had been told that most of the Saudi F-15 pilots were highly placed in the royal family. This pilot flew into position expertly and to my surprise had his oxygen mask hanging and smoking a cigarette. For whatever reason, the flammable oxygen in his mask and the nearby fuel going into his aircraft posed no threat to him. When he had his fuel, he put out his cigarette, connected his oxygen mask, and dropped back so his wingmen could get fueled. Soon they left us and headed north towards Baghdad. We flew in an orbit for an hour and then the fighters returned for a fuel top off before we all headed back to Riyahd. After landing we found that the cooks had outdone themselves and prepared an amazing Thanksgiving feast. The only thing I noticed

different was the turkey came in loafs rather than the traditional bird with drumsticks. It was all good, however.

Most days were focused on scheduled missions and processing arriving and departing aircrews. Most crews were there for a month, but the reserve and national guard crews were limited to a week or two. That caused some grumbling among the active crews, but at the end of the day it meant more flying time towards a combat support medal that was awarded for accomplishing a certain number of flights in a combat zone. One of my jobs was to pin on such medals when a crew was about to redeploy to the US.

A week before Christmas we received orders for a joint operation to strike a suspected buildup in Iraqi forces. In addition to F-15 and F-18s there would be a formation of British Tornado aircraft. Three tanker aircraft were involved and I would be flying the number two aircraft and commanding the tanker cell. The operation was fairly complicated as aircraft would take off from three different locations and rendezvous at a point about 150 miles northeast of Riyahd. All three-tanker aircraft checked in on the radio and then we started engines and taxied for takeoff. The takeoff was uneventful and by thirty miles out we joined up in formation, stacked up 500 feet vertically, and two miles separation on a 60-degree line from the lead aircraft. The lead navigator calculated the airspeed to reach the rendezvous on time, about 310 knots indicated. In addition to a visual reference to the lead aircraft, I used our aircraft radar to maintain exact position off the lead and the third tanker did the same. Soon, my navigator advised we were approaching the join up point. It was a hot, sunny day without a cloud in sight. Extra crew members were looking over my shoulder and that of my copilot to spot incoming aircraft. Someone called out a high formation of aircraft descending towards us from our 2 o'clock position, I spotted another group passing by on our left, and the boom operator in the refueling pod reported others coming up from behind. About that time the lead tanker started a port turn to help with the join up and it seemed like aircraft were coming at us from every direction in the turn. Somehow it all worked out and soon I saw a pair of F-15s slide in to about fifteen feet off my left wingtip. My copilot reported a similar sighting on our right wing. Below and to the left I could see a formation of Tornados moving up to the lead tanker. The lead tanker

called that he was accelerating to refueling speed, 350 knots, and individual fighters began to cycle behind their tankers to top off their tanks. Below, the rippling sand was unbroken by structure or foliage as far as I could see.

It took about an hour to get all the fighters refueled. My copilot controlled the fuel panel and recorded how much gas each plane got. When refueling was complete, all the fighters dropped back, formed up in tight groups and headed north into Iraq to do whatever fighters do. We settled back to routine boredom for the next hour, reviewing our flight planned fuel burn, systems operations, and the radios for any unusual traffic. When we departed Riyahd, we had advised the local air traffic control that we would be going 'due regard'. That mean we no longer monitored their radio frequencies and would be going wherever we wanted without getting clearance. When we were done with our military business, we would advise ATC where we were and that we would once again follow their instructions. This was the standard way of doing business in a combat zone and we had operated the same way during the Vietnam War.

After we had orbited for about an hour the fighters reappeared, got refueled as we headed back south. Then they headed back to their operating locations and we separated our tanker aircraft for individual clearance and landing. This was just another day in my life in the desert.

Days went by and soon it was Christmas time. Because of the restrictions on any display of Christianity in the Kingdom, any religious services or displays were held in the dining hall. Our chaplain had to remove any religious emblems from his uniform while in country. An arriving tanker brought a Christmas tree and decorations from the states, but we had to cover it with a tarp and smuggle into the dining hall. I decided to have an open house for all the officer at my quarters in Eskan village. My second in command brought in about ten cases of near beer and the dining hall cooks prepared a bunch of tasty snacks. Someone brought a bunch of cassette carols and they played throughput the evening. I think all had a good time and I ran everyone off around 10pm as we had flights on the schedule for the next day. An interesting footnote is that the Saudi two-star general who commanded in the region sent me a Christmas card. I guess the higher-ranking officers in the Saudi military were more politically oriented and were tactfully able to recognize the customs of their allies without generating unrest among the lower Saudi ranks.

My chief of maintenance had an idea to build a miniature golf course near the tennis courts. We sent a request for putters and golf balls on a redeploying tanker and the next arriving tanker brought us the equipment. During off time volunteers began construction of the course. It was pretty fancy and I am not sure where they got all the cement, lumber, and paint to construct the course. It was ready in about ten days, complete with blue painted plywood to represent water hazards. The only catch was it had to be played after dark due to the ridiculous daytime heat. Portable lighting was installed and the course was well used for the rest of my time in the desert.

As it got closer to my departure time in January, my second in command suggested we go into Riyahd to do some shopping for things to take home. We had a down day coming up and it seemed like a good idea. On the evening of the day off we headed into town. Our goal was to find the various souks or marketplaces that held things we were interested in buying. Each was in a different alleyway and contained around thirty or forty shops that specialized in in common items. We found souks for electronics, basket ware, carpets, and gold and silver items. The downtown area was a little intimidating and swarming with Saudi citizens. Women were completely covered with black robes and veils, and the Saudi men wore white robes and head coverings. There were a few in western wear, but we clearly stood out. The streets were well lit and we saw a number of beggars, many with missing hands or feet. In the Kingdom, theft and other crimes were rewarded by losing body parts to the sword. As a result, the streets were safe, even late at night.

In the electronics souk it was surprising to find the radios and tape players along with a selection of the latest US rock and roll cassette tapes for only a dollar each. With no copyright laws in the Kingdom, such items were massed produced on the black market. We had already been informed that we could not bring these items back to the states, but we made good use of them while in the desert. In the gold and silver souk, the array of precious metals and gems in each shop was breathtaking. Each shop was a room about the size of a typical living room in the states and the counters and shelves were loaded. Spread across one counter was a pile of rubies, emerald, and diamonds that must have been worth tens of thousands of US dollars. The prices of gold and silver items were determined by weight on a handy scale and workmanship did not seem to count for much. At the price of these metals, most were well out of my reach, but I did negotiate for a solid silver cartouche for my wife. For a little extra they would add her initials in Arabic on one side and hieroglyphics on the other side. We next walked a short distance to the carpet souk. There we were greeted by the shop owner who would not discuss prices until we sat down for tea. We went to a corner in his shop and were

seated on cushions while he brought forth an elaborate gold tea service. While we sat there he brought out pictures of his many famous civilian and military customers and let us know how pleased his customers were with his goods. Then he took us around his very large shop that held several hundred carpets, some on wall racks and some rolled up, most were sized nine by twelve feet. He knew that we were not allowed to bring carpets made in Iran or Iraq back to the states so he showed us goods that were primarily from Pakistan or India. My second in command selected three carpets and I found a gorgeous blue one that I wanted. I was shocked by the price at nearly $1,000 dollars each when I was expecting to pay around $100. My number two assured me that this was a good deal and the carpets would be worth three times that amount back home, a price I later confirmed. We closed the deal with the understanding that payment and carpets would be exchanged when they were delivered to the base. We stopped off to get a late-night snack of tasty shawarmas at a local stand and then headed back to Eskan village.

A couple of weeks later our replacements arrived and we prepared for departure by showing them our operation. That afternoon our goods arrived from downtown Riyadh, and we loaded everything on our airplane. Early the next morning we departed the desert and the flight back home was uneventful with an overnight stop in England. The experience in the desert was very memorable and we were happy to share our stories with all back at our home base. At the time, we had no idea that war would break out again in the region, ten years later.

The Road Back

Standing in the back yard, with my hands as far in my vest pockets as I can get them, I watch the winter clouds race by and feel the coming snow of another bitter Montana winter. A gust of wind brings smoke from the chimney down over the edge of the roof and reminds me that life is a lot more comfortable inside. Most people stay inside where life is more ordered and the days pass in an endless routine of business dealings and social responsibilities. Out here the eye is drawn to scattered wind rows of fallen leaves and patchy yellow grass that quit growing two months ago. Only the fir trees remain unchanged and firmly attached to the ground. The brisk wind gusts seem to be blowing everything else on by like so much dust in the wind. The thought creates a deep, familiar chill as lyrics from an old song by the group Kansas drift in from behind some long-closed door. "I close my eyes, only for a moment and the moments gone." The memory comes easily. It was a long time ago and yet just yesterday…

…the Scout momentarily loses traction on the washboard gravel of the shoreline road, knocking my head against the window and bringing me groggy and chilled out of my catnap to low radio music and the musty smell of damp hip boots. Tony glances over and then turns his concentration back to the road. The seat between us is littered with junk food wrappers, two half empty thermos bottles, and red and green shotgun shells in assorted loads. The debris trail of those things critical to serious expeditions spreads across the dash which is buried in maps, coffee cups, gloves, hats, and binoculars. Even the muddy floorboards have barely enough room for our feet. Gear bags, hip boots, and extra layers of cold weather clothing take up every inch of floor space, making it a challenge to secure a share of the heater's welcome output.

As we drift through the forest primeval, on our way to the next as-yet-undecided destination, I can see that most of the leaves have fallen from the roadside hardwoods since our last trip, allowing visibility into parts of the forest that would not normally open to view. If you look closely you might catch a glimpse of a deer, a porcupine or other animal that will notch a memory and maybe secure a lasting name for a particular stretch of road. Maybe today we will christen the Big Eagle Tree or Sandy Yellow Ridge. At a minimum, any such sighting will guarantee the success of the expedition and elevate it above the long list of unremarkable journeys down nameless dirt roads.

The water is dead calm along the passing Lake Superior shoreline, but that belies the brisk winter breeze ripping the last leaves from the hardwoods. The effects can be seen in the foamy, steel gray chop that starts out there past the sheltered first hundred yards of water. There are probably waterfowl swimming out there somewhere; but only the large, chunky Golden eye ducks will put up with such rough water. And they are probably looking for shelter. As I try to shake the cobwebs from my brain, I catch a reflection of myself in the window that reveals a three-day growth of dark beard, hair twisted in all directions by the knit cap I have been wearing, and bloodshot eyes due to our early morning start. As I set up and look around, I remember the Winchester autoloader and the Remington pump in the back seat, on top of their cases, with the actions open. I should be watching for grouse on the road ahead. We are near the cranberry thickets that old Henry the trapper frequents. And grouse are drawn to this boggy area like a magnet. The road ahead is clear, however, and seems to stretch forever. The sameness of the passing forest is hypnotizing. If we did not occasionally check the mileage and the map, we could drive due west forever, run out of gas, and never arrive at wherever it is we are headed.

There are few cabins or other structures in the Forest Primeval and those few are clustered together against the almost painful loneliness that cloaks this part of the woods. I try to remember the number of the county road turnoff that will take us south to Rice Lakes. Maybe 3146 or 3150. I know the road number will not be as significant as a nearby strange tree, a remembered animal encounter, or maybe an unusual building along the last half mile of road before the turn. In this part of the woods, everything looks the same and we could easily miss the turn. I ignore that possibility and concentrate on my last memory of the Rice Lakes road. At this time of year, I wonder if four-wheel drive will be enough to get us all the way to the shoreline. If we find fresh car tracks in the soft, sandy lane, it will mean that some other hunters have found our secret hunting spot. But if the tracks are more than a few hours old, any disturbed game will probably have returned.

Rice Lakes is located in a remote part of the Forest Primeval. Waterfowl use it for a stopover after their flight south across southern Canada and Lake Superior. We have had good luck there fairly often. If the ducks are not on the small, narrow front lake, then we will sneak through the thin scrub pines and over the marshy peat to the back lake. I think of stepping carefully from hummock to hummock with my load of gun, shells, daypack, and many layers of clothes. If you break through the soggy peat surface and get water in your boots, you have bought a trip back to the car for dry socks and maybe the end of hunting for the day. And there are places where a man could break through and go in over his head. The thought of getting wet reminds me that earlier today we found the road to Pendills Lake flooded. I'm hoping good weather will dry that road out soon. The early and late seasons at Pendills have provided some of the best shooting around, but heavy rains in the spring and fall frequently make the drive in to the lake impassible. Our setup on the small island at Pendills is about three hundred yards from the canoe launching site. It is a nearly perfect location. On a day like today, the action would be hot and heavy and roast duck would soon be on the menu.

The Scout motors on and Tony occasionally downshifts for curves. We pass over the small concrete bridges for Pendills, Halfaday, and Naomikong Creeks. Ahead lay the waters of Angadosh and Roxbury. Then the Whitefish Bay Shoreline vista will open up in the trees. It is a familiar journey, but the anticipation of new sights and sounds still breeds anticipation. I wonder if we should be fishing today and if the stormy fall weather has driven the big fish from the deep Lake Superior waters to the creeks, as many locals believe. The water is murky in the streams we pass and recent storms have eroded the sandy banks. In some cases, heavy water flow has caused a creek mouth to relocate along the lakeshore. But, it is too cold today to be sitting by a stream and the fish would probably ignore our time-tested offerings of blue and silver Cleo lures. Today, even a #3 Mepps spinner wouldn't even cause interest. I roll down the window to test the air temperature and am rewarded with a blast of frigid air that encourages me to quickly roll it back up. The prospect of iced up fish pole guides and wet, numb hands causes me to shiver and move my damp, stockinged feet closer to the heater duct.

We still have about fifteen more minutes until we reach Lumberjack's Bar and Grill. The old guy who runs the place makes a great hamburger, but we always seem to be the only customers. Other landmarks for the approaching turn to Rice Lakes begin to come into view. Soon it will be time to put on the damp hip boots and leave the Scout behind as we move into the dense cedar swamps and peat bogs that protect the lakes from accidental discovery. But we have a few miles to go yet, and Tony looks rock-steady behind the wheel, so I settle back with my head against the window, sink deeper into the collar of my vest, and close my eyes…

...standing in the back yard, the connection broken, I cannot remember why I came outside. I search for the mental link back to the Scout, the north woods, and escape. The damp smell of the north woods is fresh in my mind as I fight to return……the emotion that drives me is painfully strong…I have to get back to the north woods and breathe deeply of the cold, pine-scented air.

www.ingramcontent.com/pod-product-compliance
Ingram Content Group UK Ltd.
Pitfield, Milton Keynes, MK11 3LW, UK
UKHW022028190726
13853UKWH00005B/2153

9 798740 281971